Cyberstalking

Cyberstalking
Harassment in the Internet Age
and How to Protect Your Family

PAUL BOCIJ

PRAEGER

Westport, Connecticut
London

Library of Congress Cataloging-in-Publication Data

Bocij, Paul.
    Cyberstalking : harassment in the Internet age and how to protect your family / Paul Bocij.
        p. cm.
    Includes bibliographical references and index.
    ISBN 0–275–98118–5 (alk. paper)
        1. Computer crimes.   2. Stalking.   3. Harassment.   I. Title.
    HV6773.B63   2004
    613.6'6—dc22   2003068988

British Library Cataloguing in Publication Data is available.

Library of Congress Catalog Card Number: 2003068988
ISBN: 0–275–98118–5

First published in 2004

Praeger Publishers, 88 Post Road West, Westport, CT 06881
An imprint of Greenwood Publishing Group, Inc.
www.praeger.com

Printed in the United States of America

The paper used in this book complies with the
Permanent Paper Standard issued by the National
Information Standards Organization (Z39.48–1984).

10 9 8 7 6 5 4 3 2

To my wife, Helen

Contents

Acknowledgments   ix

Introduction   xi

1   What Is Cyberstalking?   1

2   Stalking or *Cyber*stalking?   19

3   The Incidence and Prevalence of Cyberstalking   33

4   Who Are the Cyberstalkers?   49

5   Who Are the Victims of Cyberstalkers?   71

6   What Motivates Cyberstalkers?   89

7   Threats to Young People   107

8   Cyberstalking and Organizations   137

9   Cyberstalking and the Law   163

10 Dealing with Cyberstalking   177

Further Readings   205

Notes   217

Glossary   229
Bibliography   243
Index   263

Acknowledgments

The author would like to acknowledge the advice and assistance of Helen Bocij and Leroy McFarlane. Many thanks to Suzanne Staszak-Silva, editor Greenwood Publishing. Also thanks to copyeditor Alison Auch, and House of Equations, Inc. for their typesetting and production services.

The author would also like to acknowledge the following publications for permission to reproduce sections of his earlier published work: *The Prison Service Journal* (HMSO), http://www.hmprisonservice.gov.uk/ library; *The Police Journal* (Vathek Publishing), http://www.vathek.com/ pj/index.shtml; *Community Safety Journal* (Pavilion Publishing), http://www.pavpub.com/pavpub/journals/.

The author would like to acknowledge the following publication and organization for permission to reproduce materials: *New Media and Society* (SAGE Publications), http://www.new-media-and-society.com; Australian Institute of Criminology, http://www.aic.gov.au/.

The publisher and the author acknowledge the intellectual rights of others, including all trademarks and registered designs.

Introduction

We are constantly told that technology enriches our lives: the Internet provides learning opportunities for our children, cell phones allow us to keep in touch with our relatives while we're on the move, and laptop computers allow us to work almost anywhere at any time. But we are also constantly warned about the dangers of technology, especially the Internet: hackers can steal our credit card numbers, pedophiles can target our children, and racists can spread messages of hate. We take these dangers seriously because technology permeates almost every aspect of our lives. For instance, it is not an exaggeration to suggest that virtually every child in the United States, Europe, and any number of other technically advanced nations will come into regular contact with the Internet. It is for this reason that parents, teachers, law enforcement agencies, and others constantly monitor the safety of the young people in their care.

People victimizing and harassing others is by no means a new phenomenon. However, it is only over the past few decades that one particular form of harassment—stalking—has captured the public's attention through a small number of high-profile cases, usually involving celebrities. When the communications revolution of the 1990s brought the Internet and other technology into the home, it took little time for stalkers to discover that technology offers new ways to pursue victims and avoid detection. Cyberstalking is a relatively new threat that can affect any Internet user, no matter where he or she is located. Adults and young people, males and females, expert computer users and novices are all equally vulnerable to this form of harassment. Nevertheless, there seems to be a common perception that cyber-stalking does not result in serious outcomes—many people think of it as little more than one person sending abusive e-mail messages to another. In addition, the distance that tends to separate a cyberstalker from his victim is seen as a safety mechanism that protects the victim from any real harm. However, this view is wrong and is unfair to vic-tims who often suffer for years without any real prospect of receiving help. When a cyberstalker targets a victim, the outcomes can include serious emotional and mental harm, physical and sexual assault, kid-napping, and even murder. One of the aims of this book is to correct some of the misconceptions about cyberstalking and to encourage the view that cyberstalking poses a serious threat to Internet users. It is my hope that encouraging such a view will eventually result in new efforts to help victims of cyberstalking.

Another reason for writing this book was to address a lack of aca-demic materials dealing with this subject. Despite its importance, only a handful of research papers dealing with cyberstalking have been published. In addition, although several books claim to deal with cyberstalking, they tend to be "how-to" titles that offer advice to victims of stalking or accounts of personal experiences. This book draws together the bulk of the available literature in an attempt to describe the state of current knowledge about cyberstalking. Further-more, this work is the first to focus entirely on cyberstalking and the first to provide a scholarly discussion of this subject. Such a discus-sion is considered valuable since one of its goals is to indicate gaps in knowledge and to highlight areas where further research is ur-gently needed.

I've written this book to be accessible to both those with a profes-sional interest in cyberstalking, such as teachers, students, and police officers, and those who simply have an interest in the topic. No prior technical knowledge is needed, except for a basic understanding of how people use the Internet. Although it may be helpful if readers know what web browsers, e-mail, and chat rooms are, they need not know the inner workings of computer viruses, anonymous remailers, and firewalls.

It is worth taking a few moments to consider how certain terms are used within the text. I have chosen to distinguish between stalking and cyberstalking by arguing that cyberstalking represents a new form of behavior that uses technology to harass one or more individuals.

A more comprehensive description and a formal definition of *cyberstalking* are offered in chapter 1; however, throughout the text, *stalking* refers to offline stalking, and *cyberstalking* means harassing people with technology. I also describe stalking and cyberstalking in terms of harassment because all forms of stalking involve an element of threat or aim to cause the victim distress. The distinction between stalking and cyberstalking may seem trivial, but I see it as being so important that chapter 2 is devoted entirely to this issue. Until we are able to focus on cyberstalking as an area of study in its own right instead of as an extension of offline stalking, we are unlikely to learn more about its specific nature.

I have also chosen to refer to cyberstalkers as males and victims as females in order to improve clarity. Of course, this convention also recognizes the fact that most cyberstalkers (and stalkers) are male, and that most victims are female, as chapters 4 and 5 will demonstrate.

Much of the literature on stalking and cyberstalking tends to refer to a victim of harassment as a "target." Presumably this is because it is more comfortable to talk about stalking and cyberstalking using a term usually reserved for an object rather than a person. However, I feel it is important to understand that stalking and cyberstalking affect real people, causing a great deal of suffering and distress. It is for this reason that I have chosen to use the word *victim* throughout the book. I make no apology for adopting a viewpoint that is sympathetic to victims of cyberstalking and hope that this text will make some small contribution toward understanding and reducing cyberstalking.

STRUCTURE AND OVERVIEW

Each chapter in the book sets out to answer important questions about the nature of cyberstalking. Chapter 1 addresses the first of these questions by explaining what cyberstalking means. This introductory material examines common definitions of stalking and cyberstalking in order to draw out common threads and highlight important features. The chapter also describes some of the behaviors commonly associated with cyberstalking. Chapter 2 looks at the differences between offline stalking and cyberstalking, arguing that although they may be related, they should be treated as different phenomena.

Chapter 3 tries to estimate the number of cyberstalkers and cyberstalking victims within the United States and other countries and argues that existing estimates related to cyberstalking are unreliable. As a result, we know very little about the number of cyberstalkers active in the world today.

Chapters 4 and 5 provide an overview of what is known about stalkers, cyberstalkers, and victims of harassment. In addition to looking at recent research findings, the chapters also discuss the impact of stalking and cyberstalking on victims.

Chapter 6 explores some of the motivations behind cyberstalking. It tries to explain some of the reasons a "normal" person chooses to become a cyberstalker, or why a person intending to cause distress to another chooses technology as the medium of harassment.

Chapter 7 looks at forms of cyberstalking that affect young people, placing a special emphasis on the activities of pedophiles and child pornographers. The chapter also considers some of the ways in which young people may place themselves at risk.

Chapter 8 focuses on a range of cyberstalking behaviors known as corporate cyberstalking, revealing that the motives behind corporate cyberstalking can be very different from those associated with cyberstalking individuals.

Chapter 9 discusses some of the legislation that can be used to deal with stalking and cyberstalking. The chapter also looks at the effectiveness of the legal system in preventing and punishing harassment.

Finally, chapter 10 describes strategies for dealing with cyberstalking. It presents material that is practical and provides specific guidelines for adults, young people, and organizations.

ADDITIONAL RESOURCES

Additional resources supporting this book are available from the author's web site at http://www.cyberstalking.info.

DISCLAIMER

To provide readers with a broader understanding of the material presented throughout this book, many software companies and software applications are discussed and referenced. However, mention of any company or its product in no way implies an endorsement of such by either the author or the publisher of this book.

1

What Is Cyberstalking?

THE JAYNE HITCHCOCK STORY

In January 1996, Jayne Hitchcock[1] responded to an advertisement on a Usenet newsgroup for the Woodside Literary Agency. Within a week of sending her book proposal to the company, Hitchcock received a reply complimenting the professionalism of her work and asking for a $75 reading fee. When Hitchcock reminded the company that it was unusual for a literary agency to charge any fees at all, her proposal was promptly returned to her.

A few months later, posts began to appear on Usenet warning writers about approaching the Woodside Literary Agency. In a kind of contest, a group of regular readers sent the agency examples of the poorest writing they could find to see if it would be accepted. Almost every piece of work was accepted by the agency, and each writer was asked for money. Many people, including Hitchcock and Jack Mingo, posted messages warning that Woodside had been investigated by a number of Usenet contributors and seemed suspect.

These messages caused Woodside's owner, James Leonard (who sometimes called himself James Lawrence), to retaliate. Leonard began by sending out hundreds of copies of his advertisements using a number of different e-mail accounts. Such a practice is known as spamming and is usually considered unethical. Leonard also used an alias to post a message attacking Mingo and suggesting that Mingo would be sued for libel.

In December 1996, Leonard began to impersonate Hitchcock in various messages posted to Usenet. Many of these messages contained inflammatory comments and were obviously intended to provoke other users to flame[2] Hitchcock. In one case, a message claiming that Hitchcock was interested in sadomasochism and containing her address and telephone number was posted to dozens of newsgroups. As a result, Hitchcock sometimes received as many as twenty calls a day from men replying to the advertisements (McCord, 1998). In the same month, an attempt was made to render useless e-mail accounts belonging to Hitchcock, her husband, her literary agent, and her employer by bombarding them with traffic, a technique known as e-mail bombing.

In January 1997, Hitchcock began legal action against the Woodside Literary Agency. However, Hitchcock and her supporters continued to be harassed. Some of the incidents reported by Hitchcock include

- A mail hoax was set up in which magazine and CD club memberships were forged in Hitchcock's name.
- Ursula Sprachman, one of the owners of the Woodside Literary Agency, alleged to the FBI that Jack Mingo had made a death threat against her. Fortunately, Mingo had recorded his telephone call to the literary agency and was able to prove that he had not made any threats.
- Ursula Sprachman also contacted the Maryland State Police concerning a fund established to help Hitchcock with her legal expenses. Sprachman alleged that Hitchcock was defrauding contributors, but she was unable to provide any evidence.
- An unknown telephone caller threatened to kill Hitchcock's lawyer, John Young, unless he withdrew from her case. However, Young was not intimidated and continued to represent Hitchcock.
- Woodside allegedly contacted Hitchcock's neighbors in an attempt to find her new telephone number. The company also wrote to her employers in order to gain more information about her. Hitchcock's employers immediately contacted her and the matter was reported to the authorities.

In 2000, James Leonard and Ursula Sprachman were arrested on charges of conspiracy to commit mail fraud and perjury by a U.S. postal inspector, John McDermott. The federal trial of Sprachman and Leonard was scheduled for May 2000, but it was cancelled when the pair decided to plead guilty and agreed to pay restitution to writers who had paid for services they never received. Sprachman and Leonard were sentenced in December 2001, with Leonard receiving the maximum penalty of eight months in prison and three years' probation, and Sprachman receiving three years probation in view of her age and health. They also settled with Hitchcock, although the details of the agreement were not released. It is worth noting that Leonard was able to delay serving his sentence until September 2002, more than six years after he first harassed Hitchcock.

INTRODUCTION

Why is it necessary to have a definition of cyberstalking? What are the difficulties in arriving at a definition of cyberstalking? How can cyberstalking be defined? What behaviors constitute cyberstalking? This chapter sets out to answer some fundamental questions regarding the nature of cyberstalking. In offering a broad introduction to the subject, a number of themes are introduced that will be returned to in later chapters. This chapter moves through a number of topics in order to provide a detailed discussion of the nature of cyberstalking. I begin by discussing the need for a comprehensive definition that can be used to meet the needs of different groups, such as academics and legislators. I then look at how stalking is defined before exploring some common definitions of cyberstalking.

Examining some of the behaviors commonly seen in cases of Internet harassment can provide another way of looking at cyberstalking. In addition to improving our understanding, this approach may also help us to develop a behavioral definition of cyberstalking. Finally, I propose and discuss a new definition of cyberstalking that is both practical and comprehensive.

THE NEED FOR A DEFINITION

As technology has advanced, completely new forms of deviant and criminal behavior have started to emerge. Many of these behaviors only become possible when technology reaches a certain level or when it becomes widely used. Computer viruses, for example, are a problem that simply did not exist before the early 1980s. It was only when the IBM PC became common in homes and offices that viruses began to pose a serious threat. Today, computer viruses affect many millions of computer users each year and are responsible for business losses that can be measured in the billions of dollars.[3] In the same way, cyberstalking—the use of information and communications technology (ICT) to harass individuals—has recently emerged as a new and growing problem. Incidentally, the term *harassment* is used interchangeably with stalking and cyberstalking since all forms of stalking involve an element of threat and/or aim to cause the victim distress.

A major difficulty in starting to deal with the problem of cyberstalking is that it means different things to different people. Unfortunately, the definition used by one body, whether a government agency or a scientific discipline, is often unsatisfactory when applied to other circumstances. A good example can be drawn from the field of information systems. Although academics can provide a coherent and logical definition of an information system, legislators have found that such a definition is inappropriate when formulating new laws (Bocij et al., 1999). This is largely because technology is evolving so rapidly that today's definition might be completely outdated in a matter of a few years.

Throughout this book, I make a distinction between physical stalking and cyberstalking. From this point onward, then, the act of physically stalking a person will be referred to as offline stalking or simply stalking. Although some writers view cyberstalking as nothing more than an extension of offline stalking, the argument made here is that cyberstalking should be regarded as an entirely new form of deviant behavior, albeit one that is related to offline stalking. This is an important theme that will be discussed throughout this book. Just as computer viruses did not exist until technology allowed them to be created and distributed, the view taken here is that cyberstalking has arisen as the result of new technologies, such as instant messaging and bulletin boards. The argument that there are major differences between cyberstalking and offline stalking seems difficult to dispute. As an example, a report prepared by the U.S. attorney general on behalf of the then vice president[4] lists several major differences between offline stalking and cyberstalking:

> Offline stalking generally requires the perpetrator and the victim to be located in the same geographic area; cyberstalkers may be located across the street or across the country.
>
> Electronic communications technologies make it much easier for a cyberstalker to encourage third parties to harass and/or threaten a victim (e.g., impersonating the victim and posting inflammatory messages to bulletin boards and in chat rooms, causing viewers of that message to send threatening messages back to the victim "author").
>
> Electronic communications technologies also lower the barriers to harassment and threats; a cyberstalker does not need to physically confront the victim. (Reno, 1999)

The necessary challenge, then, is to create a definition of cyberstalking that can meet the needs of a wide range of stakeholders. Stakeholders are all those with an interest in cyberstalking, including law enforcement agencies, Internet Service Providers (ISPs), clinicians, researchers, and victims. Each stakeholder has a different set of needs that must be catered to. Law enforcement agencies want to catch cyberstalkers, ISPs want customers to feel safe using their services, clinicians want to treat cyberstalkers, researchers want to explain the nature of cyberstalking, and victims want to be protected. However, although all of these objectives are important, an emphasis needs to be placed on protecting victims—an area that currently is sorely neglected. For instance, chapter 9 demonstrates that existing legislation may not provide the reassurance and protection needed by some people. Similarly, the definitions employed by some researchers and organizations tend to focus on offline stalking, thereby marginalizing the experiences of cyberstalking victims.

Most people would agree that in every field of study a problem must be defined before it can be examined. Without a common understanding of a given concept, any research undertaken may not address the actual problem and is unlikely to be of any real value. In addition, it becomes difficult to draw together the work carried out by different individuals and organizations because each is working under a different set of preconceptions and expectations.

WHAT IS STALKING?

It was said earlier that although cyberstalking represents a new form of deviant behavior, it bears many similarities to offline stalking. In working toward a definition of cyberstalking, it is important to understand something of the nature of offline stalking.

Many writers have adopted a relatively narrow definition of stalking, preferring to describe it only in terms of following or pursuit, for example by stating that "stalking behavior typically consists of intrusive following of a 'target': for example, by placing one's self in front of the target's home, or other unexpected and unwelcome appearances in their private domain" (Kamphuis and Emmelkamp, 2000, p. 206). In a similar vein, other writers have described how people tend to see stalking in terms of pursuit, for instance: "As a concept stalking possesses sinister and threatening connotations. It implies being hunted and harassed, whilst powerless and unable to stop a relentless and threatening pursuit" (Ogilvie, 2000, p. 2).

J. Reid Meloy is a recognized authority in the field of stalking and defines it in terms of obsessional following: "[Stalking is] an abnormal or long term pattern of threat or harassment directed toward a specific individual." He goes on to define a pattern of harassment as "more than one overt act of unwanted pursuit of the victim that was perceived by the victim as being harassing" (1998a, pp. 2–3).

Meloy's definition suggests that many people see stalking as being pathological. However, as will be argued in chapter 6, not all cyberstalkers can be described as having mental health issues. It is also interesting that Meloy defines stalking in terms of harassment. This is important because harassment implies a broad range of behaviors that go beyond simply pursuing the victim.[5]

Meloy's view is shared by Mullen, Pathé, and Purcell, who are also well-known writers and researchers in the field. Although they support Meloy's definition of stalking, they offer their own definition as "a constellation of behaviors in which one individual inflicts on another repeated unwanted intrusions and communications." Intrusions are characterized as "following, loitering nearby, maintaining surveillance and making approaches" (2000, p. 7). Although not considered a core part of stalking behaviors, they also list several related activities, such as ordering goods on the victim's behalf and making false accusations.

Some additional behaviors that can be associated with stalking are also discussed by other researchers, such as Sinwelski and Vinton, who provide an excellent summary:

> Stalking behaviors range on a continuum of severity and intensity. They may begin with acts that individually may seem insignificant, such as repeated, unwanted contact in the form of telephone calls, beeper codes, e-mail messages, or letters. If left unchecked, these contacts may escalate to unwanted physical contacts or the stalker's "coincidental" appearance wherever the victim goes. Sometimes the contacts are in the form of unwanted gifts, such as flowers or jewelry. At other times, stalkers spread false rumors about their victims to the victims' family members, friends, or employers or lie to frighten or coerce their victims. One stalker, for instance, falsely informed the victim, his ex-girlfriend, that he had AIDS. In addition, many stalkers go to the extreme of vandalizing, stealing, or destroying the victims' personal property. (2001, pp. 49–50)

Hence, stalking often involves more than simply following a victim. There is a wide range of behaviors that a stalker can adopt in order to bring about a sustained campaign of harassment. It is also worth highlighting the common belief that a stalker's behavior may escalate unless action is taken.

The descriptions of stalking described so far are those that have been developed by academics. However, a great deal can also be learned by looking at how industry deals with the problem. Many organizations are placed in the position of accepting responsibility for the safety of their employees or the people they serve. Universities, for example, have a responsibility for the safety of their students. In order to fulfill this responsibility, some organizations create formal codes of conduct that define prohibited activities and the sanctions that will be used to enforce compliance. Johns Hopkins University is a good example of an organization that has taken action to ensure the safety of its students. According to the university:

> Stalking is the willful, malicious, and repeated following or harassment of another person and making credible threats of harm. Stalking most often occurs after a woman or man has broken up with a partner or if one person wants a romantic relationship and the other does not. Stalking, however, can occur for other reasons, and the stalker may or may not be known by the victim.[6]

The definition used by the university is based on legal definitions of stalking (see chapter 9). However, it is important to remember that the university's definition emphasizes the fact that the stalker may not be known by the victim and that there are motivations other than romantic for stalking. Note also that this university's definition implies that most stalking victims are women.

WHAT IS CYBERSTALKING?

This question can begin to be answered by looking at recent efforts to define cyberstalking and by attempting to identify the behaviors commonly reported in cyberstalking cases.

Meloy, a leading U.S. expert on offline stalking, argues that the term *cyberstalking* implies "a paranoid tinged world of malicious and intrusive activity on the Internet" (1998a, p. 10). Meloy's explanation of cyberstalking is as follows:

> The Internet as a means of stalking can be used for two criminal functions:
>
> 1. to gather private information on the target to further a pursuit; and
> 2. to communicate (in real time or not) with the target to implicitly or explicitly threaten or to induce fear. (Meloy, 1998a, p. 10)

Meloy's definition is interesting in that it allows for activities such as data theft, in which an individual may use the Internet to gather information about the victim. In addition, Meloy allows for relatively new developments, such as instant messaging,[7] and does not concentrate solely on e-mail as the medium for contact between the harasser and the victim. However, though Meloy's definition is undoubtedly clear, it does not appear to be comprehensive. As an example, it does not deal explicitly with some of the activities associated with cyberstalking, such as real-time monitoring.[8]

Meloy's comments suggest that cyberstalking and paranoia go hand in hand. This view appears to be shared by many others; for instance, the Dating Detectives web site[9] provides a complete guide to dealing with cyberstalking and contains the following definition:

> Where an individual or a group of individuals contrive to use personal information and the Internet and modern technology, to take away another individual's personal rights, freedom and safety, usually by covert or anonymous methods, and pursue and monitor the victim in such a manner as to create paranoia and fear within the said victim.

It seems unfair to suggest that victims of cyberstalking may experience paranoia as a result of harassment. Paranoia is defined in basic terms as "an extreme and *unreasonable* [emphasis added] feeling that other people are going to harm you or that they have a bad opinion of you."[10] In suggesting that the fears of cyberstalking victims may be unreasonable, there is a danger that victims may not be taken seriously.

Mullen, Pathé, and Purcell (2000) do not offer a definition of cyberstalking, limiting their discussion of this area to the use of e-mail as a means of transmitting threats or making approaches to victims. However, their work on stalking raises several points that may help to improve our understanding of cyberstalking.

As mentioned earlier, Mullen, Pathé, and Purcell (2000) believe that making false accusations is not one of the core behaviors associated with stalking. However, it can be argued that such behavior *can* be considered one of the key behaviors associated with cyberstalking. It can also be argued that making false accusations can have more serious results in cyberstalking cases than in offline stalking cases. Accusations posted to bulletin boards and other services are likely to be seen by a larger audience and may be accessible for a long period of time. Similarly, ordering goods on the victim's behalf may have more serious effects in cyberstalking cases since it is fairly easy to make a number of large orders in a very short period of time. In addition, cyberstalkers may find it easy to create a convincing impersonation of the victim.

As an example, it would be quite simple for a male cyberstalker to pose as his female victim when ordering goods via the Internet.

Another important issue raised by Mullen, Pathé, and Purcell (2000, p. 261) concerns time constraints and the frequency with which incidents must occur before they are treated as stalking behavior. They make the point that setting such a threshold may have serious consequences. If the threshold is too low, it becomes difficult to determine whether a given case is genuine. As an example, some of the current legislation described in chapter 9 suggests that as few as two incidents may constitute stalking. If this is accepted, then a request for dinner that is turned down, followed by another request for a different date would constitute stalking. On the other hand, if the threshold is set too high, then victims may be forced to suffer needlessly. In some studies, for example, the threshold has been set at ten or more incidents in order to ensure that the cases examined are genuine. However, if this threshold were to be enacted by law, it would be very difficult for victims to take any action until the situation became extremely serious. Of course, it is noted that *any* attempt to set a threshold raises significant difficulties.

In terms of cyberstalking, the use of thresholds becomes even more difficult to support. It is possible, for example, for a cyberstalker to use software that automatically transmits messages over a period of time. Once the software has been configured, an abusive or threatening message might be sent each day, week, or month without any further intervention on the part of the harasser. In this case, it is difficult to determine whether this action constitutes a single incident or a number of separate incidents.[11]

Some definitions describe cyberstalking only in terms of the typical behaviors; for instance: "Cyberstalking refers to harassment on the Internet using various modes of transmission such as electronic mail (e-mail), chat rooms, newsgroups, mail exploders, and the World Wide Web" (Deirmenjian, 1999, p. 407). Although this definition is undoubtedly useful, it only describes a few of the behaviors commonly seen in cyberstalking cases and fails to explain what is meant by "harassment."

Perhaps one of the most useful definitions of cyberstalking comes from CyberAngels,[12] a highly regarded Internet safety organization. The CyberAngels web site lists a number of factors that must be considered when attempting to identify cases of cyberstalking:[13]

When identifying cyberstalking "in the field," particularly when considering whether to report it to any kind of legal authority, the following features or combinations of features can be considered to characterize a true stalking situation: Malice, Premeditation, Repetition, Distress, Obsession, Vendetta, No Legitimate Purpose, Personally Directed, Disregarded Warnings to Stop, Harassment, and Threats.

Not all of the factors listed must be present in every case of cyberstalking. In addition, each of the factors has been described in detail so that it becomes easier to identify genuine cases.

CyberAngels' material[14] has two important strengths. First, all of the material is directly relevant to cyberstalking. This is in contrast to most of the other definitions examined in this section, which are focused on offline stalking and have merely been extended to cover cyberstalking. Second, the material demonstrates a clear understanding of the behaviors associated with cyberstalking and of issues concerning modern technology. An example may help to make these points clearer. With regard to Premeditation, part of the explanation is as follows:

> Some kinds of harassment can be set in motion instantly and without preparation. Others take time to prepare. Some require the setting up and use of special hostile computer attack programs. Others may require extensive research into your personal information on the Internet.

However, victims of cyberstalking might object to some of the comments and clarifications made by CyberAngels. As an example, the following appears under Disregarded Warnings to Stop:

> You cannot claim that you are being stalked online if you have never said "Leave me alone" to the stalker. One standard defense used by stalkers in court is to claim that you were encouraging their attentions, and that you never said "NO."

This statement reduces the value of the guidelines since it raises three significant difficulties. First, the notion that victims of harassment should warn their harassers to stop contradicts the advice offered by other organizations. Internet Service Providers, for example, often advise users not to respond if a threatening or abusive message is received. Second, this view does not take into account other factors that might prevent a victim from issuing such a warning. As an example, a victim might be so frightened by messages received in chat room that he or she leaves immediately or disconnects the computer. Clearly, for these people, it would be unacceptable to suggest that they remain in the chat room so that they could ask the harasser to stop. Finally, perhaps the most obvious criticism of this statement regards the use of anonymous e-mail or false identities: if one cannot identify or contact the harasser, it becomes impossible to ask that person to stop the behavior.

Another area of criticism concerns the idea that harassment is always directed at a single individual. In the material published by CyberAngels, for example, the description for Personally Directed states: "Personal means: the harassment is directed at YOU personally" (original emphasis). However, there have been a number of cases in which a single individual has harassed groups of people. For example, the circumstances surrounding the allegations of harassment made by Cynthia Armistead and her family are fairly well-known, having been the subject of both criminal and civil legal action (Cynthia Armistead's story is described later in this chapter).

Despite these criticisms, the definition offered by CyberAngels makes an extremely important point. One of the factors that can help distinguish cyberstalking from offline stalking is the relationship between cyberstalking and the sexual abuse of children. According to CyberAngels, "CyberStalking usually occurs with women, who are stalked by men, or children who are stalked by adult predators."

A number of cases involving predators using the Internet as a means of contacting and locating children have garnered public attention. The arrest of Patrick Naughton, an InfoSeek executive, in 1999 is a typical example of such a case.[15] In many of these cases, the Internet has been used as a research tool, allowing an abuser to gather a great deal of information about the intended victim. Once a relationship has been established between the abuser and the victim, it becomes possible for the abuser to arrange a physical meeting. This form of behavior is very different from that typically associated with offline stalking and represents a threat that is just as serious.

The link between cyberstalking and the sexual abuse of children is also recognized by the U.S. government. As an example, in a report prepared by the U.S. attorney general on behalf of then vice president Al Gore, the following comments are made:

Although the Internet and other forms of electronic communication offer new and exciting opportunities for children, they also expose children to new threats. For example, Federal law enforcement agencies have encountered numerous instances in which adult pedophiles have made contact with minors through online chat rooms, established a relationship with the child, and later made contact for the purpose of engaging in criminal sexual activities. (Reno, 1999)

Perhaps the least helpful definitions of cyberstalking are those that consider it as nothing more than a variation on offline stalking. For example:

> Cyberstalking, which is simply an extension of the physical form of stalking, is where the electronic mediums such as the Internet are used to pursue, harass or contact another in an unsolicited fashion. (Petherick, 1999)

If this view is accepted, then cyberstalking represents nothing more than an additional behavior that may or may not be associated with physical forms of stalking. However, one of the main arguments made in this book is that cyberstalking represents a form of behavior that is distinct from offline stalking. As has been said, the differences between stalking and cyberstalking are such that both forms of behavior should be viewed as separate, but related, phenomena.

BEHAVIORS ASSOCIATED WITH CYBERSTALKING

Although there has been relatively little research into the behaviors associated with cyberstalking, it is possible to identify common themes by examining some of the personal accounts published via the Internet and news stories published by the media.

All of the behaviors listed in this section are easily found within the individual stories presented throughout this book. As an example, many of the behaviors described appear in Jayne Hitchcock's story. Her story is significant in that it is often considered to be the first cyberstalking case to receive national—and international—publicity. It should be noted that the descriptions given here are fairly brief since each behavior is discussed in more detail throughout the book.

Making threats. Most cyberstalking incidents involve the cyberstalker making threats against the victim, her family, or colleagues. In general, threats are made by e-mail or via instant messaging. Occasionally, a cyberstalker may use other methods, such as fax or text messaging.

False accusations. Many cyberstalkers attempt to harm the reputation of victims by posting false information about them. Often, the cyberstalker will use e-mail to make direct contact with relatives, friends, or colleagues of the victim. Sometimes, the cyberstalker will post false information to a newsgroup, chat room, or web site. There have also been cases of cyberstalkers establishing their own web sites in order to publish information about victims. In addition, some cyberstalkers attempt to escape blame for their actions by falsely claiming that their victims have harassed them. This is usually known as *false victimization* and has been noted in a number of well-known cases.[16] In fact, Mullen, Pathé, and Purcell devote a whole chapter to this topic in their book, *Stalkers and Their Victims* (2000).

Abusing the victim. Many cyberstalkers send their victims abusive or offensive messages via e-mail or instant messaging. E-mail messages are often accompanied by pornography or other offensive materials.

Attacks on data and equipment. Cyberstalkers may sometimes attempt to damage a victim's computer system, usually by transmitting a computer virus or other destructive program.

Attempts to gather information about the victim. Cyberstalkers use a variety of different methods in order to gather information about their victims. Some cyberstalkers may try to access information on the victim's computer through hacking or by using special software. Others may approach the victim's friends, relatives, or colleagues, posing as an old friend or business acquaintance. In some cases, cyberstalkers have even been known to hire private detectives or advertise for information via the Internet.

Impersonating the victim. Cyberstalkers often attempt to impersonate their victims in chat rooms and messages sent to newsgroups. This is usually done with the intention of humiliating the victim or encouraging other people to take part in the harassment. They may also impersonate the victim for other reasons, such as making fraudulent orders for goods or services.

Encouraging others to harass the victim. Many cyberstalkers find ways of using third parties to harass their victims. For instance, a common technique involves advertising a description of the victim together with her telephone number and a message suggesting that she is sexually available. Some victims have reported receiving hundreds of telephone calls and e-mail messages in reply to such ads. Cyberstalkers may also enlist the help of their friends or relatives, often by convincing them that the victim has harmed the cyberstalker or his family in some way. Involving third parties in harassment is usually called stalking-by-proxy.

Ordering goods or services on behalf of the victim. Some cyberstalkers cause annoyance or distress by ordering items on behalf of the victim. For instance, a cyberstalker may subscribe the victim to pornographic magazines or make multiple orders for expensive goods, so that the victim has to take the time and trouble to return them. Cyberstalkers have also been known to humiliate their victims by ordering embarrassing products, such as sex toys, and having them delivered to the victim's place of employment.

Arranging to meet the victim. There have been many cases in which cyberstalkers have traveled to meet their victims or vice versa. Young people face particular risk from pedophiles and other predators. (This topic is covered in more detail in chapter 7.)

Physical assault. Although such incidents are rare, cyberstalkers have sometimes attacked their victims.

A NEW DEFINITION OF CYBERSTALKING

As has been seen, any coherent and comprehensive definition of cyberstalking must take into account a wide range of issues. The definition must also try to meet the varying needs of a number of stakeholders, such as law enforcement agencies and academics. With this in mind, the following definition has been created:[17]

> A group of behaviors in which an individual, group of individuals, or organization uses information and communications technology to harass another individual, group of individuals, or organization. Such behaviors may include, but are not limited to, the transmission of threats and false accusations, identity theft, data theft, damage to data or equipment, computer monitoring, solicitation of minors for sexual purposes, and any form of aggression. Harassment is defined as a course of action that a reasonable person, in possession of the same information, would think causes another reasonable person to suffer emotional distress.

The first thing to note about this new definition is that it does not mention the Internet and does not use the term *computer*. This is in recognition of the fact that not all harassment involves a personal computer. Other forms of technology, such as fax machines and cell phones, can also be used. Similarly, not all threatening messages and other communications are sent via the Internet. For instance, company networks often feature when people are stalked in the workplace.

As mentioned earlier, all definitions of offline stalking assume that harassment is always carried out by a single individual. The definition provided here recognizes that harassment may be carried out by a group of people or an organization. Similarly, this definition recognizes that there may be more than one victim in a given case of cyberstalking, such as a family. The possibility that an organization, such as a government agency, can become a cyberstalking victim is also acknowledged. (Chapter 8 looks at corporate cyberstalking in more detail.)

The definition here provides a list of behaviors typically associated with cyberstalking for four main reasons. First, the list is intended to provide some guidance for those unfamiliar with ICT. Second, the behaviors described help to underscore the fact that cyberstalking is distinct from offline stalking. Third, the list is comprehensive, so that it includes all of the behaviors that one might expect to discover when investigating a typical incident. Finally, by emphasizing the behaviors associated with cyberstalking cases, I hope to reinforce the idea that not all cyberstalkers have mental health issues.

It is worth noting that some of the terms used in this definition are industry terms that are easily defined. The term *identity theft*, for example, refers to a range of activities that involve impersonating an individual or organization. Other terms have been selected to cover a variety of activities. For instance, *damage to data or equipment* includes acts ranging from vandalism to the transmission of a computer virus. In addition, the terms used have been chosen so that they are likely to remain relevant for a relatively long period of time.

The final section of the definition deals with issues arising from antistalking legislation, such as the notion that a credible threat must be made. Note that by imposing a test of "reasonableness," it becomes possible to avoid the difficulties associated with identifying genuine cases of cyberstalking. This approach is widely used and forms the basis of much of the legislation used in countries such as the United States and the United Kingdom.

This definition also acknowledges that some cases of cyberstalking may involve the solicitation of children for sexual purposes. The possibility that some cases of cyberstalking may eventually result in physical or sexual assault against the victim(s) is also covered. However, it should be noted that only a small number of cases are likely to involve any form of physical violence.

None of the definitions described within this chapter addresses the fact that offline stalking may sometimes develop into cyberstalking and vice versa. For instance, a person who sends poison-pen letters to his victim might eventually begin sending abusive e-mail messages. Alternatively, having harassed a work colleague via e-mail, a cyberstalker may choose to take more direct action, such as vandalizing the victim's car. The potential connection between the two is an important omission since it tends to reinforce the notion that stalking and cyberstalking are essentially the same. The definition given here should be taken to include a distinction between stalking and cyberstalking. This distinction is made by suggesting that a cyberstalking case is one in which the stalker begins to harass the victim via ICT and/or in which *most* of the harassment is based on the use of ICT.

CONCLUSION

We need a definition of cyberstalking to make sure that researchers, clinicians, law enforcement agencies, and others are all talking
about the same phenomenon. Unfortunately, there are many difficulties in arriving at a suitable definition. For instance, it is often difficult
to reach agreement over whether a given behavior can be associated
with cyberstalking.

Existing definitions of cyberstalking fail to address a number of
important issues, including the fact that many cases may involve attempts to solicit children for sexual purposes. In addition, all of the
definitions in common use assume that the victims of stalking are individuals. However, there is evidence to suggest that cyberstalking
sometimes involves small groups of people, such as individual families. Furthermore, organizations, such as companies, may also become
involved in cyberstalking.

Some people believe that cyberstalking is just another behavior that
can be associated with offline stalking. Put in more simple terms,
cyberstalking is just another way for a stalker to harass his victim.
Others, however, believe that cyberstalking is a completely new form
of deviant behavior, an idea supported by evidence suggesting that
some behaviors associated with offline stalking are seen more often or
have more serious effects in cyberstalking cases. In a cyberstalking
case, for example, spreading rumors about the victim is likely to result in more harm.

THE CYNTHIA ARMISTEAD STORY

Cynthia Armistead and her five-year-old daughter, Katie, were subjected to a sustained campaign of harassment that started in July 1996,
following an online argument with a man named Richard Hillyard.
According to Armistead, Hillyard began his vendetta by sending her
numerous messages that she felt were threatening. When she complained to Hillyard's Internet Service Provider, the company responded
by closing his account, but she then started to receive messages origi-
nating from the Centers for Disease Control and Prevention in
Atlanta—Hillyard's employer.

Armistead also began to receive obscene messages sent via anonymous remailers.[18] Someone using the nickname Dick Coward began
posting prostitution advertisements and other messages that gave
Armistead's e-mail address. Some messages were accompanied by
pictures of a nude woman with Armistead's photograph and name
attached (Raphael, 2000b). As a result, Armistead began to receive

sexually explicit messages from people responding to the ads. Someone also impersonated Armistead on IRC channels,[19] giving the impression that she was interested in having sexually explicit conversations with men. Furthermore, the ads suggested that she wanted to take part in phone sex or was willing to meet in person for sex. Consequently, Armistead received sexually explicit e-mail messages, including some containing pornographic images.

When the family began to receive strange telephone calls at all hours of day and night, Armistead changed her number several times, but the calls continued, suggesting that Dick Coward had found a way to obtain the family's unlisted telephone numbers.

The fear and distress suffered by Armistead and her daughter forced the family to move three times within a single year. Armistead also limited her activities on the Internet because she was concerned that there might be further attempts to harm her reputation. Eventually, Armistead became so concerned about her family's safety that she learned to use a firearm and obtained a permit to carry a concealed weapon.

Although Armistead had contacted the police early on, they seemed unable or unwilling to take action. However, when Armistead received an e-mail message claiming that she had been followed from her mailing address to her home, it became clear that the harassment had moved into the offline world, and the police began to take matters more seriously. In July 1997, Richard Hillyard was tried on charges of Harassing Phone Calls and Stalking. He was found not guilty on the charge of Harassing Phone Calls, and the charge of Stalking was dismissed (*Beloit Daily News*, 1997).

As of 2001, Armistead continued to be harassed from time to time. Her web site provides a detailed chronology of events and links Hillyard to a number of incidents.[20] Both Hillyard and Dick Coward maintain their own web sites that dispute Armistead's account of events. For instance, Hillyard claims that Armistead is harassing him and that her web site has endangered his family by publishing his address and telephone number.

2

Stalking or *Cyber*stalking?

THE JOHN ROBINSON (SLAVEMASTER) STORY

The case of John Edward Robinson, also known as the Slavemaster,[1] touches upon public fears that have been fueled by countless newspaper stories, television dramas, and feature films. Robinson was tried in June 2000 for the murder of five women he was alleged to have contacted via the Internet. However, it was suspected that he may have been responsible for as many as eleven deaths, including that of a baby girl (Milburn, 2000). In a strange turn of events, it was later found that although Robinson had murdered the mother, he had arranged for the child to be adopted by his brother for a fee of $5,500 (Wiltz, 2002).

Using a screen name of Slavemaster, Robinson contacted women who might be willing to act as "sex slaves" for him. The women were encouraged to meet Robinson through various inducements, including money and jobs. For example, one woman was offered $60,000 to move to Kansas to look after Robinson's diabetic, wheelchair-bound father. After murdering his victims, Robinson hid the bodies in barrels on his property (ABCNews.com, 2000a).

Robinson was caught after separate incidents involving two Texas women who had traveled to meet him to engage in sadomasochistic sex. Both women, who had originally made contact with Robinson via the Internet, complained that he had been more brutal than they had imagined. One of the women also claimed that Robinson stole sex toys worth more than $500 from her. As a result of the women's complaints, Robinson was arrested for aggravated sexual battery and felony theft. When investigators searched his rural property, they found the bodies he had hidden, and Robinson was then charged with murder. Following his trial in late 2002, Robinson was sentenced to the death penalty in early 2003 (CourtTV.com, 2003).

An unusual development related to the Slavemaster case concerns a chain letter that is occasionally circulated across the Internet. The letter is usually presented as an official warning from a law enforcement organization and recipients are encouraged to send copies of the document to all female friends, relatives, and colleagues. Clearly, many people would find the warnings contained within the letter extremely distressing:

> If a person with the screen-name of Slavemaster contacts you, do not reply. Do not talk to this person; do not answer any of his/her instant messages or e-mail. Whoever this person may be, he/she is a suspect for murder in the death of 56 women (so far) contacted through the Internet.[2]

These kinds of chain letters do a great deal to fuel public concern. However, it must be remembered that such chain letters often contain an element of truth. After all, the Slavemaster did actually exist and was responsible for a number of deaths.

The idea that a serial killer may have operated via the Internet is, understandably, one that has resulted in a great deal of public anxiety. Robinson's case demonstrates the relative ease with which the Internet can be used to locate victims. Furthermore, given that Robinson was fifty-six years old and not considered particularly attractive, his case also shows the ease with which an individual can construct a new, more attractive identity in order to entice potential victims.

INTRODUCTION

Is cyberstalking distinct from stalking? If so, what are the main differences between the two? In this chapter, I set out to distinguish between stalking and cyberstalking. Although the questions asked seem simple, they encourage discussion of some very complex issues.

In his interesting and influential book, *Crime and Everyday Life* (2002), leading U.S. criminologist Marcus Felson begins by listing ten fallacies about crime. By looking at common misconceptions about crime, he shows how easy it is to accept things at face value without really thinking about them. However, when these fallacies are named and described, it is both easier to identify them and easier to resist them.

Although this book does not claim to be in the same league as Felson's engaging discussion of the causes of crime, I make no apology for borrowing his idea and applying it in this chapter. In reading about cyberstalking, several ideas come up time and time again. First, there is the view that cyberstalking is just another behavior related to stalking. Those who support this view tend to argue that cyberstalkers are just stalkers who use modern technology as part of an overall pattern of harassment. Second, many people believe that cyberstalking is not as harmful as offline stalking, a perception often linked with the belief that cyberstalkers do not physically assault their victims. Finally, some people argue that cyberstalking is pathological in nature, implying that all cyberstalking results from some form of psychological problem, such as mental illness.

These fallacies are harmful in that they play down the scale and seriousness of the cyberstalking problem. In addition, they encourage people to divert attention and—even more important—resources away from the real problem. In this chapter, I hope to dispel seven common fallacies related to cyberstalking by encouraging readers to think for themselves about some of the claims made by various "experts."

SEVEN FALLACIES ABOUT CYBERSTALKING

The sections that follow are presented in no particular order, but taken as a whole, the seven fallacies make the case that cyberstalking should be seen as a unique form of deviant behavior. The list may eventually be expanded or condensed as the field of research advances in this area. Although it may be possible to counter some of the arguments, others remain difficult to dismiss. For instance, the view that cyberstalking can involve harassing a victim "sight unseen" is difficult to dispute and is a behavior not seen in cases of offline stalking.

1. Cyberstalking Is an Extension of Offline Stalking

As mentioned in chapter 1, some writers think of cyberstalking as nothing more than an extension of offline stalking. For these people, cyberstalking represents just another method used by stalkers to pursue their victims. For instance, a stalker might send an e-mail message instead of sending a handwritten poison-pen letter. However, there are several ways to argue that cyberstalking is a completely new form of deviant or criminal behavior.

First, the public, the press, and even governments seem to have made a distinction between stalking and cyberstalking. In personal web pages, victims describe themselves as cyberstalking victims, not as stalking victims. Similarly, in 1999, the U.S. Congress commissioned a report on cyberstalking, not stalking. This means that cyberstalking is accepted as being distinct from other forms of stalking.

Second, if cyberstalking is nothing more than an extension of offline stalking, it is difficult to explain the fact that many cyberstalkers harass their victims exclusively via the Internet. Put simply, how can cyberstalking be an extension of offline stalking if no offline stalking actually occurs?

Finally, the perception that cyberstalking is an extension of offline stalking seems to ignore the fact that as new forms of technology emerge, they are exploited through new forms of criminal or deviant behavior (Thomas and Loader, 2000; Smith, 1998). For instance, computer viruses simply did not exist prior to the early 1980s. They only began to appear once various circumstances became conducive to the creation and dissemination of such destructive programs. These circumstances included high levels of personal computer ownership and the availability of suitable distribution channels (such as e-mail).

Those who would argue that cyberstalking is merely regular stalking behavior that makes use of technology[3] must first explain why cyberstalking does not appear to have existed during the 1980s and early 1990s. After all, several writers have suggested that stalking has existed as a form of deviant behavior for many centuries (see Gallagher, 2001, p. 2, and Meloy, 1998b, p. xix). If so, then stalkers would have had the opportunity to make use of modern computer and telecommunications technology from the very beginning of the computer boom in the mid-1980s. It is also worth pointing out that although Internet use did not become common until the mid-1990s, networked computer systems have existed for several decades. It is likely that some stalkers would have adopted this technology for harassing people in the workplace. If cyberstalking is just stalking with modern technology, then the question that must be answered is simply this: Why did it take almost two decades for stalkers to start using modern technology such as e-mail, chat rooms, newsgroups, bulletin boards, and cell phones?

2. Cyberstalkers Are "Obsessional"

Some definitions of stalking suggest that cases must demonstrate some form of obsessional behavior on the part of the stalker. In general, this behavior is proven to exist when the stalker ignores one or more warnings related to his behavior. However, in the case of the

Internet, it is often impossible to contact a cyberstalker, as he will have protected his identity in various ways, for example by using an anonymous remailer. This raises two important points. First, some definitions of stalking assume that the stalker has mental health issues since his pursuit of a victim is described as "obsessional." There is a growing body of evidence to suggest that not all stalkers—and certainly not all cyberstalkers—have mental health problems.

Second, there is an assumption that stalkers and their victims are able to communicate with one another, otherwise it would not be possible to warn a stalker about his behavior. What is not dealt with is the notion of a stalker arranging circumstances so that only one-way communication is possible. For instance, as mentioned, a cyberstalker may use an anonymous remailer to issue threats, making it impossible for the victim to respond. And whereas it is true that many cases of offline stalking involve a stalker who attempts to remain anonymous, by acting in the physical world, for example by painting graffiti on the victim's house, the stalker risks being seen and possibly captured. These risks are much smaller when a cyberstalker operates via the Internet. To begin with, there is no risk of being "seen" while committing a criminal or deviant act. Furthermore, the time, effort, and expense involved in tracing an anonymous e-mail message may make it impossible to locate and capture the cyberstalker.

3. Cyberstalkers Know Their Victims

One of the most important differences between offline stalking and cyberstalking is that there is *always* some kind of relationship between the offline stalker and his victim. However, this is not necessarily the case in cyberstalking incidents.

> In general, stalkers always have had, or have, some form of physical or emotional relationship to their victims. For instance, the authors are not aware of any reported case where a stalker has not at least *seen* their victim, whether in a photograph, on television or in person. In contrast, there are many reported cyberstalking cases where the stalker has never seen the victim and where he may not have known even the most basic information—such as the age, gender or ethnicity of the victim. (Bocij and McFarlane, 2003b, p. 22)

A good example of this involves the case of a serial cyberstalker I dealt with a few years ago (Bocij, Bocij, and McFarlane, 2003). In this case, the cyberstalker selected his victims based solely on the information provided in an online directory. The ICQ (I-Seek-You) service allows people to chat with friends, family, and colleagues all over the world. A key feature of the service is the ability to create a personal profile in a special directory called the "white pages." Other ICQ users can then search the directory to find information on a given person or find people with similar interests. The cyberstalker used this directory to find victims who lived close to him and who had certain characteristics, such as belonging to a certain age group. There are two points that are important to note about this case. First, the cyberstalker relied completely on the white pages information to locate his victims. Although members can place pictures in the directory, none of his victims did so. This means that all the victims were chosen without the stalker ever setting eyes on them.

Second, the information entered into a white pages directory entry is not checked for accuracy. Hence, members can report a false gender, age, location, and so on. This means that the cyberstalker was able to present himself as an entirely different person because most of the people he dealt with relied only on the information in the white pages. Of course, this also meant that the cyberstalker could not be certain that his victims really were, say, females who lived in a certain area. This type of situation simply does not occur in the offline world. If this seems unclear, a simple example may help. It may seem nonsensical at first, but imagine the case of a mature male stalker posing as a teenage girl—talking to a mature male posing as a teenage girl. Of course, this could only happen in the online world, where it is often necessary to rely on the information given, rather than on what is observed firsthand. In fact, these kinds of situations already happen more often that might be imagined. For instance, an example from the United States was described like this: "One FBI agent pretending to be a teenage girl signed on to a chat room as the 23rd participant. All of the other 22 'teenagers' turned out to be adults seeking inappropriate contact with a teenage girl" (Hughes, 1999, p. 29).

4. Cyberstalkers Cause Less Harm Than Offline Stalkers

In cases of offline stalking, the concern is usually with two main types of harm. The first is physical assault. There have been many cases of stalking that have ended in a physical attack or even murder. The second is the emotional and psychological harm caused by an overall pattern of harassment that may include following the victim, vandalizing her property, or making silent phone calls.

It seems clear that cyberstalking victims are likely to suffer just as much psychological and emotional harm as victims of offline stalking.

Furthermore, it is important to understand that cases can end in a physical attack upon the victim. Sometimes, as in the tragic cases of Amy Boyer (discussed later in this chapter) and the serial killer known as the Slavemaster, cyberstalking can even result in murder. Fortunately, such attacks seem less common than in cases of offline stalking. There is no real evidence to support this observation other than the fact that newspapers seldom carry stories of cyberstalking cases that ended in murder. When such cases occur, they are rare enough to receive national—and even international—attention.

The emotional and psychological harm suffered by cyberstalking victims may often take different forms from that caused by offline stalking. In addition, there are likely to be many cases in which the harm caused by a cyberstalker is either more or less serious than the harm caused by an offline stalker. For instance, the use of the Internet as a means of harassing another person automatically places limitations on what can be done. If separated by a huge distance from his victim, a cyberstalker's choices are usually reduced to making threats, trading insults, or attempting to embarrass. Embarrassing or humiliating a person by posting rumors or other false information about her to a bulletin board, newsgroup, or chat room is sometimes called cyber-smearing. Cyber-smearing can also involve sending rumors and false information to the victim's friends, relatives, or work colleagues. The harm caused by cyber-smearing is often greater than equivalent offline acts, such as spraying graffiti on walls or sending poison-pen letters (Bocij, 2002).

5. Cyberstalkers Seldom Use Stalking-by-Proxy

If separated by distance, a cyberstalker may try to encourage others to pursue a victim for him. This behavior is known as stalking-by-proxy (Sheridan, Davies, and Boon, 2001; Pathé and Mullen, 1997). Although stalking-by-proxy is often carried out by friends and relatives of the stalker, some cyberstalkers are able to recruit complete strangers to help them. In some cases, for instance, stalkers have hired private detectives to help them find information about their victims (Pathé and Mullen, 1997).

On the other hand, the offline world offers relatively few opportunities to find people willing to participate in stalking-by-proxy. Stalking is like other forms of criminal or deviant behavior, such as the sexual abuse of children, in that it is generally seen as a solitary activity. For instance, I am unaware of any cases in which two or more stalkers have combined forces to pursue their victims. This is because opportunities to meet like-minded people are rare, and employing out-siders, such as private detectives, carries a great deal of risk. The Internet, however, makes it much easier for some people, such as pedophiles, to group together so that they can share resources and offer each other support and encouragement (Bocij and McFarlane, 2003a). It is also much easier for cyberstalkers to recruit complete strangers to help in pursuing a victim. This is often achieved by impersonating the victim in a newsgroup or message board and sending out abusive or inflammatory messages. By encouraging other users to become hostile to the victim, the cyberstalker is often able to incite a "flame war" that can quickly get out of hand.

Cyber-smearing and stalking-by-proxy can be thought of as being more serious than their equivalent offline acts because they can be carried out on a huge scale. For instance, the act of writing twenty poison-pen letters pales in comparison to a single e-mail message that might be read by thousands—or even millions—of people.

Scale is also relevant to the number of stalking versus cyberstalking victims. One of the arguments made throughout this book is that it is easier to become a cyberstalker than it is to become an offline stalker. This idea has many implications, such as raising the possibility that some cyberstalkers might pursue more than one victim at a time. If so, then there are likely to be more cyberstalkers and more cyberstalking victims than their offline equivalents. Earlier, it was mentioned that some people feel that the victims of offline stalking tend to suffer more harm than the victims of cyberstalking. Although this is not the view taken throughout this book, it helps to raise an important question concerning the harm suffered by victims of stalking and cyberstalking. The question to consider is this: Which is more serious, a smaller group of people suffering a great deal of harm or a larger group of people suffering a little less harm? Of course, the answer proposed here is that neither situation is acceptable.

6. Cyberstalkers Do Not Make "Credible Threats"

A major difference between stalking and cyberstalking is that it is possible for a cyberstalker to pursue a victim located in another coun-try. Assuming that the cyberstalker and the victim share a common language, it is just as easy for a cyberstalker to harass a victim in New York as it is for him to pursue someone in Paris. Most behaviors asso-ciated with stalking, such as vandalism, can be replicated via the Internet. For instance, vandalism can take the form of damaging the victim's data, usually with the help of a virus or Trojan horse program.

Perhaps the only behavior that cannot be duplicated via the Internet is a physical assault on the victim. However, as will be shown, distance is not necessarily a reliable barrier between a cyberstalker and his victim.

Those who believe that cyberstalking is not as serious as offline stalking often draw on the notion of a "credible threat" to support their arguments. In the United States, many state antistalking laws mandate that a credible threat of violence must be made against the victim before any action can be taken against a stalker. In a report to Congress on stalking and domestic violence, U.S. Attorney General John Ashcroft noted:

> In the context of cyberstalking, a credible threat requirement would be even more problematic because the stalker, sometimes unknown to the victim, may be located a great distance away and, therefore, the threat might not be considered credible. (Ashcroft, 2001, p. 45)

This argument can be broken down into two parts. First, a victim of cyberstalking may not know the identity of the stalker. Second, if there is a great distance between the victim and the cyberstalker, it is assumed that the cyberstalker is unlikely to make a physical attack on the victim.

The first part of this argument can be dealt with very easily by suggesting that not knowing the identity of the criminal does not mean that the crime cannot be investigated. For example, a person reporting a break-in would not be expected to name the burglar before the police agreed to investigate. In addition, it can be argued that investigators should err on the side of caution. Only when the cyberstalker has been identified should the credibility of any threats made be assessed.

The second part of the argument is also easy to deal with. There have been a number of cases in which cyberstalkers have traveled long distances to attack their victims or—perhaps more significantly—in which victims have traveled long distances to meet their cyberstalker. For example, in the case of John Edward Robinson—the notorious Slavemaster—some of his victims traveled from as far away as California and Texas to Kansas, where they were murdered. In another case, Lindsay Shamrock ran away from home, traveling all the way from Florida to Greece in order to be with a cyberstalker she believed she was in love with (see chapter 7). In an unusual case, it is alleged that an Australian cyberstalker waited a number of years for his Canadian victim to come to *him* (Stangret, 2001). Sara Ballingall, a

Canadian actress who appeared in the hit TV show *Degrassi High*, alleged that Brian Andrew Sutcliffe of Melbourne had stalked her while she was in Australia. Although Sutcliffe was not prosecuted, a Canada-wide warrant for his arrest was issued in case he followed the actress back to Canada.

The increase in low-cost airfares also makes it easier for cyber-stalkers to physically confront their victims. In Europe, for example, even those receiving unemployment benefits can probably afford the cost of a plane ticket from, say, London to Rome.[4]

7. Cyberstalkers Share the Same Motivations as Offline Stalkers

The literature dealing with stalking and cyberstalking gives the overwhelming impression that all of those engaged in stalking-related activities have mental health issues. This is understandable as most of the available literature stems from the field of psychology and tends to focus on the most unusual cases. Meloy's work, for example, focuses on areas such as the stalking of clinicians by their patients, and Mullen, Pathé, and Purcell concentrate almost exclusively on the cases referred to their clinic. However, it is important to emphasize that, more than likely, not all of those involved in activities such as cyberstalking have mental health issues. There is a great deal of evidence to support the view that cyberstalking is often used as a tool intended to achieve specific goals.

For example, cyberstalking can involve companies and organizations as both victims and cyberstalkers. The motives behind corporate cyberstalking can be very different from those behind offline stalking (Bocij, 2002). Corporate cyberstalking involves an individual, a group, or an organization pursuing another individual, group, or organization. Sometimes, the motive behind corporate cyberstalking can be political, for profit, or for competitive advantage. (See chapter 8 for a detailed discussion of corporate cyberstalking.)

Politically motivated cyberstalking can involve acts that some people might describe as terrorism. For instance, "hacktivism" can involve attacking company or government web sites in order to make a political point.

Some cases of corporate cyberstalking involve actions designed to make profits or protect a company's business activities. For example, some forms of online stock fraud can include posting false rumors to financial web sites, chat rooms, bulletin boards, and newsgroups in order to artificially inflate or deflate prices.

Furthermore, an organization can use cyberstalking to achieve a strategic advantage over another. For example, a dispute between British Airways and Virgin Atlantic allegedly involved "poaching Virgin's passengers, hacking into computers and feeding stories to the media" (BBC Online Network, 1999).

Some writers have suggested that some people may begin cyberstalking for relatively trivial reasons, such as a desire for attention. Some of these motives are not seen in cases of offline stalking. For instance, one writer notes:

> Looking for similarities with real-life stalkers can be misleading. A stalker usually has a real perceived relationship of love or hate with the person they're stalking. A cyberstalker may be simply playing games, trying to demonstrate how clever they are at your expense, or merely killing time. Protected by one of a hundred fake identities and email addresses, they seem to possess infinite patience and relentless energy. In many ways, they have more in common with hackers. (Anderiesz, 2002)

It is also important to remember that many people link cyberstalking with the sexual abuse of children. As mentioned, this link has been formally recognized by the U.S. government. Although this quotation also appeared in chapter 1, it is critical enough to bear repeating:

> Although the Internet and other forms of electronic communication offer new and exciting opportunities for children, they also expose children to new threats. For example, Federal law enforcement agencies have encountered numerous instances in which adult pedophiles have made contact with minors through online chat rooms, established a relationship with the child, and later made contact for the purpose of engaging in criminal sexual activities. (Reno, 1999)

CONCLUSION

The fallacies associated with cyberstalking tend to divert attention away from important issues, such as the harm caused to victims. Perhaps the most important of these is the claim that cyberstalking is an extension of offline stalking. However, there are several questions that must be answered before such an assertion can be accepted.

There is a common misconception that all stalkers and cyberstalkers are obsessional, implying that they have some form of mental health problem. However, some cyberstalkers can be described as being very rational since they may be motivated by a desire to make a financial profit or to achieve a political goal.

In general, cyberstalkers harm their victims in the same ways as offline stalkers. However, cyberstalking places a natural emphasis on certain forms of behavior that are easier to carry out or that cause more harm to the victim. For instance, cyberstalkers are less likely to confront their victims in person but are more likely to use cyber-smearing because it is easier to carry out and tends to cause the victim more distress than equivalent offline acts (such as sending poison-pen letters). However, it is crucial to keep in mind that cyberstalking *can* move to the offline world.

The notion of a "credible threat" requires that the victim be in fear of being physically attacked. Many people feel that cyberstalkers cannot make credible threats because they are often separated from their victims by long distances. However, as many cases have shown over the past few years, this is simply untrue. The case of John Edward Robinson is just one example in which distance did not prevent a cyberstalker from luring his victims to meet him in person.

Having looked at the nature of cyberstalking, and having shown that some cases can result in very serious outcomes, as in the case of Amy Boyer, the next chapter attempts to show the size of this problem.

THE AMY BOYER STORY

The tragic murder of Amy Boyer was one of the first cyberstalking cases to gain widespread media attention.[5] Boyer's case is also credited with encouraging attempts to introduce legislation intended to combat cyberstalking and protect personal privacy.

Amy Boyer was a twenty-year-old student in her final year of dental hygiene school. Boyer was widely regarded as a well-liked and highly motivated young woman. She had a regular boyfriend and was supporting her studies by working two part-time jobs. In October 1999, a fellow student, Liam Youens, waited for Boyer to leave work, then drove his car so that it was positioned directly opposite to Boyer's, preventing her from being able to open her door. He called her name to draw her attention and then shot her through the car window. A few moments later, he turned the gun on himself and ended his own life (Spencer, 2002).

As Boyer's family, the police, and the media began to look into the murder, a number of disturbing facts emerged (Spencer, 2002; ABCNews.com, 2000b). First, it was discovered that Youens, unbeknownst to Boyer, had been following her movements for more than four years. Although Boyer never knew Youens, he had become infatuated with her after seeing her once at school (Hitchcock, 2000). Second,

Youens had been able to obtain confidential information about Boyer from various Internet services, including her social security number and her work address. Third, Youens had been keeping a diary on the World Wide Web that detailed his obsession.[6] The diary contained information about how Youens had been watching Boyer for several years and how he felt about her. Furthermore, it appeared that the diary had been online for at least two years. Finally, the most disturbing fact of all was that Youens's plan to murder Boyer was also contained on the web site. The plan was explained in detail and was eventually carried out exactly as described. It is not known whether there were any visitors to the web site, but if there were, none seems to have taken the plan seriously enough to contact the police.

3

The Incidence and Prevalence of Cyberstalking

THE DIANA NAPOLIS (CURIO) STORY

"Curio" was the nickname used by a woman who harassed a group of people over a period of five years. Curio's harassment grew out of a number of ritual abuse scandals that emerged in the 1980s and early 1990s. Many people, including psychotherapists and police officers, believed they had evidence that secret cults had taken over many day-care centers and were abusing young children in horrific rituals. It was claimed that many of these cults were made up of satanists and that their rituals involved human sacrifice, torture, cannibalism, and sexual abuse (Sauer, 2000). In addition to a number of cases in the United States, similar incidents took place in Canada, the United Kingdom, and Australia. In the mid-1990s, mental health experts and law enforcement agencies finally discredited the idea of widespread satanic ritual abuse. A number of highly publicized trials had ended in acquittals for lack of evidence, and several studies had found no sign that organized groups, satanic or otherwise, were taking part in ritualized abuse. For example, a ten-year investigation by the FBI found little evidence to support the notion of any widespread conspiracy.

Despite the evidence, Curio still believed that children were being subjected to ritual abuse and claimed to be able to document fifty cases worldwide. In her view, many of those working to discredit the idea of satanic ritual abuse were doing so because they themselves were child abusers or part of a larger conspiracy to mislead the public. In order to protect young victims, Curio began to post information about these people to the Internet.

One of Curio's targets was Carol Hopkins, a former school administrator and a member of a San Diego County grand jury that criticized the child protection system after investigating allegations that social workers had removed children from their homes without good reason. Hopkins later formed the Justice Committee and publicized what she felt were false allegations of child abuse around the United States. Curio blamed Hopkins and two reporters for misleading the public about ritual abuse in San Diego for almost six years. Over time Curio made a number of allegations against Hopkins, including that she was a child molester and was attempting to protect other molesters. As a result of the harassment, Hopkins eventually gave up the Justice Committee and moved to Mexico. However, she still remained a target for Curio, who continued to post messages about her.

Another of Curio's targets was Elizabeth Loftus, a professor of psychology at the University of Washington. Loftus had written articles and books challenging the idea that the traumatic experiences of child abuse victims can act to repress memories of the abuse. Loftus had also testified in several trials, in which she explained how the memories of young people could be easily manipulated, even by those with good intentions.

On one occasion, Loftus traveled to address the New Zealand Psychology Society but found herself involved in an argument concerning an allegation that she was conspiring to help child molesters. The argument was partly caused by Curio's postings, which had influenced a story in the *Wellington Evening Post* and had been discussed on various talk shows. According to Loftus, some of the people attending her speech were met by individuals carrying twenty-seven-page booklets that made a number of allegations against her. Much of the information contained within the booklets had been compiled from the Internet and postings made by Curio.

Curio was careful to protect her identity by using computers located in public places, including cybercafés, libraries, and health centers. However, she was eventually caught in 2000 by Michelle Devereaux, a woman with twenty years of experience in the computer field and who had once believed herself to have been a victim of ritual abuse. Devereaux was able to trace Curio's posts to specific computers and even devised a way of monitoring Curio's messages, so that a message was sent to her pager each time a new post was made. Working with the San Diego State University (SDSU) police, Devereaux eventually managed to catch Curio in a computer lab on campus.

Curio was revealed to be Diana Napolis, a forty-four-year-old woman from La Mesa, California. Napolis had been a child protection worker for a number of years but had left that position in 1996. This matched information given in some of Curio's posts, where she had revealed that she had worked in the child abuse field for ten years and had a personal background in the occult. When questioned about her behavior, Napolis denied that she had harassed other people, insisting that all she had done was post messages and information. Although no charges were filed against Napolis, many of those she had harassed no longer considered her a serious threat because her identity was now known.

Little more was heard from Napolis until late 2002, when she was arrested on charges of (offline) stalking and making death threats against actress Jennifer Love Hewitt. In court, Napolis accused both Steven Spielberg and Jennifer Love Hewitt of being part of a satanic conspiracy, suggesting that they were manipulating her body through "cybertronic" technology (Sauer, 2002). In March 2003, Napolis was committed to a state hospital for up to three years, or until deemed fit to stand trial (SignOnSanDiego.com, 2003).

INTRODUCTION

How many cyberstalkers are there? How many victims of cyberstalking are there? Many estimates have been produced that claim to describe the prevalence of cyberstalking within the United States and other countries. Although some of these estimates have become accepted through being published in official government reports, they can be criticized for being little more than guesses.

This chapter discusses many of the cyberstalking estimates commonly cited by government departments, Internet safety organizations, the media, and researchers. It is shown that all of these estimates are flawed in one way or another, usually because they are based on assumptions that have not been proven to be true.

Having looked at figures describing the extent of stalking and cyberstalking in the United States, the United Kingdom, and other countries, I conclude by offering a more conservative estimate of the number of cyberstalking incidents that take place each year. Although the figure proposed may fall far short of the actual number of incidents, it supports the view that cyberstalking represents a significant problem.

THE EXTENT OF OFFLINE STALKING

Cyberstalking is clearly distinguishable from offline stalking. It tends to be easier and less risky than offline stalking. For instance, the offline stalker must physically follow his victim, perhaps taking time away from work to do so and possibly raising the suspicions of colleagues or the employer. This kind of surveillance may involve a high risk of being seen or caught. It may also become expensive, for example, if the stalker needs to follow the victim to a distant location. On the other hand, most of a cyberstalker's activities can be carried out from the comfort of his own home. Gathering information about a victim, for example, becomes a case of accessing various databases or intercepting e-mail messages. The risk of detection is relatively low and the cyberstalker can actually use technology to reduce the work involved in his pursuit of a victim.

A good example of this involves the case of a serial cyberstalker I worked on a few years ago. The cyberstalker made use of technology in order to find out a great deal of information about his victims. For instance, the cyberstalker was able to follow the movements of a victim by using Trojan horse software to monitor e-mail messages and other communications. In writing about this case, I argued that cyberstalking

> might easily involve a single individual harassing a relatively large number of victims over a comparatively short period of time. More disturbingly [is] . . . the prospect of a single individual harassing a number of victims simultaneously. Related to this point is the possibility that technology may serve to remove potential barriers for stalkers, enabling them to conduct their activities with a business-like efficiency. (Bocij, Bocij, and McFarlane, 2003, p. 32)

If cyberstalking is easier to carry out than offline stalking, this might be reflected in the figures provided in this chapter. On the one hand, if offline stalking and cyberstalking are closely related, the figures that show how common each activity is might be similar. On the other hand, if cyberstalking is significantly different from offline stalking, one activity might be shown to be more common than the other one. In both cases, it is worth taking a little time to see how common stalking incidents are in the United States and other countries.

The United States

A 1999 report prepared by former attorney general Janet Reno and the U.S. Department of Justice, *Cyberstalking: A New Challenge for Law*

Enforcement and Industry, is often cited in newspaper, magazine, and journal articles about cyberstalking. In addition to providing various statistics, the report attempts to link offline stalking with cyberstalking by suggesting that "data on offline stalking may provide some insight into the scope of the cyberstalking problem" (Reno, 1999). However, this argument needs to be viewed with caution because there seems little evidence to suggest that stalking and cyberstalking are directly comparable. However, it is accepted that gaining an insight into offline stalking may provide a *context* for a discussion of cyberstalking.

The Department of Justice report draws on a National Violence Against Women Survey[1] and presents some of the findings. Essentially, the report suggests that "one out of every 12 women (8.2 million) and one out of every 45 men (2 million) have been stalked at some time in their lives." Furthermore, the report states that "one percent of all women and 0.4 percent of all men were stalked during the preceding 12 months."

Brian Spitzberg (2002), a researcher from San Diego State University, has suggested that stalking may be more widespread than commonly thought. In a meta-analysis of 103 studies of stalking, he found that stalking had affected 23.5 percent of women and 10.5 percent of men. His findings suggest that 20 percent of the population have been stalked at some time in their lives. Spitzberg's findings are given weight by the fact that the studies he has analyzed represent a total of almost 70,000 participants.

There is some evidence to suggest that the number of stalking incidents may vary from one part of the United States to another. For instance, the Massachusetts Medical Society (2000) reported on a study showing that 15 percent of women in Louisiana had been stalked during their lifetime. This value is significantly higher than for the National Institute of Justice survey, which found that only 8 percent of women had been stalked at some time in their lives (Klein, 1998).

There is also evidence to suggest that the frequency of stalking may vary according to age and gender. A study of college students, for example, found that 26.67 percent of females and 14.7 percent of males reported that they had been stalked (Fremouw, Westrup, and Pennypacker, 1997). A second study by the same researchers found even higher rates of stalking: 35.2 percent for females and 18.4 percent for males.

The United Kingdom

Few sources exist on which to base the extent of stalking within the United Kingdom. Perhaps the best known source of statistics is the

British Crime Survey (BCS), an annual survey of approximately 15,000 adults living in England and Wales. The 1998 BCS paid specific attention to stalking and published a number of useful statistics. It was reported that 2.9 percent of the population had been victimized in the previous year, equivalent to approximately 900,000 individuals (Budd and Mattinson, 2000). However, since the survey used a broad definition of stalking, the number of incidents that might represent a criminal offense was somewhat smaller, ranging between 2.6 percent and 1.9 percent, depending on whether the incident resulted in distress or fear or involved a threat of violence (Budd, Mattinson, and Myhill, 2000).

In general, 11.8 percent of the population had been stalking victims. This compares well with statistics reported earlier for the United States. For instance, the National Institute of Justice survey suggests that 10.3 percent of the population have been victims of stalking in their lifetimes (Reno et al., 1998). In fact, a little before the BCS figures were released *The* (London) *Times* stated:

> Statistics from America suggest that 8 per cent of women and 2 per cent of men have been stalked at some time in their lives. There are no figures for Britain but there is no reason to think they would be substantially different. (Ahuja, 2000)

As in the United States, the BCS data indicate that women and young people are more likely to become victims of stalking: "Women (4.0%) were more likely to have experienced persistent and unwanted attention than men (1.7%). Risks were particularly high for young women aged between 16 and 19 (16.8%)" (Budd and Mattinson, 2000, p. 1).

It is disappointing to find that the 1998 British Crime Survey fails to take into account modern technology, such as fax machines, e-mail, pagers, and so on. This omission makes it difficult to estimate how many people use technology to harass their victims. Furthermore, it is not possible to estimate how many individuals use the Internet as the *only* instrument by which they carry out harassment. However, it might be suggested that the use of e-mail, instant-messaging software, and other services to harass victims could be compared to silent or threatening telephone calls. If this is the case, then it may be possible to gain some idea of the scale of cyberstalking within the United Kingdom. According to the 1998 survey, some 43 percent of victims reported receiving ten or more silent telephone calls, and 26 percent reported receiving ten or more threatening telephone calls. This might be taken to suggest that cyberstalking occurs far less frequently than offline stalking, although the number of potential victims remains relatively high. However, in offering this comparison, it is recognized that such an approach is similar to the "back of the envelope" method mentioned later and that it should be treated with a great deal of caution.

Canada

Canada does not have a specific stalking offense. Instead, stalking is dealt with under the offense of Criminal Harassment.

Official figures show a year-on-year increase in the number of stalking cases dealt with by the police. For instance, cases of criminal harassment rose by approximately one-third over the period 1996 to 1999, increasing from 4,071 to 5,382 (Humphreys, 2000). Between 1999 and 2000, a further increase of 16 percent was recorded, representing a total increase of 50 percent between 1996 and 2000 (Statistics Canada, 2001).

Given the size of Canada's population,[2] stalking appears to be less common than in the United States, United Kingdom, and Australia. However, all of these figures must be treated with caution. First, the figures relate only to incidents dealt with by the police—there were likely many unreported cases. Second, the figures cited were drawn from only part of Canada's police services (41 percent in 2000). Finally, in terms of the increases described, the Canadian Center for Justice Statistics warns: "It is difficult to determine if this represents a real increase in stalking behavior or reflects greater awareness and reporting of this relatively new offence" (Statistics Canada, 2001).

Australia

A survey conducted by the Australian Bureau of Statistics found that 15 percent of women reported being stalked at some time in their lives. A further 2.4 percent reported being stalked in the twelve months preceding the survey. Women aged eighteen to twenty-four were more likely to be stalked than older groups (Mullen, Pathé, and Purcell, 2000, p. 30).

More recent figures come from a study of 3,700 adults carried out by Purcell, Pathé, and Mullen (2002). This study found that 23.4 percent of respondents had been stalked at some time in their lives. In keeping with the trends described for the United States and the United Kingdom, women were twice as likely as men to report being stalked, and younger people were more likely to be stalked than older people.

THE EXTENT OF CYBERSTALKING

The report prepared by Reno and the U.S. Department of Justice is careful to avoid presenting any firm figures with regard to cyberstalking:

> Assuming the proportion of cyberstalking victims is even a fraction of the proportion of persons who have been the victims of offline stalking within the preceding 12 months, there may be potentially tens or even hundreds of thousands of victims of recent cyberstalking incidents in the United States. (Reno, 1999)

This relatively simplistic observation is supported with the use of estimates prepared by CyberAngels, arguably the largest and best-known Internet safety organization in the world. The organization is supported by thousands of volunteers and reportedly deals with as many as 500 cases of cyberstalking each day (Dean, 2000). According to CyberAngels, there are approximately 63,000 stalkers on the Internet, pursuing approximately 474,000 victims (Aftab, 2001).

Unfortunately, when one looks more closely at how CyberAngels arrived at these figures, doubt must be cast on their validity. Indeed, even the attorney general's report advises caution:

> Although such a "back of the envelope" calculation is inherently uncertain and speculative (given that it rests on an assumption about very different populations), it does give a rough sense of the potential magnitude of the problem. (Reno, 1999)

CyberAngels argues that statistics related to offline stalking can be applied directly to the Internet. The group's discussion on the subject begins by suggesting that there are 200,000 stalkers active in the United States today out of a population of approximately 250 million. In addition, approximately 1.5 million Americans have been or are currently stalking victims. These figures already differ from those quoted within the attorney general's report. However, they are worth examining further as they can be used to illustrate the logic behind CyberAngels' argument.

By manipulating the values described, CyberAngels manages to arrive at some simple ratios that can be used to describe the situation a little more clearly:

- Approximately 1 in every 1,250 persons is a stalker, equivalent to approximately 0.08% of the population.

- Approximately 1 in every 166 persons is a victim of stalking, equivalent to approximately 0.6 percent of the population.

These ratios are then applied directly to the Internet, based on an estimated global user base of 79 million. The result suggests that there are approximately 63,000 stalkers and 474,000 victims in the world today. These estimates raise a number of difficulties that seem to have been overlooked by other writers and researchers.

As mentioned earlier, it is common to assume that *stalking* and *cyberstalking* are synonymous and that the meaning of each term has a clear definition. However, this is not necessarily the case. Cyberstalking can involve many different forms of behavior and has numerous unique characteristics that can be used to differentiate it from offline stalking. For instance, in cases of cyberstalking, the use of the Internet allows the victim and the stalker to be located in different countries. Even assuming that the population of the United States shares a common meaning for terms such as *stalking*, *harassment*, and *cyberstalking*, other countries do not. This makes it difficult to generalize findings from the United States to other nations, such as the United Kingdom and Australia.

The estimates produced by CyberAngels also appear to be based on a number of other assumptions. As an example, the assertion that there are 200,000 stalkers in the United States is not accompanied by any supporting evidence. Given some of the other estimates available from various sources, it can be argued that this figure may be an extreme value. For instance, the National Institute of Justice has reported that "estimates of the number of stalkers in the United States vary from 20,000 to 200,000" (Travis, 1996).

Similarly, the suggestion that 1.5 million Americans have been or are currently stalking victims is not in keeping with other, more accepted estimates. It has already been pointed out, for example, that the U.S. Department of Justice reported in 1998 that 0.4 percent of men and 1 percent of women are stalked each year (Reno et al., 1998). Based on a population of approximately 250 million people, this is equivalent to 3.5 million victims each year.

Returning to the issue of how cyberstalking can be defined, the report also makes the point that a less rigid definition would result in vastly different figures. Using a more relaxed definition, it can be suggested that 6 percent of women and 1.5 percent of men are stalked each year. Based on a population of approximately 250 million people, this is equivalent to 18.75 million victims each year.

CyberAngels' claim that the global number of Internet users stands at approximately 79 million is also open to dispute. NUA Internet Surveys[3] collects and distributes survey information via a web site and a series of regular newsletters. The company has collected a number of estimates concerning the number of Internet users throughout the world and within individual countries. As of August 2001, the company estimated the total number of Internet users across the world at approximately 513 million (NUA Internet Surveys, 2003). If the estimates offered by CyberAngels are applied to this figure, the number of cyberstalkers operating in 2001 stood at approximately 410,000, and the number of victims stood at approximately 3.1 million.

NUA also supplies figures for the total number of Internet users in the United States. As of August 2001, this figure stood at 166.14 million users. If the estimates offered by CyberAngels are applied to this figure, the number of cyberstalkers operating in the United States in 2001 stood at approximately 132,000 and the number of victims at a little over 1 million.

In defense of CyberAngels, the figure of approximately 79 million Internet users in the United States was accurate up to August 1998 (NUA Internet Surveys, 2003). However, it must be noted that Cyber-Angels' estimates do not appear to have been updated since that time, yet they continue to be published via the Internet and other sources. Even if one accepts that the estimates were accurate as of 1998, they are clearly no longer valid.

As of February 2003, NUA reported the total number of Internet users in the world at 605.6 million and the number of U.S. users at 165.75 million.[4] Using the method employed by CyberAngels suggests a world total of approximately 484,000 cyberstalkers and approximately 3.6 million victims. In the United States, there would be approximately 132,000 cyberstalkers and 1 million victims.

The impact of the alternative values of CyberAngels' estimates is significant. On the one hand, the number of stalkers may be many times larger or smaller than suggested by CyberAngels. More disturbingly, most of the alternative values discussed suggest that the number of victims may be many times higher than claimed.

It has already been argued that the Internet removes many of the barriers that might normally prevent a stalker from pursuing a victim, such as allowing the stalker to obtain confidential information about a victim inexpensively, quickly, and easily (Bocij and McFarlane, 2002b). These factors might encourage some people to harass others using the Internet, even though they might not contemplate such action in the offline world. If this is the case, then it might be expected that there would be a higher proportion of stalkers operating via the Internet than in the real world. It might also be expected that cases of serial stalking or even cases where a single person pursues a number of victims simultaneously would be found. The Diana Napolis case provides a good example of someone who might be described as a serial stalker.

The estimates provided by CyberAngels should be treated with caution because of the way in which they have been produced. By relying on unproven assumptions and suspect statistics, the organization may have served to misinform the public about the true extent of the problem. This might result in the problem of cyberstalking being overlooked or—more likely—becoming a moral panic. As an example, a journalist named Lewis Koch (2000a, 2000b) has argued that there is little justification for the public hysteria he claims has become associated with cyberstalking. He argues that many of the estimates that have appeared in the media are inaccurate, misleading, or simply not supported by evidence. Estimates cited in newspapers and on television programs provide a good example.

> The alleged number of stalkers in the U.S. is 200,000. That number has been floating around for eight years. The reporter who first reported it in 1992 can't exactly recall his source. Oprah Winfrey and Sally Jessy [sic] Raphael picked it up that year. (Koch, 2000a)

Koch (2000a, 2000b) also criticizes the Department of Justice and CyberAngels for relying too heavily on a telephone survey carried out by the University of Cincinnati that addressed the sexual victimization of female students. According to Koch, the study found that 24.7 percent of stalking incidents involved e-mail, but the finding was interpreted as meaning that approximately 25 percent of all stalking incidents involved cyberstalking. Furthermore, the survey only contained a few questions relevant to cyberstalking, was not based on a representative sample, and collected no corroborating data, such as copies of e-mail messages. Koch suggests that those who have relied on the results of the survey may have contributed to the hysteria surrounding cyberstalking, effectively confusing the issues that are of real concern. With regard to the study itself, he states:

> What we're left with is a suspicious statistical extrapolation and a nearly nonexistent, shockingly weak study of cyberstalking that wasn't even a study of cyberstalking in the first place. (Koch, 2000a)

The ability to produce somewhat dubious estimates related to cyberstalking is more widespread than might be imagined. A good example is an article produced by TheGuardianAngel.com, in which a series of crude calculations similar to those performed by Cyber-Angels results in the somewhat shocking claim that there are more than 10 million cyberstalking victims in the United States and Canada alone (Hook, 2000). Oddly, the material seems to contradict itself by then suggesting that there are only 225 victims of cyberstalking each day (Hook, 2000).

PREVALENCE OF CYBERSTALKING

If it is accepted that existing estimates of cyberstalking may not be reliable, then a simple question remains unanswered: How common are cyberstalking incidents? Furthermore, how many victims of cyber-stalking exist and how many cyberstalkers are active in the world to-day? Clearly, given that very little research has been conducted in this field, it is impossible to provide firm figures related to the number of cyberstalking incidents that occur each year. At best, it is possible to arrive at only some very crude estimates that may help to illustrate the overall scale of the problem.

One way to develop an estimate of the scale of the cyberstalking problem is by considering the number of cases dealt with by two of the largest Internet safety organizations, CyberAngels and Women Halting Online Abuse (WHOA). As mentioned earlier, CyberAngels deals with approximately 500 cases of cyberstalking each day, of which 65 to 100 represent genuine cases. WHOA reports dealing with ap-proximately 100 new cases each week.[5] Taking the lower value for CyberAngels, this means that approximately 30,000 cases of cyber-stalking are dealt with each year by these organizations.

Another source of statistics is InterGOV International, a division of which is the relatively well-known Web Police organization. Web Police maintains branches around the world and is represented in most major countries, including the United States, Canada, the United King-dom, Australia, and Europe. Established in 1986, Web Police is one of the oldest, largest, and well-respected Internet safety organizations in the world.

According to its own figures,[6] Web Police receives 3,704 criminal and civil complaints each day, amounting to more than 1.3 million incidents each year. Of these incidents, only 31 percent are considered valid in terms of being Internet related. Of the remaining total, 17 percent of complaints concern child pornography, 11 percent stalking, 9 percent harassment or threats, and 2 percent chat-room abuse. It is unusual that Web Police sees the behaviors listed as entirely separate from one another. For instance, it seems reasonable to suggest that harassment is similar to stalking.

Upon closer examination, the figures reveal that 1,148 valid complaints are received every day by the various branches of Web Police. Of these, 195 concern child pornography, 126 stalking, 103 harassment or threats, and 23 chat-room abuse. In total, around 46,000 stalking-related complaints are received each year. Encouragingly, Web Police reports a success rate of 87 percent, meaning that most valid complaints are resolved satisfactorily.

Taking into account all of the figures derived from CyberAngels, WHOA, and Web Police, there are at least 76,000 complaints related to cyberstalking each year. By extending the figures from Web Police to include harassment and chat-room abuse, there are approximately 122,000 cyberstalking incidents each year. However, in order to avoid claims of exaggeration, the lower of these two values will be used here.

Several points must be kept in mind when considering these figures. First, it should be remembered that both CyberAngels and WHOA are based within the United States and that the majority of the cases they deal with will involve Internet users living there. Although the figures given here go some way toward illustrating the extent of the problem in the United States, they do not necessarily apply to other nations. It is also worth noting that without additional data it is impossible to separate out the stalkers and victims who may live in other countries. Some of the incidents reported to U.S. Internet safety organizations, for example, may involve stalkers who are based in other countries. With this in mind, it might be that the figures provided by Web Police provide a truer picture of the extent of cyberstalking around the world. However, without more information, this can not be said with any real certainty.

Second, CyberAngels, Web Police, and WHOA represent only three of the numerous Internet safety organizations located around the world. Clearly, the figures given here likely represent only a fraction of the actual number of cases that occur each year. Similarly, for each incident reported to these organizations, there are likely to be several cases that are not reported at all.

Third, although these figures concern the number of victims reporting incidents each year, they do not necessarily reflect the number of cyberstalkers currently active. It is important to remember that a single cyberstalker may pursue several victims simultaneously or may move from one victim to another over a fairly short period of time.

Finally, as use of the Internet continues to grow, it is likely that the number of incidents that take place each year will also grow. This means that although it is possible to estimate the minimum number of cyberstalking cases that take place each year, estimates concerning the maximum number will need to be revised upward continuously.

Adopting the estimate derived from the three organizations has much to recommend it. First, it is fairly certain that each of the 76,000 cases reported each year is a genuine cyberstalking case. This is because the determination of whether a case represents a genuine cyberstalking incident is made by an organization with specialist expertise in this area.

Second, there will be a body of evidence to support the assertion that 76,000 cases take place each year. CyberAngels, Web Police, and WHOA will undoubtedly generate thousands of documents, e-mail messages, and other electronic records during the course of their work.

Third, unlike the figure of 200,000 active stalkers publicized by television talk shows, the source of this new estimate is known and the details of the estimate can be verified. It should be remembered that even the report prepared by the Department of Justice warns us of "statistics from unspecified sources."

Finally, the figure of 76,000 cyberstalking incidents each year can be taken to represent a relatively safe value that is unlikely to fuel claims that the problem's scale has been exaggerated. This is important when one considers that research in this field is likely to be influenced by public perception and that there have already been claims that concern about cyberstalking is nothing more than hysteria (Koch, 2000a, 2000b).

CONCLUSION

Many studies have looked at offline stalking in the United States and the United Kingdom. In general, these studies are seen as being fairly accurate and reliable. However, although figures related to offline stalking may provide an insight into cyberstalking, care must be taken when considering them as it cannot be assumed that the terms *stalking* and *cyberstalking* are interchangeable.

In terms of offline stalking, some statistics suggest that women are more likely to be victimized than men and that younger people are more likely to be victimized than older people. In the United States, up to 10.3 percent of the population have been victims of stalking in the past. Similar figures have been reported for other countries; for instance, UK official statistics suggest that 11.8 percent of the population have been victims of stalking.

There are many problems that need to be faced when trying to estimate the prevalence of cyberstalking in the United States and the United Kingdom. These include using outdated or inaccurate figures as the basis for new statistics or simply applying figures related to offline stalking directly to the Internet.

Estimates of the number of cyberstalkers and cyberstalking victims can vary wildly. For instance, estimates of the annual number of cyberstalking victims in the United States range from 1 million to 10 million, and the annual number of cyberstalking victims across the world could range from 474,000 to 18.75 million.

In considering cyberstalking estimates, it is important to remember that there are still many areas about which very little is known. For instance, it is not known whether a typical cyberstalker may harass more than one victim or if some cyberstalkers pursue several victims simultaneously. These issues will have an impact on how cyberstalking is viewed and on any efforts to reduce the number of incidents reported each year.

The next chapter begins to explore some of the characteristics of cyberstalkers, looking at how they can be classified and the behaviors they use.

4

Who Are the Cyberstalkers?

THE KERRY KUJAWA STORY

Kerry Kujawa was a twenty-year-old student at Texas A&M University. Kujawa developed a relationship with a young woman named Kelly McCauley via the Internet (Chan, 2000). Over a period of months, Kujawa became attached to McCauley and eventually arranged a face-to-face meeting that apparently took place on 7 April 2000. A week or so after the meeting, Kujawa's relatives and friends received an e-mail supposedly written by Kujawa himself. The message stated that Kujawa was fine and had decided to stay with McCauley a little longer. At roughly the same time, McCauley began telling people in the online chat room that she and Kujawa used that they were engaged and planned to marry soon. Some time later, Kujawa's friends became concerned that they had heard nothing further from him and filed a missing persons report. A day before the report was filed, the police had found Kujawa's body but had been unable to identify him.

After a thorough investigation, the police were able to identify Kujawa's killer. Kenny Wayne Lockwood was a thirty-one-year-old male who was over six feet tall and a former McDonald's assistant manager. The investigation found that Lockwood had invented the personality of Kelly McCauley in order to meet with young men. The deception was assisted by a story that many men would find appealing; McCauley was in a destructive relationship and needed someone to help her. To complete the illusion, Lockwood sent photographs of an attractive young woman that was supposedly McCauley.

Lockwood met Kujawa at the agreed time and place but, in order to allay Kujawa's suspicions, pretended to be McCauley's brother. Later on, he shot and killed Kujawa, then disposed of the body. The messages sent to the chat room and Kujawa's friends were to delay suspicion (Hight, 2000).

Kujawa's case was one of the first cyberstalking incidents to come to public attention in which the stalker assumed another identity in order to pursue his victim. Lockwood clearly invested a great deal of time and effort into constructing the Kelly McCauley identity, even going as far as inventing a "history" that he felt would be attractive to the young males he was pursuing as victims.

INTRODUCTION

How do people classify stalkers? Which classifications of stalkers are most useful in describing cyberstalkers? In what other ways can cyber-stalkers be classified? What else is known about cyberstalkers? Having looked at the nature of cyberstalking, this chapter examines those who carry it out.

In this chapter, I describe how researchers have attempted to classify stalkers and their behaviors. As will be shown, most researchers have focused on the relationships between stalkers and their victims, psychiatric classifications, or common behaviors exhibited by stalkers. Although the classifications in common use are undoubtedly helpful, each provides only limited detail about a set of groups identified by a particular researcher. Fortunately, a more detailed understanding of stalkers can be gained by looking at some of the research into stalking that has been done over the past decade.

Having looked at some of the characteristics of stalkers, I move on to consider how cyberstalkers can be classified. As will be seen, there are no accepted classifications of cyberstalkers and only limited research has been conducted in this area.

SOME CLASSIFICATIONS OF STALKERS

It is worth pointing out that there is no universally accepted typology of stalkers (The Information Centre, 2000). In addition, there are no accepted typologies of cyberstalkers. Most writers and researchers have extended existing classifications of offline stalkers to cover cyber-stalking. However, there are some obvious problems with this approach, not least of which is the likelihood that stalking and cyberstalking can be seen as distinct behaviors.

I have chosen the typologies described in this section because each seems to have some relevance to cyberstalking. For instance, the work of Harmon, Rosner, and Owens (1995) may help to explain why some people engage in behavior such as flaming when they believe that they have been insulted in some way. Similarly, the intimacy seeker described by Mullen, Pathé, Purcell, and Stuart (1999) may also help to explain some of the affection-seeking behavior often seen in chat rooms.

It is important to note that there are several other well-known typologies that have not been covered here. For example, one typology suggests that stalkers can be classified as psychotic or nonpsychotic (Kienlen et al., 1997). However, these other classifications are considered to be beyond the scope of this discussion.

Australian criminologist Emma Ogilvie has described how typologies of stalkers have developed around three basic themes (2000b). First, classifications created by government departments or agencies tend to focus on the relationship between the stalker and the victim. The classification used by the U.S. National Institute of Justice, for example, moves from "stranger" to "intimate." This is similar to the classification used by the British Home Office, in which the relationship between stalker and victim is described as simply "intimate" or "nonintimate."

Second, some writers have focused on psychiatric classifications of stalkers, usually concentrating on obsessional behavior. For example, a typology developed by Zona, Sharma, and Lane (1993, p. 893) includes erotomania, which they define as "the delusional belief that one is passionately loved by another."

Finally, a third group of typologies focuses on the behavior of stalkers. The work of Mullen, Pathé, Purcell, and Stuart (1999), for example, looks at the motivations behind stalking. One of the categories used by Mullen and his colleagues is the intimacy seeker, described as a person with "the aim of establishing a loving relationship with the object of their unwanted attentions" (Mullen, Pathé, and Purcell, 2000, p. 117).

Table 4.1 is derived from Ogilvie's work and provides a useful overview of the classifications in common use.

Erotomanics, Love Obsessionals, and Simple Obsessionals

Michael Zona and his colleagues have the distinction of being the first to propose a typology of stalkers. Their work was based on a

Table 4.1
Selected Stalking Typologies

Authors	Classification
Zona, Sharma, and Lane (1993)	Erotomanic
	Love obsessional
	Simple obsessional
Harmon, Rosner, and Owens (1995)	Affectionate/amorous
	Persecutory/angry
Geberth (1996)	Psychopathic
	Psychotic
Roberts and Dziegielewski (1996)	Domestic violence
	Erotomania/delusional
	Nuisance
Wright, Burgess, Burgess, Laszlo, McCrary, and Douglas (1996)	Nondomestic (organized or delusional)
	Domestic
De Becker (in Orion) 1997	Attachment-seeking
	Identity-seeking
	Rejection-based
	Delusionally based

Kienlen, Birmingham, Solberg, O'Regan, and Meloy (1997)	Psychotic
	Nonpsychotic
National Institute of Justice (1998)	Intimate or former intimate
	Acquaintance Stranger
Emerson, Ferris, and Brooks Gardner (1998)	Unacquainted
	Pseudo-acquainted
	Semi-acquainted
	Intimately-acquainted
Mullen, Pathé, Purcell, and Stuart (1999)	Rejected
	Intimacy seeking
	Incompetent
	Resentful
	Predatory
Budd, Mattinson, and Myhill (2000)	Female victim—intimate relationship with offender
	Female victim—nonintimate relationship with offender
	Male victim—intimate relationship with offender
	Male victim—nonintimate relationship with offender

Source: E. Ogilvie. 2000B. Stalking: Policing and prosecuting practices in three Australian jurisdictions. *Trends and Issues in Crime and Criminal Justice* No. 176 (Canberra: Australian Institute of Criminology). Reproduced with permission.

review of case files from the Threat Management Unit of the Los Angeles Police Department and found three types of stalker: erotomanics, love obsessionals, and simple obsessionals (Zona, Sharma, and Lane, 1993).

Erotomanics were those who were convinced they were loved by the people they stalked. Most erotomanics were female and had had no prior relationships with the people they stalked. The attention of erotomanics tended to focus on people in the entertainment industry.

Love obsessionals also tended to believe the people they stalked loved them. However, love obsessionals could be distinguished from erotomanics because their delusions arose from a more serious psychotic illness. Some love obsessionals showed intense infatuation with the people they stalked but did not claim their feelings were reciprocated. Most love obsessionals were male and most focused on people in the media, such as celebrities. As with erotomanics, there had been no prior relationships between most love obsessionals and their victims.

Simple obsessionals tended to pursue victims with whom they had had a previous relationship of some kind. Although many victims were ex–intimate partners, other groups were also represented, such as neighbors and work colleagues. The group of simple obsessionals studied was made up of equal numbers of males and females. Most simple obsessionals had begun to stalk their victims after a relationship broke down or sometimes in revenge for what they saw as mistreatment by the victim.

Affectionate/Amorous and Persecutory/Angry Stalkers

A study of stalking by Harmon, Rosner, and Owens (1995) uses two axes to look at the nature of the attachment between stalker and victim and also the nature of any prior relationship between them.

The nature of the attachment between stalker and victim is classified as either affectionate/amorous or persecutory/angry. The affectionate/amorous classification is described as follows:

> In the affectionate/amorous type, the object is pursued initially for amorous reasons, although the emotion of love may turn to hostility and even aggression in reaction to perceived rejection by the loved one. Third parties may also be victimized because of the obsession. (Harmon, Rosner, and Owens, 1995, p. 189)

The persecutory/angry attachment is described as follows:

> In the persecutory/angry attachment, the object is pursued because of some real or imagined injury generally related to a business or professional relationship, and may in fact not be a person but an institution. Again, multiple individuals may be victimized because of the obsession. (Harmon, Rosner, and Owens, 1995, p. 189)

The story of David Cruz presented at the end of this chapter could be taken to provide a good example of an affectionate/amorous cyberstalker.

The second axis used by Harmon, Rosner, and Owens (1995, p. 190) describes any prior relationship between the stalker and his victim. Six types of prior relationship have been identified. In brief, these are:

Personal: There was a known romantic or other personal attachment.

Professional: The stalker had at one time retained the professional services of the victim (for example, a dentist, an attorney, a veterinarian, a therapist).

Employment: The stalker was either the employer or employee of the victim.

Media: The victim is a well-known public personality with no other connection to the stalker.

Acquaintance: The stalker and the victim have met on a superficial level.

None: There is no discernible connection between the stalker and the victim, and there is no clear reason for the selection of the victim.

Nondomestic and Domestic Stalking

Wright and his colleagues developed a typology of stalkers based on the nature of the relationship, the content of communication, the level of aggression, and the motive of the stalker (Wright et al., 1996). Since Wright and his colleagues were affiliated with the FBI, their work is considered highly influential in terms of how stalking is viewed in the United States.

This classification divides stalkers into two basic groups, nondomestic and domestic (Wright et al., 1996, p. 496). Nondomestic stalkers have no interpersonal relationship with their victims, and, in general, victims cannot identify the stalker when they first become aware of being stalked. Nondomestic stalkers can be divided into two further groups: organized and delusional. The victims of organized stalkers have often come into contact with the stalker in the past without realizing it. Wright and his colleagues describe organized stalkers as follows:

> An organized stalker is one who targets and communicates with the victim through hang-up, obscene, or harassing telephone calls; unsigned letters; and other anonymous communications. The stalker's identity may remain unknown, or at some point the individual may make his or her identity known through continuous physical appearances at the victim's residence, place of employment, or other location. It is unlikely that the victim is aware of being stalked prior to the initial communication or contact. (Wright et al., 1996, p. 496)

The delusional stalker fantasizes about his relationship with the victim:

> This fantasy is commonly expressed in such forms as "fusion," where the stalker blends his or her personality into the target's, or erotomania, where a fantasy is based on idealized romantic love or spiritual union of a person rather than sexual attraction. (Wright et al., 1996, p. 497)

Domestic stalking involves a prior relationship between the stalker and the victim. Wright et al. provide a disturbing description:

> Domestic stalking occurs when a former boy/girl friend, family, or household member threatens or harasses another member of the household. . . . The domestic stalker is initially motivated by a desire to continue or reestablish a relationship that can evolve into an attitude of "If I can't have her no one can." (1996, p. 499)

Wright and his colleagues note that domestic stalking often ends in a violent attack upon the victim. Such an attack can occur in various locations but commonly takes place in the victim's home or place of work.

A Classification Based on Motive

Mullen, Pathé, Purcell, and Stuart (1999) proposed a classification of stalkers based on motivation, the context in which stalking emerged, the nature of any prior relationship with the victim, and any psychiatric diagnosis. Five basic types of stalkers were identified: rejected, intimacy seeking, incompetent, resentful, and predatory.

A *rejected stalker* pursues an ex-intimate, such as a former spouse or girlfriend. Sometimes, a close friend or relative may also become the victim of a rejected stalker. Rejected stalkers are motivated by a desire to achieve some kind of reconciliation or a desire for revenge against the victim. However, it is not uncommon for rejected stalkers to display both kinds of behavior. This type of stalking tends to last for a long period of time, possibly because the stalker does not wish to end the relationship with his victim.

The *intimacy seeker* hopes to establish a relationship with the object of his affection. He often believes that the victim reciprocates his feelings and that a romantic relationship is destined to happen. Intimacy seekers tend to reinterpret rejection as a more positive response.

Unlike the intimacy seeker, the *incompetent stalker* is not in love with his victim and is merely trying to establish contact with her, perhaps by asking for a date or coming to her attention in another way. The harassment experienced by victims stems from the fact that the incompetent stalker tends to have poor social skills. Although this type of stalking seldom lasts very long, it may be repeated frequently with a new victim each time.

The *resentful stalker* is seeking revenge for some kind of hurt or injury, whether real or imagined. The purpose of the harassment is to frighten the victim so that the stalker feels he has exacted retribution. Resentful stalkers sometimes present themselves as victims who are simply fighting back against what they perceive as unjust treatment.

The *predatory stalker* is often regarded as the most dangerous type of stalker. Mullen, Pathé, and Purcell describe this kind of stalker as follows:

> The predatory stalker stalks preparatory to launching an attack, usually sexual in nature. The stalking is a combination of information gathering, rehearsal in fantasy and intrusion through surreptitious observation. The stalking is a means to an end, the end being the assault, but is sustained by the gratifying sense of power and control, often augmented by the pleasures of voyeuristic intrusions. (2001, p. 11)

Kenny Lockwood, the murderer of Kerry Kujawa, could be described as an example of a predatory cyberstalker.

A Classification of Stalking Behaviors

Although not a classification of stalkers per se, Brian Spitzberg's typology of stalking behaviors is relevant to any study of stalking or cyberstalking. Spitzberg's meta-analysis of 103 studies of stalking has resulted in a classification of the behaviors commonly found in stalking incidents. These behaviors take one of seven basic forms:

1. hyperintimacy, or behaviors displaying excessive interest in developing a relationship;
2. proximity/surveillance, or following types of behavior;
3. invasion, in which the stalker trespasses on the victim's property, space, or privacy;
4. proxy, in which the stalker involves associates of the victim or third parties to pursue the victim;
5. intimidation and harassment, whereby the stalker threatens or otherwise attempts to psychologically manipulate the victim;
6. coercion and constraint, through which the stalker controls the victim through extortion, threat, or force;
7. aggression, which takes the form of violence, whether sexual or nonsexual. (Spitzberg, 2002, p. 262)

A number of studies have looked at the behaviors often found in stalking incidents (see, for example, Sheridan, Davies, and Boon, 2001; Mullen and Pathé, 1994; Kienlen et al., 1997), but few seem to have found such a simple and elegant way of grouping them together. Spitzberg's classification can also be applied to cyberstalking incidents with little difficulty. For instance, "invasion" might describe attempts to compromise the victim's computer system.

WHAT RESEARCH REVEALS ABOUT STALKERS

Although there have been numerous studies on stalking, most have focused on victims rather than stalkers. This means that much of what is known about stalkers has been inferred from the victims' experiences. In some cases, researchers have even asked stalking victims to estimate or guess at the characteristics of their stalkers, making for some very unreliable findings.

This section summarizes the results of a small number of studies that have looked at both victims and stalkers. The studies described have been selected for a number of different reasons. For instance, some studies have been chosen because they are representative of a given population. In general, studies that have used very small samples have been avoided, as have studies that seem to add relatively little to existing knowledge.

The first study explored is Tjaden and Thoennes's survey (1998) of 8,000 men and 8,000 women, since it is often cited by academics, government agencies, and journalists as a key resource describing the nature and extent of stalking in the United States.

In looking at the gender of stalkers, Tjaden and Thoennes (1998) found that 87 percent of the stalkers identified by victims were male. Most victims knew their stalkers since only 23 percent of females and 36 percent of males were stalked by strangers. Over 59 percent of females were stalked by ex-intimates compared with 30 percent of males. Interestingly, it was found that 21 percent of women were stalked before the relationship ended, and that 36 percent were stalked both before and after the relationship ended, suggesting that most women are stalked by intimate partners while the relationship is intact.

According to the survey, men are more likely to be stalked by male strangers and acquaintances than women. In addition, homosexual men are at greater risk of being stalked than heterosexuals. The report suggests that some stalking may be motivated by homophobia.

The motivation behind stalking was also examined by looking at victims' perceptions of why they were stalked:

> It appears that much stalking is motivated by stalkers' desire to control, or instill fear in, their victim. The survey results dispel the myth that most stalkers are psychotic or delusional. Only 7 percent of the victims said they were stalked because their stalkers were mentally ill or abusing drugs or alcohol. (Tjaden and Thoennes, 1998, p. 8)

One of the most important findings of the survey was a link between stalking and other forms of violence, such as domestic violence. For instance, 81 percent of those stalked by a husband or ex-husband were also assaulted by him (Tjaden and Thoennes, 1998).

A study by Burgess and his colleagues (1997) looked at stalking in the context of domestic violence. The study gathered data from 120 male and female batterers who had been charged with domestic violence. The main findings were:

> Stalkers tended to live alone, were less likely to be married, not living with children, and used more alcohol than nonstalkers. They also tended to have had a history of prior stalking offenses and of being abused themselves. Factor analysis found three stalking groupings: one in which discrediting was the key, a second revolving around love turning to hate, and a third with violent confrontation with the ex partner. (1997, p. 389)

Harmon, Rosner, and Owens (1995) studied a group of forty-eight people who had been charged with harassment and referred for evaluation to a Forensic Psychiatry Clinic. This group was compared to all of the cases referred to the clinic over a one-year period. Most stalkers (70 percent) were between thirty-one and fifty years old, with a mean age of forty. With regard to gender, two-thirds of the group were male. In terms of ethnicity, over two-thirds of the group were white, 13 percent were black, and 10 percent were Hispanic. All of the stalkers had received at least some high school education, 80 percent had completed high school, and 40 percent were college graduates.

In more recent work, Harmon, Rosner, and Owens (1998) studied the records of stalkers referred to the Bellevue Hospital Center Forensic Psychiatry Clinic for the New York County Criminal and Supreme Courts between 1987 and 1996.[1] A total of 175 records were identified as meeting the criteria for inclusion in the study. In brief, their chief findings were that most stalkers were male (78 percent) and single (59 percent) or previously married (31 percent). Only 9 percent of stalkers were married. The majority of stalkers were aged thirty to thirty-nine (37 percent) or forty to forty-nine (26 percent).

In terms of ethnicity, most stalkers were white (47 percent), black (27 percent), or Hispanic (18 percent). The remainders were classified as "other" or "unknown." Around a quarter of the group had received at least some high school education and another quarter had graduated high school or received an associate degree. A relatively large number of people were college graduates (19 percent) or held graduate degrees (8 percent).

Surprisingly, a large number of stalkers were found to have mental health problems. For example, 32 percent were diagnosed with personality disorders, 24 percent with schizophrenia or other psychotic disorders, 15 percent with delusional disorders, and 21 percent with adjustment or mood disorders. Although this appears to contradict Tjaden and Thoennes's findings (1998), it may simply be a reflection of the sample used.

It is also worth noting that Harmon, Rosner, and Owens (1998) found that many of the stalkers studied exhibited violent behavior—on average, 47 percent. Oddly, stalkers they classified as amorous (48 percent) were slightly more likely to exhibit violent behavior than persecutory stalkers (45 percent).[2]

Paul Mullen and his colleagues studied 145 stalkers who had been referred to an Australian forensic psychiatry unit for treatment (Mullen et al., 1999). Most of the stalkers studied were male (79 percent) and ages ranged from fifteen to seventy-five, with a median age of thirty-eight. Although most of the stalkers were employed (56 percent), a substantial number were unemployed (39 percent). Over half of those studied had never had a long-term relationship, and another 30 percent were currently separated or divorced. The victims of these stalkers included ex-partners (30 percent), professional or work contacts (34 percent), and strangers (14 percent). Most stalkers (63 percent) made threats against their victims, and 36 percent committed assault. Referring back to Mullen, Pathé, Purcell, and Stuart's (1999) classification of stalkers, resentful stalkers were more likely to make threats and damage property, but rejected and predatory stalkers committed more assaults.

Fremouw, Westrup, and Pennypacker (1997) studied the prevalence of stalking among approximately 600 college students. They found that more than 80 percent of stalking victims knew the identity of their stalker. More females (43 percent) had "seriously dated" the stalker than males (24 percent), and fewer than 20 percent were stalked by strangers. There were only a few incidents in which a victim was stalked by someone of the same gender. Interestingly, it was found that only 1 percent of students admitted to having stalked another person. Fremouw, Westrup, and Pennypacker explain such a low figure by observing that students were probably reluctant to admit to behavior that can be described as socially undesirable.

In the United Kingdom, the 1998 British Crime Survey included a stalking questionnaire that was distributed to approximately 15,000 adults living within England and Wales. The size of the sample and the methodology used make the results highly credible. In brief, the survey found that most incidents were carried out by men (81 percent) (Budd and Mattinson, 2000). Men committed 90 percent of incidents against women and 57 percent of incidents against men. In terms of age, men between twenty and thirty-nine committed half of the incidents. Over a third of incidents involving male victims were carried out by stalkers under twenty.

Most incidents (79 percent) involved a single stalker acting alone. For men, 66 percent of incidents involved only one stalker. For women, the figure was 84 percent. Some 20 percent of incidents against men involved three or more people.

In almost a third of cases (29 percent), the stalker was an ex-intimate of the victim (such as a spouse or boyfriend). In another third of cases (34 percent), the identity of the stalker was not known. The remaining incidents were carried out by neighbors, friends, work colleagues, relatives, and others. Women were more likely to be stalked by a stranger than were men. The most common reasons given for stalking were: to start a relationship (22 percent), to annoy or upset the victim (16 percent), or to continue a relationship (12 percent).

Still focusing on the United Kingdom, Sheridan, Davies, and Boon (2001) conducted a survey of ninety-five stalking victims referred to them through a victim support organization. Although their work centered on the victims of stalking, they were also able to gather information about the stalkers. Most stalkers (87 percent) were male and 7 percent were female. The remaining cases involved mixed groups of multiple stalkers. The ages of the stalkers ranged from eleven to seventy-three,[3] with the average age being thirty-five. In terms of employment, the largest groups were professionals (26 percent) and the unemployed (23 percent). Regarding any prior relationship between the stalker and his victim, it was found that the stalker was an ex-partner in 48 percent of cases and a former acquaintance in 37 percent of cases. The identity of the stalker was not known in 12 percent of cases.

When asked to identify the reason they were being stalked, the victims responded as follows:

- Forty-six percent said they were being harassed by an ex-partner after ending a relationship
- Twenty-four percent said that the stalker believed himself to be in love with the victim
- Fifteen percent could offer no explanation for the harassment
- Seven percent said that the stalking had escalated from an argument with a neighbor
- Two percent said that they were being stalked by the new girlfriend of a former husband
- One percent said that the stalker believed himself to be protecting the victim

The work of Sheridan, Davies, and Boon (2001) resulted in three findings that are of particular relevance and importance to cyberstalking. The first finding was that 41 percent of the sample believed their stalker had harassed another person in the past or was currently doing so. This supports the idea of a serial stalker, a person who moves from one victim to another in order to repeat a cycle of harassment. The second important finding concerns the extent to which other people become involved in stalking. In this study, 40 percent of victims said that friends or relatives of the stalker had also been involved in the harassment. The third finding was that harassment is not always confined to the victim—it can be extended to include the victim's family and friends:

Almost 80% of stalkers had made attempts to obtain information on their victim from the victim's family and friends. Further, over half had actually stalked members of the victim's family, 40% had threatened those close of the victim and 17% had actually carried out assaults on the same. (Sheridan, Davies, and Boon, 2001, p. 244)

WHAT RESEARCH REVEALS ABOUT CYBERSTALKERS

Despite growing interest in cyberstalking, few academic studies have focused all of their attention on this subject. Occasionally, researchers looking at offline stalking may include one or two survey questions dealing with cyberstalking, but few seem interested in examining the topic in more depth. For this reason, there is relatively little literature on the subject, and what exists is difficult to find.

In a recent paper, Spitzberg and Hoobler (2002) reported on three pilot studies and a larger study dealing with cyberstalking victimization. One of the strengths of this work is that it accepts cyberstalking as distinct from offline stalking. However, since the paper focuses on the victims of cyberstalking, it reveals only a little about cyberstalkers themselves.

The three pilot studies reported within the paper were used to develop a comprehensive questionnaire dealing with the behaviors experienced by cyberstalking victims. The way in which these behaviors can be classified was described earlier in this chapter.

The main study concentrated on the extent to which behaviors associated with offline stalking can be translated to the online world and vice versa. A questionnaire was given to 235 students, and the results were analyzed to examine the behaviors commonly experienced by cyberstalking victims. Table 4.2 provides a summary of the behaviors.

An interesting point that Spitzberg and Hoobler (2002) make is that some of the behaviors assumed to happen frequently are actually quite rare: "Results indicate that very few students are victimized by some of the more devious types of cyberpursuit (e.g. stealing persona, directing others to threaten, etc.)" (p. 86).

In discussing how people cope with cyberstalking, Spitzberg and Hoobler (2002) also suggest that the cyberstalker's behavior may be influenced by his level of computer literacy:

> It may be that the types of pursuer who resorts to more extreme forms of cyberpursuit are also the people who can circumvent most typical coping responses. In other words, people who simply send messages that plead for greater intimacy may be merely as computer-savvy as the object of the affections. . . . In contrast, the more extreme pursuer, who resorts to threat and spatial pursuit, may be able to work around the more mundane coping responses so as to render such responses relatively moot. (2002, p. 86)

These are both important points and are echoed in some of my own research, described later in this chapter.

Table 4.2
Summary of Behaviors Associated with Cyberstalking

Has Anyone Ever Undesirably and Obsessively Communicated with or Pursued You Through Computer or Other Electronic Means By:

1	Sending tokens of affection (e.g., poetry, songs, electronic greeting cards, praise, etc.)	31
2	Sending exaggerated messages of affection (e.g., expressions of affections implying a more intimate relationship than you actually have, etc.)	31
3	Sending excessively disclosive messages (e.g., inappropriately giving private information about his/her life, body, family, hobbies, sexual experiences, etc.)	26
4	Sending excessively "needy" or demanding messages (e.g., pressuring to see you, assertively requesting you go out on a date, arguing with you give him/her "another chance," etc.)	25
5	Sending pornographic/obscene images or messages (e.g., photographs or cartoons of nude people, or people or animals engaging in sexual acts, etc.)	19
6	Sending threatening written messages (e.g., suggesting harming you, your property, family, friends, etc.)	9
7	Sending sexually harassing messages (e.g., describing hypothetical sexual acts between you, making sexually demeaning remarks, etc.)	18
8	Sending threatening pictures or images (e.g., images of actual or implied mutilation, blood, dismemberment, property destruction, weapons, etc.)	18
9	Exposing private information about you to others (e.g., sending mail out to others regarding your secrets, embarrassing information, unlisted numbers, etc.)	5
10	Pretending to be someone she or he wasn't (e.g., falsely representing him- or herself as a different person or gender, claiming a false identity, status or position, pretending to be you, etc.)	17
11	"Sabotaging" your private reputation (e.g., spreading rumors about you, your relationships, or activities to friends, family, partner, etc.)	20
12	"Sabotaging" your work/school reputation (e.g., spreading rumors about you, your relationships, or activities in organizational networks, electronic bulletin boards, etc.)	12

64

13	Attempting to disable your computer (e.g., downloading a virus, sending too many messages for your system to handle, etc.)	3
14	Obtaining private information without permission (e.g., covertly entering your computer files, voicemail, or the files of coworkers, friends, or family members, etc.)	10
15	Using your computer to get information on others (e.g., stealing information about your friends, family, coworkers, etc.)	7
16	"Bugging" your car, home or office (e.g., planting a hidden listening or recording device, etc.)	7
17	Altering your electronic identity or persona (e.g., breaking into your system and changing your signature, personal information, or how you portray yourself electronically, etc.)	1
18	Taking over your electronic identity or persona (e.g., representing himself or herself to others as you in chat rooms, bulletin boards, pornography or singles sites, etc.)	3
19	Directing others to you in threatening ways (e.g., pretending to be you on chat lines and requesting risky sex acts, kidnapping fantasies, etc.)	2
20	Meeting first online and then following you (e.g., following you while driving, around campus or work, to or from the gym or social activities, etc.)	1
21	Meeting first online and then intruding (e.g., showing up unexpectedly at work, front door, in parking lot, intruding in your conversations, etc.)	3
22	Meeting first online and then threatening you (e.g., threatening to engage in sexual coercion, rape, physical restraint, or to harm himself or herself, your possessions, pets, family or friends, etc.)	3
23	Meeting first online and then harming you (e.g., corresponding with you through an online dating service and then following, harassing, or otherwise stalking you)	1
24	First meeting you online and then stalking you (e.g., corresponding through an online dating service or as acquaintances and then following, harassing, or otherwise stalking you)	1

Source: B. H. Spitzberg and G. Hoobler. 2002. Cyberstalking and the technologies of interpersonal terrorism. *New Media and Society*, 14 (1), 71–92. Reproduced with permission.

Another important point made by Spitzberg and Hoobler is that activities on the Internet may place people at more risk of becoming victims of cyberstalking: "The more everyday mundane activities a person is exposed to on the world wide web, internet, and cyber-based world of electronic communications, the more at risk the person is for experiencing unwanted pursuit through those very same media" (2002, p. 86). This suggests that people changing the way in which they use the Internet may reduce the risk of experiencing harassment. Put another way, there may be certain activities that attract cyberstalkers.

In a pilot study I conducted (Bocij, 2003), 169 Internet users were asked to complete a questionnaire concerning cyberstalking. As with the work of Spitzberg and Hoobler (2002), this research was concerned with the experiences of victims and reveals relatively little about the cyberstalkers themselves. There are also many methodological issues that mean it is crucial to interpret the results carefully. Despite these issues, it is still worth considering the study's findings.

Over 80 percent of respondents had experienced some of the behaviors commonly associated with cyberstalking, but only 21.9 percent were considered to be genuine cases of cyberstalking (see chapter 5 for a detailed discussion of this study's findings). However, the criteria used did not allow for the possibility of group cyberstalking (several cyberstalkers pursuing one or more victims) or stalking-by-proxy (cyberstalker recruits others to pursue a victim on his behalf). If some cases involved more than one stalker, then up to 33.9 percent of respondents might have been genuine victims of cyberstalking. In the context of the study, this appears to show that a relatively high number of cases may involve group cyberstalking or stalking-by-proxy, suggesting many cyberstalkers may prefer not to work alone.

The victims of cyberstalking were divided into three groups according to their level of computer literacy: novice, intermediate, or expert. It was found that novice computer users reported receiving more threats than expert users. On the other hand, expert users were more likely to see more sophisticated attacks on their data, hardware, and software. This may suggest that computer literacy influenced the behaviors cyberstalking victims experienced. Put another way, it may have been that, in general, the more knowledgeable and experienced the computer user, the more knowledgeable and experienced the cyberstalker. Although this seems to tie in with the results reported by Spitzberg and Hoobler (2002), it must be remembered that the suggestion is highly speculative.

The behaviors experienced by cyberstalking victims also help to shed a little light on cyberstalkers. Table 4.3 shows that the most com-

Table 4.3

Proportion of Respondents Who Experienced Behaviors Associated with Cyberstalking

Behavior	%
Sent you threatening or abusive e-mail messages	39.88
Made threats or abusive comments via instant-messaging software, such as MSN	38.69
Made threats or abusive comments in chat rooms	47.62
Posted false information (e.g., rumors) about you to a bulletin board or chat room	24.40
Impersonated you in e-mail messages to your friends, family, or work colleagues	8.93
Encouraged other users to harass, threaten, or insult you (e.g., other members of a chat room)	23.81
Ordered goods or services in your name, possibly charging items to your credit cards	2.98
Attempted to damage your computer system by sending malicious programs to you, such as a computer virus	40.48
Attempted to monitor your actions by inserting Trojan horse software (e.g., key logging programs) on your computer system	26.79
Attempted to access confidential information stored on your computer, such as credit card numbers, e-mail messages, etc.	17.26
Any other behavior you found distressing in any way	27.98

Source: P. Bocij, 2003. Victims of cyberstalking: An exploratory study of harassment perpetrated via the Internet. *First Monday*, 8 (10). Available at www.firstmonday.dk/issues/issue8_10/bocij/index.html.

mon behaviors experienced included making threats, posting false information about the victim, or attempting to infiltrate the victim's computer system. It is worth noting that some of the figures given are at odds with the results reported by Spitzberg and Hoobler (2002). However, in general, both studies seem to agree that behaviors such as issuing threats tend to occur very often, whereas behaviors such as identity theft tend to happen less often.

It was also found that a large proportion of victims (42 percent) did not know the identity of their harassers. Some of these cases might be explained by suggesting that the victim did not know how to find the identity of the stalker. If the victim had been able to trace the stalker, then she may have known him, but the fact remains that a lot of cyberstalkers remain anonymous. This is contrary to what is known about offline stalking, for which research has shown that the majority of stalkers know their victims (McGrath and Casey, 2002). When the identity of the stalker was known, it was found that the cyberstalker was often an ex-intimate (8.8 percent), friend (15.8 percent), or work colleague (1.8 percent). Again, this does not seem to fit with other studies, such as Tjaden and Thoennes's work (1998), where they found that over 59 percent of females had been stalked by ex-intimates. However, it must be remembered that the study did not use a representative sample and that the findings must be viewed with some caution.

CONCLUSION

Although a number of studies have looked at the characteristics of stalkers, very few have looked at cyberstalkers. Consequently, our knowledge of cyberstalkers is very limited.

Although a number of typologies have been proposed, there is no universally accepted classification of offline stalkers. Most classifications of offline stalkers tend to be based on three themes: the relationship between stalker and victim, psychiatric classifications, and the behavior of stalkers. It may be possible to extend some of these classifications to include cyberstalkers, but there are obvious difficulties in doing so. Although new classifications of cyberstalkers are slowly starting to appear, all require further refinement and need to be supported by additional research before they can become useful.

In the next chapter, the focus moves away from cyberstalkers and begins to examine the characteristics of cyberstalking victims. However, this does not mean that there is nothing more to learn about cyberstalkers. Criminologists argue that it is possible to learn a great deal about the perpetrators of crimes by looking at their choice of victim and the results of their actions.

THE DAVID CRUZ STORY

In 2003, David Cruz received a prison sentence of five months for cyberstalking Chloe Easton, a twenty-six-year-old reflexologist. Cruz was a U.S. citizen who had come to live in the United Kingdom and first met Easton through mutual friends. He quickly became infatuated with her and invited her to help him train an American football team that he coached. Easton, who was going through a messy divorce, found Cruz very supportive and soon began to confide in him. However, when Cruz made romantic advances toward her, Easton made it clear she only wanted to be friends. Angered, he began a campaign of harassment against her and her family that lasted for seven months (BBC News, 2003).

Throughout much of the harassment, Cruz gave the appearance of a concerned friend who was trying to help Easton find the person stalking her. For instance, he would use various nicknames to enter chat rooms and post made-up details of Easton's sexual activities. He would then tell Easton that he had accidentally found this information and offered to show it to her (South London Press, 2003).

Easton began to receive up to forty sexually explicit phone calls and text messages each day. Cruz also sent abusive and obscene e-mails to Easton, her relatives, and her colleagues. In one incident, Cruz e-mailed the health club where Easton worked, posing as a client and claiming that Easton had offered him sexual services for £30 (approximately $50). On another occasion, Cruz posted Easton's personal details on a web site that invites visitors to "rate" prostitutes, advertising her services as costing £45 (approximately $75) and commenting, "Not very pretty, fit body—she giggles a lot" (South London Press, 2003). It was reported that Easton's details were accessed 700 times by visitors to the site and she received more than thirty calls asking about her services (Wilkins, 2003; South London Press, 2003).

Cruz also targeted Easton's parents. On one occasion, he sent Easton's father a message with a pornographic video attached, which showed a woman who looked like Easton engaged in group sex (Wilkins, 2003). Another message threatened gang rape, telling her parents that four men were waiting to attack Easton when she had finished working out in Finsbury Park (South London Press, 2003).

Police claimed that Cruz had left nothing to chance and had even developed a five-point plan to help him stalk Easton. It was clear that Cruz had taken great care to protect himself against exposure. For instance, he made phone calls and sent text messages using five different phones. In addition, Cruz used passwords and encryption to protect data on his computer system, although investigators were eventually able to discover his password—"Abuser." According to police, Cruz also attempted to cover himself by fabricating evidence that would point to his roommate. Furthermore, when Easton accused Cruz of harassment, he made a counterclaim, saying that she had sent various messages to him. In reality, he had forged the messages after breaking into Easton's e-mail account.

After Cruz's arrest, investigators learned that he had been involved in a very similar incident involving a student from Tennessee (BBC News, 2003). Cruz had a brief relationship with the student when they met in England in 1998. When the student broke off the relationship and returned to the United States, Cruz began to harass her using some of the methods he employed against Easton. Although police attempted to investigate the case, they were unable to locate Cruz in order to question him. Unfortunately, the statute of limitations ran out before Cruz could be located and charged, so police could not take the case further.

5

Who Are the Victims of Cyberstalkers?

THE KACIE WOODY STORY

Kacie Rene Woody, a thirteen-year-old girl from Arkansas and the daughter of a police officer, was abducted from her home by David Fuller, a forty-seven-year-old man from San Diego, California. Fuller took Woody to a storage garage he had rented around fifteen miles from Woody's home, where he may have sexually assaulted her. When police arrived at the storage garage to search for Woody, they heard a gunshot from inside. A SWAT team spent more than two hours attempting to negotiate before storming the building. When they entered, they found that Fuller had shot Woody to death before committing suicide. Officers believed that the shot heard when they first approached the storage units was Fuller taking his own life (MostlyCreativeWorkshop, 2002).

Further investigation revealed that Fuller had met Woody in a chat room several weeks before her murder. A month before he abducted Woody, Fuller had traveled to Arkansas from his home in San Diego, apparently to rent a camper and the storage unit where he planned to take her. Investigators were certain that Woody had not invited Fuller to meet her and that she did not know he was coming. However, on the day she was kidnapped, Woody confided to a friend in a chat room that she thought she was being followed. She also told her friend that she had been receiving calls from someone she had been chatting with online for the past month (*North County Times*, 2002).

Woody's brother raised the alert when he was unable to find her after four hours. Woody's online friend, who lived in Georgia, also contacted his local police when she suddenly stopped answering his messages. Police officers suspected Woody had been kidnapped when they realized that she appeared to have left the house without her shoes (NBCSandiego.com, 2002). Officers also found signs of a struggle— Woody's eyeglasses were broken and a chair was out of place (TheSanDiegoChannel.com, 2002).

When investigators checked Woody's computer, they learned that she had been in contact with someone calling himself David Fagan, who claimed to be an eighteen year old from California. However, Woody had actually been talking to David Fuller, a Persian Gulf War veteran and former used car salesman. When police contacted local motels to find people who had checked in before Woody's disappearance, they came to suspect that David Fuller and David Fagan were the same person. This was confirmed when it was found that Fuller's motel registration information contained a phone number matching a cell phone that had been used to call Woody's home. Checking Fuller's credit card information led to the rented camper and the storage unit (*North County Times*, 2002).

Following Fuller's death, police became concerned that Woody may not been his first victim (MSNBC, 2002; NBCSandiego.com, 2002). This was because Woody's abduction seemed to have been well planned and Fuller had made few mistakes.

INTRODUCTION

Who are the victims of cyberstalking? Who is most at risk of cyberstalking? What is the impact of stalking/cyberstalking on victims? As with the previous chapter, I begin by looking at research related to offline stalking. As will be shown, it is possible to identify those groups most at risk by looking at some of the characteristics of stalking victims. The same approach is used when discussing research related to cyberstalking victims. Although victims of offline stalking and cyberstalking share many similarities, there are also significant differences. In terms of similarities, for example, it seems clear that most stalking and cyberstalking victims are female. In terms of significant differences, it may be that fewer cyberstalking victims know the identity of their harasser.

In the last section of the chapter, I attempt to provide an understanding of the impact of stalking and cyberstalking on victims. Once more, the discussion concentrates on recent research related to the effects of stalking and cyberstalking. As will be shown, many victims are profoundly affected by their experiences, often making major lifestyle changes because of the fear, anxiety, and distress they have suffered as a result of harassment.

WHAT RESEARCH REVEALS ABOUT VICTIMS OF OFFLINE STALKERS

The National Violence Against Women Survey reported on by Tjaden and Thoennes (1998) is considered highly influential and has helped to shape the official U.S. response to stalking. This nationally representative telephone survey of 8,000 women and 8,000 men is considered to offer a very accurate view of stalking in the United States.

As might be expected, the survey found that most stalking victims were women (78 percent). In terms of age, the majority of victims were eighteen to twenty-nine (52 percent) or thirty to thirty-nine years old (22 percent). The average age of stalking victims was twenty-eight.

In general, there was no difference in stalking rates between white women and those from ethnic minorities. However, when specific ethnic groups were taken into account it was found that American Indian/Alaska Native women reported significantly more victimization. On the other hand, Asian and Pacific Islander women were much less likely to be stalked than women from other ethnic groups. There are several possible explanations for this finding. For example, the report suggests that women from an Asian/Pacific Islander background may be more reluctant than women of other ethnic groups to report harassment.

Most people in this survey knew their stalker. Only 23 percent of female stalking victims were harassed by strangers. In the case of women, 38 percent were stalked by a spouse or ex-spouse, 10 percent by a partner or ex-partner, and 14 percent by a date or former date. As noted in chapter 4, it was found that "contrary to popular opinion, women are often stalked by intimate partners while the relationship is still intact" (Tjaden and Thoennes, 1998, p. 6).

In general, the figures for men were significantly lower than those for women. For instance, only 13 percent of males were harassed by a spouse or ex-spouse. However, males were much more likely to be stalked by acquaintances (34 percent) or strangers (36 percent). And, as noted earlier, there was also some evidence that homosexual men were more at risk of being stalked than heterosexual men. The report speculates that this may be a result of homophobia.

Another nationally representative study of stalking was conducted as part of the 1998 British Crime Survey (see also chapter 4). As with Tjaden and Thoennes's work, the survey found that women were most at risk of being stalked. Young women in particular were at risk, especially those aged sixteen to nineteen and twenty to twenty-four (Budd and Mattinson, 2000).

The survey also found a number of factors that increased the likelihood of being stalked. The risk for women of being stalked increased if they were students (12.4 percent), single (9.8 percent), living in privately rented accommodation (7.4 percent), living in a flat or maisonette (a two-story building divided into two apartments) (6.6 percent), or living in a household with an annual income of less than £15,000 (approximately $24,000) (5.3 percent). The survey noted that some of these risks might overlap; for instance, a student might live off-campus in rented accommodation.

A number of other significant findings were reported (Budd, Mattinson, and Myhill, 2000). Women who were married or widowed were least likely to become victims of stalking. Single men were significantly more at risk than married men. In terms of employment, as mentioned earlier, students were most at risk to be stalked. However, the unemployed—especially unemployed women—were also at high risk. Those least at risk were the retired. It was also found that, in general, the more educated the person, the greater the risk of becoming a stalking victim. Finally, in almost a third of the incidents (29 percent), the stalker was an intimate or ex-intimate of the victim (e.g., wife, partner, etc.). The other incidents were committed by strangers (34 percent), acquaintances (32 percent), or relatives and friends (6 percent).

In another major study, Purcell, Pathé, and Mullen (2000) conducted a mail survey of 3,700 Australian men and women, achieving a response rate of more than 60 percent. The study found a lifetime stalking incidence of stalking of 23.4 percent. As with other studies, younger people were more likely to be stalked than older people. For instance, the lifetime cumulative incidence of stalking for those eighteen to thirty-five years old was 31.8 percent, but only 14.6 percent for those over fifty-six.

In terms of gender, women were more likely to be stalked (75 percent) than men, and 43 percent reported being between sixteen and thirty years old when the stalking began. With regard to their relationships, it was found that those who reported stalking were more likely to be separated or divorced females. It was also found that:

> The majority of those reporting stalking were pursued by someone previously known to them (57%), being a prior intimate partner in 13%, casual acquaintance in 15%, or an individual encountered in a work context (16%). Harassment by neighbours (5%), family members (4%), estranged friends (3%) and casual dates (1%) was also reported. In 42% the

perpetrator was a stranger to the victim, or someone whose identity, though suspected, was yet to be revealed. (Purcell, Pathé, and Mullen, 2000, p. 3)

Purcell, Pathé, and Mullen (2000) also looked at duration of harassment and methods used to pursue victims. Victims reported that harassment lasted from one day to forty years, with an average of almost eight months. This is a significantly shorter period of time than found by other surveys. Tjaden and Thoessen (1998, p. 12), for instance, found that stalking cases last an average of 1.8 years. However, as will be seen, Purcell, Pathé, and Mullen's figure is in keeping with that found in a study of cyberstalking. Duration of harassment was found to vary according to the relationship between the victim and her stalker. Those pursued by ex-intimates experienced a longer duration of stalking (average 16.6 months) than those pursued by strangers (average 0.8 months).

Another interesting aspect of Purcell, Pathé, and Mullen's (2000) work is the attention they paid to the number of behaviors experienced by stalking victims. Most victims (53 percent) experienced only one or two forms of intimidation. A sizeable group of respondents (37 percent) experienced three to five forms, and some people (8 percent) even experienced six or more forms of intimidation. This is significant because it appears that those stalked by ex-intimates are subjected to more forms of intimidation than those stalked by strangers (an average of 4.7 behaviors versus an average of 2 behaviors).

In the United Kingdom, Sheridan, Davies, and Boon (2001) conducted a mail survey of ninety-five stalking victims. In terms of the respondents, the survey found that most stalking victims (92 percent) were female, although the sample included a married couple who had completed the questionnaire together. In terms of age, the youngest victim was just two years old and the oldest was seventy. The average age of victims was 33.74.

The survey revealed some interesting findings regarding the victims' employment and socioeconomic status. The largest groups were professionals (27 percent), clerical (18 percent), homemakers (12 percent), and students (10 percent). The unemployed made up 6 percent of the sample, and unskilled workers accounted for a further 8 percent. Interestingly, it appears that the socioeconomic status of respondents altered as a result of stalking. This is most clearly seen by looking at changes in employment over the course of stalking. For instance, it was found that

during the course of stalking, the occupational status of the victims altered substantially. For instance, 26 were in professional occupations

when they were first stalked, and just ten described themselves as professionals when they completed the questionnaires. Similarly, the number of victims in clerical occupations dropped from 17 to just three.
(Sheridan, Davies, and Boon, 2001, p. 218)

In many cases, these changes were clearly linked to the effects of stalking, for instance some people reported that they had changed jobs as
a result of being stalked.

In keeping with other studies, most victims knew their stalker. The
stalker was an ex-intimate (48 percent) or acquaintance (37 percent) in
most cases. Only 12 percent of stalkers were strangers.

In looking at the duration of stalking, the study found that the average period was 7.71 years. This was undoubtedly influenced by one
or more extreme cases; for instance, the shortest period was six months
and the longest was forty-three years. However, these figures emphasize the fact that stalking can last a very long time, becoming part of
the daily lives of victims, their families, and friends.

WHAT RESEARCH REVEALS ABOUT VICTIMS
OF CYBERSTALKERS

Working to Halt Online Abuse (WHOA) is one of the largest Internet
safety organizations in the world. The organization began collecting
information on the cases it handles in early 2000 and has published a
selection of statistics on its web site.[1] The statistics available at this
writing described a total of 827 cases handled from January 2000 to
December 2002.

It should be remembered, however, that the data WHOA provides
are not representative since it consists of information obtained from
self-selected stalking victims. In addition, in many cases the data is in-
complete, usually because victims of stalking have been unwilling or
unable to provide various pieces of information. Despite these problems, WHOA's figures remain the *only* widely accessible statistics.

Some of WHOA's data are broken down into figures for 2000, 2001,
and 2002. Although this may sometimes provide a little extra detail,
most of the figures discussed here are the averages provided by the
organization for the period 1 January 2000 to 31 December 2002. Unless
specified otherwise, the values given here are the cumulative (average)
figures provided by WHOA.

In terms of age, 41 percent of victims were aged eighteen to thirty,
26 percent were aged thirty-one to forty, and 14 percent were aged
forty-one or above. It should be noted that many respondents (19 per-

cent) did not reveal their ages. Interestingly, the figures for 2002 show that the majority of victims were aged eighteen to thirty (49 percent) or thirty-one to forty (36 percent).

In keeping with studies of offline stalking, it was found that most cyberstalking victims were women (61.5 percent). Victims' gender was not known in 7.5 percent of cases. In attempting to explain the large number of women, WHOA makes the point that women may be more likely to report their experiences or seek help than men.

The marital status of 15 percent of victims was not known. Of the remainder, 43 percent were single, 32 percent were married or living with a partner, and 10 percent were separated or divorced.

With regard to ethnicity, almost a third of victims (29 percent) did not provide this information. Of those who revealed their ethnicity, most victims were Caucasian (62 percent), Hispanic (3 percent), Asian (2 percent), African American (2 percent), or Native American (1 percent).

Using the average figures for 2000 and 2001,[2] it was found that the majority of cyberstalking victims were found to live in the United States (57.81 percent).[3] However, it was noted that almost a third of respondents (33.98 percent) did not give their location. Smaller groups lived in Canada (1.17 percent), Australia (1.17 percent), the Netherlands (1.17 percent), and the United Kingdom (2.73 percent). All other groups represented less than 1 percent, with fewer than three victims. In the United States, the largest groups of victims lived California, Florida, Illinois, New York, Texas, and Massachusetts.

In looking at how people become victimized by cyberstalkers, victims were asked what method was used to begin their harassment. The largest groups of victims were harassed by e-mail (41.7 percent), in chat rooms (12.97 percent), message boards/forums (12.24 percent), and by instant message (10.3 percent).

The average figures for 2000 and 2001 revealed that that almost half of all cyberstalking victims were harassed by a stranger (49.26 percent). There had been prior contact of some kind between the victim and the cyberstalker in 46.31 percent of cases. In 4.43 percent of cases, the level of contact between victim and cyberstalker was not known. Figures for 2002 revealed that most victims had come to know their cyberstalkers online (28 percent), as an ex-partner or intimate (27 percent), as a friend (16 percent), through work (9 percent), or as a former customer (7 percent).

WHOA also asked respondents if they knew the gender of their harassers. It was found that most cyberstalkers (61.5 percent) were male and that 31 percent were female. In all other cases, the gender of the cyberstalker was not known. Interestingly, WHOA has observed that the number of female cyberstalkers has grown, whereas the number of male cyberstalkers seems to have declined. For instance, the proportion of female cyberstalkers grew from 27 percent in 2000 to 35 percent in 2002.

Victims were asked to indicate if the harassment escalated online. Figures for 2001 (60.6 percent) and 2002 (66 percent) show that the harassment did not escalate in most cases. However, cyberstalking often turned into offline stalking. In 2001, more than a third of victims (35.9 percent) answered "yes" to the question "Were there offline threats or stalking?" A similar figure was reported for 2002 (34 percent).

In my own research (Bocij, 2003), I conducted a survey of 169 Internet users in order to learn more about how cyberstalking affects its victims. It must be stressed that the sample used was not representative and that the findings are considered tentative.

Allowing for cases that may have involved more than one stalker, approximately a third of respondents (33.9 percent) could be considered genuine victims of cyberstalking.

Most cyberstalking victims were female (62.5 percent) and thirty years or older (60.7 percent). Only 19.6 percent of respondents were under twenty, and a further 19.6 percent were between twenty-one and thirty. More than three-quarters of respondents (76.5 percent) were married or living with a partner. In general, the younger the person, the less distressed she or he was likely to feel as a result of harassment. For instance, when asked to self-rate the level of distress felt on a scale from one to ten, those aged forty-one to fifty represented the largest group (25 percent) that reported a level of ten.

All respondents (100 percent) thirty-one or over stated that they used the Internet every day. Approximately 73 percent of those under thirty used the Internet every day.

Most respondents lived in the United States (46.4 percent) or the United Kingdom (43.9 percent). In terms of ethnicity, most respondents described themselves as being of British origin (40.3 percent) or as African-Caribbean (33.9 percent).

A large group of cyberstalking victims (42.1 percent) did not know the identity of the person who harassed them. Only a small number of respondents claimed to have been harassed by a work colleague (1.75 percent) or a former intimate partner (8.77 percent). Close to a quarter (23.81 percent) of respondents stated that their cyberstalker encouraged others to take part in the harassment. Almost 42 percent of those who did not know the identity of their cyberstalker said that the stalker had encouraged others to take part in the harassment.

Although for many the harassment had ceased, 26.3 percent reported that they were still being harassed at the time they completed the questionnaire. Respondents were asked to state how long their harassment had lasted. The shortest period of harassment was two weeks, the longest thirty-eight months. The average was 7.95 months, but most cases of harassment (63.2 percent) ended within six months.

A series of questions classified respondents as novice, intermediate, or expert computer users. Using this classification, novice computer users made up 26.8 percent of the sample, intermediate users 44.6 percent, and expert users 28.6 percent. When users self-rated their knowledge and experience of computing on a scale from one to ten, the majority (75 percent) rated themselves between five and eight, with an average of 6.62.

In general, the greater a person's knowledge and experience of ICT, the less distressed he or she was likely to feel as a result of harassment. For instance, when asked to self-rate the level of distress felt on a scale from one to ten, expert users represented only 28.6 percent of those who reported a level of ten. The average level of distress for novice users was 8.63. No novice users reported a level of distress below five, and 50 percent reported a ten. In comparison, the mean level of distress for expert users was eight, and only 30 percent reported a ten.

Differences were also noted in the behaviors experienced by novice and expert users. In general, novice computer users reported receiving more threats than expert users. For example, 87.5 percent of novice users reported being threatened via instant messaging software, compared with only 60 percent of expert users. However, expert users reported more attacks on data, hardware, and software. For instance, 70 percent of expert users reported attempts to insert Trojan horse infiltrating software, compared with only 37.5 percent of novice users.

Gauging levels of ICT knowledge and experience is helpful in examining areas such as respondents' level of distress. In general, one would expect respondents with a good knowledge of technology to feel less threatened by cyberstalking incidents. This is because such people are likely to be less vulnerable than other computer users, a view supported by the results of the study. For instance, more than 97 percent of expert users reported using a personal firewall, compared with just 31.6 percent of novice users. It seems reasonable to suggest, then, that most expert users are likely to consider themselves to be relatively safe from computer viruses, Trojans, key loggers (keystroke recorder), and so on.

One reason expert computer users might feel less threatened than novice users is because they understand more of what is and is not possible in terms of "attacks" perpetrated by computer. For instance, there are many urban myths associated with computer viruses, such as viruses that can cause a computer monitor to explode.[4] It is easy to see how such misconceptions can cause novice computer users to feel a great deal of distress.

WHAT RESEARCH REVEALS ABOUT THE IMPACT OF STALKING AND CYBERSTALKING ON VICTIMS

The harm experienced by victims of stalking and cyberstalking is often overlooked. Hence, in exploring what characterizes victims of stalking, it seems reasonable also to consider the effects of stalking and cyberstalking. Although there has been virtually no research done dealing with the impact of cyberstalking on victims, there seems little reason to believe that it is significantly more or less harmful than offline stalking. With this in mind, this section focuses on research describing the effects of offline stalking on victims.

A number of writers have noted that stalking can easily become a major part of a victim's life, influencing every aspect of her daily routine and causing tremendous psychological damage. For instance, a great deal of harm can be caused when stalking is prolonged and victims are unable to gain respite:

> It is not hard to imagine that months or years of exposure to persecution and threats can lead to serious psychological consequences. In particular, it is the constancy of threat into the private domain that causes the greatest distress to victims of stalking. The protracted and intense sense of intrusion and violation, by definition without an escape haven, is what seems to set stalking distress apart from other more or less traumatic types of stress. (Kamphuis and Emmelkamp, 2000, p. 208)

A good example of the harm caused by stalking involves the case of a woman who was harassed after a failed relationship:

> The victim suffered from depression, anxiety, guilt, shame, helplessness, humiliation, and post-traumatic stress disorder (PTSD). The stalking affected her psychological, interpersonal, and occupational functioning. Consequently, she was fired for poor work performance and poor attendance. (Abrams and Robinson, 2002, p. 468)

It is also worth remembering that stalking may affect different victims in different ways. For example, British researcher Emily Finch makes the point that individual differences may determine the harm suffered by stalking victims:

> Response to stalking is inextricably linked to the psychology of the victim and it is clear that conduct that renders one victim insensible with fear may leave another victim wholly unmoved. Victims respond in a variety of ways ranging from amusement or indifference on the one hand to more extreme reactions causing significant psychological damage at the other end of the continuum. (Finch, 2002, p. 424)

The U.S. Department of Justice prepared a special report on stalking and domestic violence for Congress in May 2001. In trying to describe how seriously stalking affects people's lives, U.S. Attorney General John Ashcroft said: "A number of victims described stalking as a nightmare that invaded all aspects of their lives. They spent a great deal of energy, time, and money just trying to stay alive" (Ashcroft, 2001, p. 23).

The report notes that many victims try to protect themselves by controlling the information kept about them by various people and groups, such as government agencies. Victims will often change their personal details such as telephone number, address, and social security number. In addition, people also try to restrict public access to information about them, for example by removing their details from mailing lists. Some people go further and attempt to screen those who try to contact them, perhaps by subscribing to a caller ID service for their telephone. In extreme cases, stalking victims may take even more drastic steps, such as

> changing their lifestyles and restricting their communication with others by, for example, altering routines, discontinuing activities, switching jobs, finding new schools for children, temporarily or permanently relocating, and ceasing communication with family and friends. (Ashcroft, 2001, p. 24)

Ashcroft's report also describes some of the emotional and psychological costs of stalking by listing some of the stalking victims' reactions reported via a focus group:

- Powerlessness/loss of control
- Feelings of desperation and isolation
- Self-blame or shame
- Hypervigilance and overreactivity

- Sleep disturbances such as nightmares and difficulty falling asleep or staying awake
- Avoidance of intimacy
- Weight loss or gain
- Substance abuse
- Intense fear of specific and general things such as being alone or in crowds
- Anxiety and depression
- Spiritual crises (Ashcroft, 2001, p. 24)

One of the most important points made by the report is that stalking affects whole groups of people, not just individual victims. The relatives, friends, and colleagues of a stalking victim may become *secondary victims* of stalking (Pathé, 2002, p. 48). For instance, a stalker may target a friend or relative as a way of controlling the primary victim. Alternatively, friends or relatives may witness acts of stalking or may suffer psychological harm as they offer comfort to the primary victim. There may also be indirect effects of stalking. For example, a child may need to take time off school. As shown by Kacie Woody's tragic murder at the hands of a cyberstalker, there is no doubt that stalking and cyberstalking can affect the lives of family and friends permanently.

There can also be financial costs associated with stalking. According to Ashcroft's report, some 26 percent of stalking victims had taken time off work as a result of stalking. Much of this time was taken "to attend court hearings, meet with a psychologist or other mental health professional, avoid contact with the assailant, and consult with an attorney" (Ashcroft, 2001, p. 25). The average time missed from work as a result of stalking was eleven days. Some 7 percent of stalking victims never returned to work at all.

In another study, Eric Blaauw and his colleagues (2002) conducted a survey of 241 stalking victims and found that all reported multiple stalking behaviors. Most respondents reported a variety of behaviors, including unwanted telephone calls and letters, surveillance, being followed, destruction of property, and physical assaults. Two-thirds (66 percent) of victims reported that their harassment had lasted for two years or more. A sizable group (13 percent) said that their stalking had lasted ten years or more.

Many victims reported that the frequency of stalking varied from day to day. For instance, some victims said that the stalking had stopped for several months and then started again. In addition, many victims (68 percent) said they were stalked more often on a daily basis at the start of the harassment than at the end (34 percent). Overall, around half of victims (47 percent) felt that the frequency of their harassment had decreased over time. Only 4 percent of victims felt that the stalking had intensified over time.

Most victims (93 percent) sought help from mental health professionals, the police (89 percent), or took legal action against their stalkers (45 percent). However, these actions often failed to bring relief, forcing victims to take other measures:

> Many victims had taken matters into their own hands by acquiring an unlisted telephone number (81%), relocating (44%), going underground (40%), quitting their job or working less (39%), changing jobs (21%), avoiding social outings (63%), taking additional security measures (65%), or even assaulting the stalker (19%). Again, many of these actions had not generated the desired results; many times the victims noted that the stalker had once again obtained the victim's telephone number or work or home address. Many victims reported that "nothing seems to work." (Blaauw et al., 2002, p. 57)

Understandably, Blaauw et al.'s study (2002) found that many respondents had suffered a great deal of harm as a result of their experiences. For instance, the General Health Questionnaire used as part of the study indicated that 78 percent of respondents might have a diagnosable psychiatric disorder. Several victims also had a history of suicide attempts, and 31 percent of respondents described repeated thoughts about committing suicide.

The work of Blaauw and his colleagues (2002) has also identified a link between the psychological harm caused to victims and the number and type of stalking behaviors experienced. It was found that victims reported more symptoms if they had been followed or had experienced theft/destruction of property. Victims also reported more symptoms if they experienced six or more forms of stalking behavior.

The 1998 British Crime Survey also looked at how the experiences of stalking victims affected their lives (Budd and Mattinson, 2000; Budd, Mattinson, and Myhill, 2000). In keeping with some of the other studies described within this chapter, this study found that many stalking cases (19 percent) lasted for a year or more. Around a third of cases lasted less than a month, and an additional 26 percent lasted between one and three months.

Victims experienced a wide range of behaviors, including being forced to talk to the stalker (49 percent), silent telephone calls (45 percent), physical intimidation (42 percent), being followed (39 percent), and the stalker waiting outside the victim's home (33 percent). The majority of victims (78 percent) experienced more than one stalking behavior. Approximately half of stalking victims experienced two to five behaviors, and a third of victims experienced six or more types of behavior. Men and women tended to have different experiences of stalking. Women experienced a wider range of stalking behaviors, but men experienced more threats of violence or actual violence. With regard to violence, many stalking victims feared being attacked (31 percent) or feared that violence might be used against a friend or relative (27 percent). Women were more concerned that violence might be used against them than men were. However, men were more concerned that violence might be used against someone they knew.

In terms of the impact of the stalking on victims, it was reported that

> 92% of victims said they were annoyed or irritated by the experience (70% "very" and 21% "fairly"). Three-quarters had found the experience distressing or upsetting (50% "very" and 24% "fairly"). Women were particularly likely to have been "very" distressed or upset (57% of women compared with 32% of men). (Budd and Mattinson, 2000, p. 3)

The majority of victims (71 percent) said that they had changed their lifestyle as a result of stalking. Most people (59 percent) now avoided certain places or people, some went out less than before (35 percent), and many started taking more personal security measures (42 percent). More than three-quarters of women said that they had changed their behavior compared with 59 percent of men.

A study by Pathé and Mullen (1997) provides a detailed and harrowing account of how stalking affected the lives of 100 Australian stalking victims. Most stalking victims were women (83 percent), and most (52 percent) were still experiencing stalking at the time they completed the questionnaire. The average length of stalking was two years, although some victims reported being stalked for as long as twenty years.

All victims experienced several forms of stalking behavior. Most reported silent, abusive, or threatening telephone calls (78 percent), unwanted letters (62 percent), direct approaches (79 percent), being followed or being kept under surveillance (71 percent), or property damage (36 percent). The majority of victims also received threats, many directed at the victim's family or friends (43 percent). Approximately a third of victims (31 percent) were physically assaulted, and 7 percent were sexually assaulted. A link was found between threats of violence and actual assaults on victims: thirty-four victims had experienced personal violence, and twenty-six of them had been threatened previously. Women were at more risk of violence than men, and the risk to both was increased if there had been an intimate relationship between the stalker and the victim.

The work of Pathé and Mullen provides a powerful description of the psychological and social impact of stalking on whole families:

> Over half of the victims had curtailed, changed or ceased work altogether. Many of those professionally employed considered their professional reputation had suffered as a direct or indirect result of the stalking. A number of victims felt compelled to shift residence, in some cases overseas, sacrificing ties with an increasingly precarious social network.
>
> The psychological suffering in this group was pronounced. Many felt powerless to change their situation and a quarter of the sample had contemplated escape through suicide. A sense of violation and inability to trust were common. Anger and guilt were experienced frequently, as victims found their own actions and those of expected sources of help ineffectual. (1997, p. 14)

In looking at the psychological suffering of victims, Pathé and Mullen (1997) found that more than half of the group studied displayed symptoms commonly associated with post-traumatic stress disorder (PTSD). Over half of the group (55 percent) said that they experienced flashbacks of their stalking experiences, usually brought on by a knock at the door or the telephone ringing. Some people even experienced flashbacks many years after the stalking had ended. Seeing someone with a familiar face, or hearing a familiar voice, also caused flashbacks. In all, 37 percent of stalking victims met the criteria for a diagnosis of PTSD.

Pathé and Mullen (1997, p. 16) also found that the effects of stalking affected the victims' physical health:

- Eighty-three percent suffered heightened anxiety levels, described as "jumpiness," "shakes," panic attacks, or hypervigilance
- Seventy-four percent experienced chronic sleep disturbance, for example due to recurring nightmares
- Forty-eight percent reported that their appetites had been affected. Almost half of the group (45 percent) reported changes in their weight. Although most people lost weight, some gained weight in an attempt to make themselves seem less attractive to their stalkers.
- Thirty percent reported persistent nausea, and 27 percent reported frequent indigestion
- Twenty-three percent increased their consumption of cigarettes or alcohol
- Fifty-five percent reported tiredness or weakness
- Forty-seven percent reported increased or more severe headaches

A common response to stalking was to make major lifestyle changes that often affected the victim's entire family (Pathé and Mullen, 1997,

p. 15). All but six victims reported making major changes, and 82 percent had changed their usual routine as a direct result of being stalked.[5]

Many people avoided going to any place the stalker might be, such as supermarkets or parking lots. Some even changed their driving habits, becoming extremely cautious and being careful to drive home by varied routes.

At home, some people took extra security precautions, for example by changing their names, obtaining an unlisted telephone number, or installing a sophisticated alarm system. Some female victims took self-defense courses or kept weapons under their beds. Some women even underwent firearms training.

Most people (70 percent) went out less often through fear of meeting their stalker. When the stalker was a neighbor, victims tended to spend as little time at home as possible. Some stalking victims forbade young children from answering the door or the telephone. One person even stopped her children from playing outside.

More than half of victims (53 percent) missed time from work or school. Some were forced to give up their jobs because of the anxiety they were suffering. Some people also lost their jobs when their work performance deteriorated or when stalkers caused problems for employers, for example by repeatedly phoning the workplace. Stalking also affected the work of friends, family, and work colleagues. In one case, for example, the husband of a stalking victim gave up working to stay at home and protect his wife.

Stalking also caused upheaval by forcing victims to change jobs or move home: "In 37% of cases, stalking necessitated a change in workplace, school or career. Thirty-nine per cent of victims relocated residence (up to five times); seven moved between states and three overseas" (Pathé and Mullen, 1997, p. 16).

Some of the findings made by researchers such as Pathé and Mullen are echoed in the work of others. For instance, in a recent study, Sheridan, Davies, and Boon (2001, p. 227) asked ninety-five stalking victims to choose from a list of adjectives the one that best described their feelings as a result of being stalked. A large group (41 percent) said that they had experienced all of the emotions on the list. Of those who chose one emotion, among the most common choices were "fear" (18 percent), "terrorized" (15 percent), "intimidation" (7 percent), "imprisoned" (5 percent), and "powerlessness" (4 percent).

Sheridan, Davies, and Boon also asked respondents if they had made any changes to their lifestyles as a result of stalking.

Just 6% (6) said that no, they had not. Nearly half (44%) said that they had altered their behaviour in such matters as taking a different route to work, or stopping going out alone in public, *and* had changed their telephone number, *and* had moved house. A further 20% (19) had made behavioural changes, and had also altered their telephone number. (2001, p. 228)

Perhaps one of the most significant and disturbing findings was that 22 percent of victims had tried to avoid their stalkers by moving to another county or even another country. However, such a strategy was not always effective owing to the sheer persistence of some stalkers. One woman, for example, described how she had moved 200 miles away without telling anyone of her new address. Despite this, her stalker somehow traced her new location after only three weeks.

CONCLUSION

Several studies have shown that most victims of cyberstalking are women. In addition, most victims live in the United States, Canada, Australia, the Netherlands, and the United Kingdom. The largest groups of cyberstalking victims appear to be aged eighteen to thirty and thirty-one to forty. A large proportion of cyberstalking victims are pursued by strangers. In many cases, victims have reported that the cyberstalker encouraged other people to take part in the harassment.

Almost a third of cyberstalking cases may turn into offline stalking. Research suggests that the average length of a cyberstalking case is almost eight months. However, most cases end within six months.

A person's knowledge and experience of ICT may influence the behaviors experienced by cyberstalking victims. In general, novice computers users experience more threats than expert users. However, expert users experience more attacks on data, hardware, and software. Knowledge and experience of ICT may also influence the level of distress felt as a result of harassment. In general, expert computer users are likely to feel less distress than novice computer users.

Many experts agree that prolonged stalking can cause severe psychological, emotional, and physical harm to victims. In terms of psychological harm, many victims come to exhibit the symptoms of post-traumatic stress disorder, and many even contemplate suicide as a way of escaping their tormenter. As well as harming psychological and emotional health, stalking can also affect victims' physical health.

Many stalking victims take drastic action in order to protect themselves against their stalkers. This can include relocating or cutting off all communication with friends and relatives. In these types of cases, the friends, relatives, and colleagues of victims are secondary victims of stalking.

It should be clear that cyberstalkers can hold a great deal of power over their victims. As has been shown, stalking and cyberstalking can cause victims to lose their jobs, become estranged from family and friends, and even become mentally ill. However, a desire for power over the victim is not the only motivation behind cyberstalking. The next chapter outlines some of the other motivations that can encourage a person to become a cyberstalker.

6

What Motivates Cyberstalkers?

THE STORY OF THE BOEHLE FAMILY

The Boehle family underwent a campaign of harassment that lasted for two and a half years and eventually forced them to move (Raphael, 2000b). The family's ordeal began when they started receiving telephone calls from men who asked to speak with the family's nine-year-old daughter. The calls were considered "menacing" by the family since they often occurred late at night and usually involved callers asking for the child by name. After receiving a number of such calls, the family asked for help from the police. They were advised to change their telephone number and keep their daughter inside the house.

Dissatisfied with the response given by the police, Mike Boehle, the child's father, decided to investigate further. He eventually came to suspect that a neighbor with whom he had argued on several occasions had organized the calls. Eventually, he was able to determine that the neighbor had been using the Internet to post messages about the child—along with the Boehle family phone number—making it appear that she was soliciting sex from strangers. Apparently, the neighbor had begun a campaign of harassment because of a number of relatively trivial incidents, such as when the child had written in chalk the word *hello* near the neighbor's driveway. The neighbor, Charles Gary Rogers, was given away by the subject line of one of his messages: "Hello on the driveway."

After moving to a new community in order to protect the identity of the child, the family contacted the Computer Crime Unit of a neighboring police department. Officers were able to compare telephone records with the date and time of each message posted to the Internet. Each time a message had been posted about the child, Rogers had been online. Following his arrest, Rogers was convicted only of transmitting obscene material, a misdemeanor for which he received only a $750 fine. On the other hand, the Boehle family was forced to move and were subjected to more than two years of harassment.

There are several points worth noting about this case. First, relatively little provocation was needed in order for the neighbor to begin what can be described as an organized, prolonged campaign of harassment. Second, it was easy for Rogers to post messages on behalf of the child to produce the results he wanted. Third, until the specialist Computer Crime Unit became involved, the police seemed to show little concern for the family's distress and provided very limited assistance. Fourth, Rogers seems to have been treated very leniently by the legal system, indicating that cyberstalking may not always be taken seriously. Such sentences are unlikely to have a deterrent effect on others and might add to the distress felt by victims. Finally, the very real sense of fear felt by the family should not be underestimated. In an interview, Deborah Boehle, the child's mother, said, "Even though he never touched my daughter . . . he literally led millions of pedophiles to her" (Raphael, 2000b).

INTRODUCTION

What makes a "normal" person become a cyberstalker? As was seen in chapter 4, many of the classifications of stalkers in common use are based on the assumption that stalkers have some form of mental health problem. Although these classifications help to explain some of the motivations behind stalking, they do not explain how people move from inaction to the active pursuit of others. For instance, one man cyberstalks his former wife following a bitter divorce, but another does not. Assuming both men are respectable citizens and have no history of mental illness, what is the catalyst for cyberstalking? Using another example, how might we explain the case of the Boehle family, in which the most trivial of incidents—a child writing with chalk on the sidewalk—resulted in a cyberstalking campaign that lasted for more than two years?

Understanding what influences a person to become a cyberstalker is essential to reducing this kind of harassment. It is important to remember that the number of potential cyberstalkers probably outnumbers the existing cyberstalkers active in the world today. In addition, the number of active cyberstalkers online is likely to grow as more people become computer literate and begin to use the Internet for work and leisure.

This chapter looks at the technological and social factors that encourage and enable cyberstalking. Although there may be many other factors that influence a person to become a cyberstalker, I have chosen to concentrate on issues related to technology and the Internet. In addition, I have avoided looking at issues that have not been examined by research. For instance, although it seems reasonable to suggest that some cyberstalkers exhibit attention-seeking behavior, this has not yet been investigated through research.

HOW TECHNOLOGY ENABLES CYBERSTALKING

Why do people become cyberstalkers? One way to approach this question is by suggesting that the Internet is a reflection of society, including some of its darker aspects, such as crime. Almost every form of deviance conceivable in the physical world is also represented on the Internet in one way or another:

> Because the Internet is as broad as the human psyche, it naturally encompasses all of the darkest manifestations of evil imaginable: every form of denigration of human dignity and antisocial behavior, from racial hatred and white supremacist ideology, to self-mutilation, torture and sado-masochism, to virulent misogynism, to violent extremism and Satanism. (Berg, 2001, p. 18)

People victimize others in many different ways. For instance, children are bullied on the playground, and some adults suffer sexual harassment in the workplace. It seems only natural that these kinds of behaviors can be transferred to the Internet. Although the methods used may change, the intent remains the same.

However, this kind of explanation cannot explain every incidence of cyberstalking, because it focuses on people who are already considered deviant or antisocial. Many of the cases we read about in the media or on web sites involve people who appear to be perfectly "normal." These people may live in respectable neighborhoods, hold good jobs, be well educated, and have no criminal record. Why do *these* people turn to cyberstalking as a means of harassing another person? Perhaps a better way of phrasing this question is this: What makes person who is reasonable and law-abiding in the offline world willing to take part in antisocial or criminal activities in the online world of the Internet?

I would argue that there is a combination of technological and social factors that encourages individuals to take part in criminal or antisocial acts such as cyberstalking. Some of the factors that might contribute to this situation are provided in Table 6.1. Although not intended to be exhaustive, this list offers a good starting point for further analysis and discussion.

TECHNOLOGICAL FACTORS

In general terms, it can be argued that technological factors encourage individuals to take part in deviant acts because they enable participation without fear of sanctions. In the Boehle case described earlier, the perpetrator received only minimal punishment for his crime. Technology provides both the mechanism through which the individual can act and the protection needed against arrest or other punishment. In this section, it is argued that part of the reason for this is that technology has become more accessible and easier to use. Furthermore, any typical person can now obtain the technical means needed to conceal his identity, obscure his actions, and do away with any evidence of wrongdoing.

Increased Access to Technology

The costs of buying, maintaining, and operating a personal computer have fallen steadily over the past two decades. For instance, it is not difficult to buy a new personal computer—complete with modem—for less than $500. Similarly, high speed Internet access is now available for the price of a standard dial-up subscription not long ago.

Even those unable to afford a personal computer can access the Internet with little difficulty through friends, relatives, cybercafés, public libraries, schools, universities, and other organizations. Although there is ample evidence to suggest the existence of a digital divide, there is also evidence to show that access to technology is improving (Bocij et al., 2002, pp. 671–72). For instance, as of September 2002, there were over 182 million people online in the United States and Canada and 34 million in the United Kingdom.[1] In the United

Table 6.1
Technological and Social Aspects of the Internet That May Enable or Encourage Deviant Behavior Such as Cyberstalking

Technological factors	Social factors
• Increased access to technology, including hardware, software, and services (e.g., through reduced costs)	• Disinhibition
• Increased familiarity with technology (e.g., use of e-mail)	• Deindividuation
• Ability to remain anonymous through technological means (e.g., anonymous remailers)	• Depersonalization/dehumanization
• Ability to disguise activities through technological means (e.g., encryption)	• Lack of policing (capable guardian)
• Ability to destroy evidence of deviant activities through technological means (e.g., secure file deletion)	• Perceptions of power and control
	• Physical and emotional distance
	• Formation of deviant groups
	• Formation of strategic identities

States alone, Internet access has grown from 18 million users in 1995 to 163 million in 2002.

The concept of a digital divide may go some way toward explaining why cyberstalking is virtually unheard of in some parts of the world. It can be argued that reduced access to technology also means fewer opportunities for technology to be abused. For instance, it is not surprising that there are no recorded cases of cyberstalking in Somalia, where there are only 200 Internet users out of a population of 7 million.[2]

Increased Familiarity with Technology

Over the past two decades, the public has become more educated concerning the use of ICT. It is not an exaggeration to suggest that education and training opportunities are now available to every member of society. Children learn to use technology as an integral part of their education. Adults attending university courses often undertake compulsory computing courses in order to gain skills such as word processing. Other learning opportunities arise from evening classes, distance learning courses, web-based training, work-based training, computer-based learning resources, books, and magazines. Even the housebound can now access training and education through schemes that make a computer, software, and training materials available on loan.

As people learn more about technology, their use of it tends to become more sophisticated. An e-mail user, for instance, may learn how to attach files to messages, use different typefaces, or forward messages to several people at a time. However, the skills and new learning acquired by computer users are not always put to harmless or practical use. The proliferation of newsgroups and web sites devoted to subjects such as hacking[3] and pornography tells us that many people have less benign goals.

Ability to Remain Anonymous

Although improved education and training have allowed the public to make better use of technology, improvements in the design of software have also played an important role. These improvements also have made it easier for cyberstalkers and others to remain anonymous when carrying out criminal or deviant acts. For instance, sending anonymous e-mail used to require a great deal of technical knowledge. Users needed to be able to create relatively complex scripts containing a series of instructions that described how to treat the message being sent.[4] Even if a user was able to create the necessary script, the overall process of sending messages—especially those containing file attachments—was slow and very unreliable. The massive expansion of the Internet has brought with it the introduction of web-based remailers, which make sending anonymous e-mail as easy as filling in a simple form on the screen. In addition, there are now many e-mail packages capable of handling anonymous e-mail that can be obtained free of charge.

A good example of a free package is QuickSilver.[5] QuickSilver is an e-mail package capable of automating the entire process of sending anonymous e-mail through a series of remailers. The program requires little technical knowledge to install and operate—it configures itself automatically and even downloads lists of working anonymous remailers, other configuration files, and program updates when needed. For all intents and purposes, the program appears as a typical e-mail package, hiding all of the complexity associated with "chaining"[6] anonymous e-mail behind a deceptively simple user interface.

Ability to Disguise Activities

Powerful, low-cost encryption software has also helped individuals to remain anonymous by concealing their activities. As with anonymous e-mail, encryption software used to be difficult to use and was often expensive. The introduction of various free encryption packages, such as Pretty Good Privacy (PGP), gave many computer users access to the most powerful encryption algorithms available.

Although encryption has many legitimate uses, criminals have been quick to adopt it as a way of avoiding detection. For instance, in many investigations involving child pornography, pedophiles have been found to be using PGP in order to disguise their activities (Denning and Baugh, 2000, p. 108).

Many people associate encryption with e-mail, believing it only of use when sending confidential messages. However, encryption can also be used to disguise the contents of files stored on a computer system. Many computer users employ file encryption to safeguard sensitive information, such as personal documents, passwords, and so on. Not surprisingly, file encryption is also used to disguise less innocent data, such as pornography or copies of abusive letters.

File encryption software has become so easy to use that it has become accessible to virtually every computer user. A good example of such a program is BestCrypt,[7] a package that creates an encrypted container file that can be used to hold confidential data. The container file appears as an additional hard disk drive on the user's computer system and can be used just like any other hard disk drive. The process of encrypting and decrypting files is completely automatic; files are encrypted when they are written to disk and decrypted in memory when they are read. This approach is called transparent encryption because users do not have to manually encrypt or decrypt files.

Ability to Destroy Evidence of Deviant Activities

An additional layer of security for those involved in deviant or criminal acts has appeared in the form of various utilities designed to delete all traces of Internet activity from an individual's computer system. For instance, packages such as Evidence Eliminator[8] erase details of any web sites visited, files downloaded, documents viewed, and so on. Files are erased securely, meaning that they cannot be recovered using forensic computing techniques. In addition, the package is comprehensive enough to deal with incriminating data that might be overlooked under normal circumstances, such as the contents of the Windows cache. The developers of the program are so confident of its capabilities that the package is advertised as "proven to defeat the exact same forensic software as used by the US Secret Service, Customs Department and Los Angeles Police Department (LAPD)."

There are many other types of software that can be used to destroy evidence of deviant or criminal behavior. File shredders are a good example of this kind of software. Under normal circumstances, when a file is deleted the data it contains is not destroyed until a new file overwrites it. This means that it is often possible to recover the contents of a file that supposedly has been deleted. File shredders ensure that deleted files are completely erased from a hard disk drive and cannot be recovered. As with encryption packages, this kind of software can be obtained free of charge and is easy to use.

SOCIAL FACTORS

The previous section argued that technology provides the means by which a person can take part in deviant or criminal activities on the Internet, such as cyberstalking. However, it can be argued that simply having the ability to do something does not necessarily motivate a person to do it. This section considers some of the social factors that may help to motivate a person to carry out antisocial or criminal acts via the Internet.

Disinhibition

Many writers have suggested that the anonymity offered by Internet creates a disinhibition effect (Griffiths, 2001; Wu Song, 2002; Joinson, 1998). In simple terms, disinhibition can be defined as follows:

1. Loss of inhibition, as through the influence of external stimuli such as drugs or alcohol, or as a result of brain damage.
2. Unrestrained behavior resulting from a lessening or loss of inhibitions or a disregard of cultural constraints.[9]

With regard to the Internet, Bubaš provides an excellent description of how disinhibition can encourage deviant behavior:

In FtF [face-to-face] communication, individuals are constrained by the social rules that govern interpersonal interaction, immediate negative feedback, and visible consequences of their inappropriate behavior, as well as by possible social sanctions. However, when using the Internet the users reside in relative anonymity and physical safety, distant from others in interaction, often unaware of their identities and personalities, as well as of the negative consequences of their risky or potentially damaging behavior. This contributes to the expression of anger or aggression, inappropriate self-disclosure, or personal use of socially doubtful material on the Internet, like pornography. (2001)

If the concept of disinhibition seems difficult to grasp, then it may be helpful to compare the influences Bubaš (2001) describes with some other, more familiar situations. For instance, all of the factors he describes also apply to the crank telephone calls sometimes made by children. One of the reasons a child may be willing to be rude or insulting to the person called is because the threat of reprisals is almost negligible. Using a telephone or cell phone can allow the caller to remain anonymous but also places a physical and emotional distance between the caller and the victim.

Another example might involve the effects alcohol has on some people. As indicated by the definition provided earlier, inhibitions are standards for acceptable behavior within society. For instance, most people are inhibited from stealing because they have been taught that theft is wrong. Research shows that alcohol tends to loosen inhibitions and impair judgment (George and Norris, 1996). In some cases, alcohol does little more than allow some people to become more extroverted, but in others, the effects can be more serious. For instance, the perpetrators of crimes such as rape and incest often blame alcohol for their behavior (George and Norris, 1996). In everyday communications, various forces control people's behavior, such as the reactions of those we talk to and the (largely unspoken) social rules that govern how we should behave with others. According to writers such as Bubaš (2001), the very nature of the Internet removes many of these controls so that inhibitions start to break down. As with the effects of alcohol, people may react in different ways when inhibitions are loosened. In writing about disinhibition and the Internet, psychologist John Suler describes how people may react:

> Sometimes people share very personal things about themselves. They reveal secret emotions, fears, wishes. Or they show unusual acts of kindness and generosity. On the other hand, the disinhibition effect may not be so benign. Out spills rude language and harsh criticisms, anger, hatred, even threats. Or people explore the dark underworld of the internet, places of pornography and violence, places they would never visit in the real world. (2003)

Deindividuation

Some writers argue that a process known as deindividuation[10] may contribute to the disinhibition experienced by many Internet users. For instance, Robert Willison (2001) from the London School of Economics describes deindividuation as "a state where an individual's self-awareness is reduced through membership of a group." He explains how a person may take part in criminal or deviant behavior when "individual identities are submerged through group membership. In such circumstances, one is susceptible to situational cues and may partake in behaviour which outside of the group context, would not occur." He goes on to state: "Taken to an extreme, private self-awareness, impaired by deindividuation, can lead to 'lynch-mob' behaviour and a 'herd' mentality."

We can interpret Willison's (2001) work as meaning that some people can begin to take on the attitudes and values of the group(s) they belong to. If a person belongs to a group with extreme values, he or she may begin to take on those values and act accordingly. For instance, it would not be surprising for a person to take on homophobic views if he or she visited homophobic web sites and took part in homophobic newsgroup discussions. With the encouragement of other like-minded people, it would also be unsurprising if this same person took part in flaming or otherwise harassing gay or lesbian Internet users.

Dehumanizing Others

One way in which individuals are able to justify treating others cruelly is by dehumanizing them: "Self-censure for cruel conduct can be disengaged by stripping people of human qualities. Once dehumanized, they are no longer viewed as persons with feelings, hopes and concerns but as subhuman objects" (Bandura, 1999, p. 8). Several powerful examples of dehumanization are provided by the Museum of Tolerance (1997), an online resource that provides comprehensive information on the Holocaust and World War II. In describing Nazi ideology, an article on the site describes how Hitler came to believe that Jews were inferior humans who were closer to apes than to "the superior races of mankind." The article also states that "Heinrich Himmler, in order to reinforce his men's motivation for their part in the Holocaust, compared the Jews to fleas and mice—obnoxious forms of life that had to be destroyed."

The disembodied nature of the Internet makes it relatively easy to begin to depersonalize individuals and entire groups. For instance, in describing the use of racist terms in newsgroups it has been stated that "depersonalisation is plainly evident on the Internet where shockingly dehumanising levels of hostility are given voice in the terms used to describe and deride people from minority ethnic groups" (Sutton, 2003). One need only look at the contents of certain newsgroups, such as those dedicated to flaming specific groups, to see how common such behavior is.

Perceptions of Power and Control

There can be little doubt that some people feel a need to exert power over others. For instance, Philip Zimbardo's work (1973) on the exercise of power and its effects on the individuals is well known, having been the subject of many articles and television documentaries. The Stanford Prison Experiment involved ordinary people taking on the roles of prisoners and prison guards and illustrated how tools of power—reflective sunglasses, handcuffs, keys, clubs—were used to degrade and dehumanize the prisoners.[11]

Applying labels to whole groups or subjecting individuals to harassment (such as racial harassment) are just two examples of how power can be exercised via the Internet. Several writers have suggested that some cyberstalkers are motivated by the desire to exert power over their victims, usually through fear (see, for example, McGrath and Casey, 2002; Deirmenjian, 1999).

It can be argued that the Internet helps to support this kind of behavior in two main ways. First, the lack of any face-to-face contact
places both physical and emotional distance between the victim and
harasser. This helps to depersonalize the victim further while reinforcing the harasser's anonymity and sense of invulnerability. For instance,
it can be argued that "it is easier to harm others when their suffering
is not visible and when injurious actions are physically and temporally
remote from their effects" (Bandura, 1999, p. 7).

Second, the harasser may feel more powerful since he is able to in-
flict a great deal of harm on another person from a distance and with
very little effort. For instance, in discussing the rise of new services that
create child pornography to order, a colleague and I used the term *virtual sex tourist* to describe a person able to cause the sexual abuse of a
young person from a distance, that is, without being physically present
(Bocij and McFarlane, 2003a).

As mentioned earlier, some stalkers reduce the effort involved in
harassing a victim by inciting others to act on their behalf through
stalking-by-proxy (Sheridan, Davies, and Boon, 2001; Pathé and
Mullen, 1997). Stalking-by-proxy may increase the stalker's sense of
power since he can manipulate a number of people instead of just a
single victim. The same behavior has also been noted in many of the
cyberstalking cases reported in the media, on personal web sites, and
within academic papers. The following is a typical example of how
cyberstalkers can use stalking-by-proxy to their advantage:

> Gary Dellapenta, a 50-year-old security guard, was arrested for his online
> activities in Los Angeles. . . . It all began when Dellapenta was rebuffed
> by his 28-year-old victim Randi Barber. As a result of this rejection,
> Dellapenta became obsessed with Barber and placed adverts on the
> Internet under the names *"playfulkitty4U"* and *"kinkygal30"* claiming she
> was "into rape fantasy and gang-bang fantasy." As a result of these
> postings, she started to receive obscene phone calls and visits by men
> to her house making strange and lewd suggestions. (Griffiths, 2000,
> p. 548)

This type of stalking-by-proxy appears in a number of the cyberstalking accounts contained within this book, including the stories
involving the Boehle family, Jayne Hitchcock (chapter 1), Cynthia
Armistead (chapter 1), and David Cruz (chapter 4).

Stalking-by-proxy may also be used to harass whole groups of
people or in pursuit of a political goal. For instance, British academic
Mike Sutton (2003) has reported that far-right groups have attempted
to use stalking-by-proxy in order to deal with their opponents. In his

work, he cites a case reported in the press where "Combat 18 activists circulated the names and addresses of prominent local anti-racist figures on their Web site, together with directions for making and storing petrol bombs." The *Los Angeles Times* reported a similar incident in 2001, when two AIDS activists admitted to publicizing the phone number of senior officials at the Centers for Disease Control and Prevention in Atlanta (Ornstein, 2001).

Little is known of the social and psychological causes for stalking-by-proxy using technology. However, in the context of groups with extreme views, one possible explanation may involve the way individuals perceive the group's authority. The influence of the group and its message may cause individuals to surrender to the group's authority, making them submissive to its suggestions and wishes.

The view that the Internet allows some people to exert power over others can also be supported by feminist arguments regarding inequalities between men and women. Many feminists contend that we live in a male-dominated society that seeks to degrade and control women by portraying them as sexual objects. For instance, a recent feminist article described how the Internet, movies, radio, and advertising all tend to portray teenage girls "as highly sexualized beings, ready to cater to the whims of men" (Asher, 2002, p. 23). The article goes on to describe how teenage girls are reduced to the status of objects: "This popular culture will not acknowledge the emotional and physical consequences of its abuse because it does not see girls as human beings; instead they are as inanimate as mountains and exist only to be conquered."

Pornography is also considered as one of the ways that men try to degrade and control women. Many studies have shown a link between pornography and violence (Malamuth, Addison, and Koss, 2000). For instance, research conducted in the 1980s found that prolonged exposure to pornography can encourage a taste for pornography that features pseudo-violence or violence. Prolonged consumption also causes people to trivialize rape as a criminal offense and "increases men's propensity for committing rape" (Zillman, 1986, pp. 27–28).

Since the Internet offers unprecedented access to all types of pornography,[12] it must be considered a particularly powerful influence. As an example, Gossett and Byrne (2002) discuss the existence of Internet rape sites—web sites that contain violent images of women being raped or assaulted. In their study, all of the sites examined showed women as the victims and men as the perpetrators. Many sites showed women being abused in various ways:

> The pain caused to the victim is a primary selling point for the sites. Many sites describe, in unflinching detail, the actual physical pain that the woman is experiencing, and some appear to focus on the expressions of pain on the victim's face. The repeated use of words such as "pain," "abuse," "brutal," and "torture" on the sites also intensifies the violent connotations. (p. 703)

Gossett and Byrne (2002) also noted that people were given almost unlimited control over the content of the material viewed. Many sites contained "jukeboxes" offering a variety of choices regarding the types of scenes available. One jukebox, for example, offered 100 choices of scene.

As can be seen, Internet rape sites give men a tremendous sense of power since they are able to dictate the exact circumstances of a violent sexual attack on a victim of their choice. Safe behind a wall of anonymity, they are able to "direct" the material viewed from a distance, producing exactly what they wish to see. Although cyberstalking seldom results in such serious outcomes, it is easy to see a number of parallels between cyberstalking and these web sites. For instance, a cyberstalker may issue threats to make his victim do as he wishes or to cause distress. It could also be argued that stalking-by-proxy allows a cyberstalker to "direct" events in almost the same way as the users of the pornography web sites described here.

A good example that demonstrates how some harassers are able to gain power over their victims is the case of Vincent Mark Santana. Santana, a registered sex offender, was able to harass nineteen women from the detention center he was held at while awaiting trial for rape (Smith, 2002). Santana made hundreds of calls at random in order to find suitable victims. He convinced his victims to stay on the phone by telling them he was next door and would kill them if they hung up. The women were then told to imagine that Santana was raping them and were forced to describe what was happening. On other occasions, Santana would force women to take part in sexually explicit conversations. Perhaps the strangest aspect of this case was that all calls made from the detention center were collect calls, meaning that Santana was able to convince all of his victims to accept the charges.

Physical and Emotional Distance

The previous section discussed circumstances in which some people may submit to the wishes of the groups they belong to. This view draws on the work of noted psychologist Stanley Milgram. Milgram's work (1963, 1965) focused on obedience, that is, a person's willingness to conform to the demands of authority, even if the demands violate that person's sense of right and wrong. Milgram's best-known study involved an exercise where "teachers" were asked to administer electric shocks to "learners." The intensity of the electric shocks administered was gradually increased until a maximum level of 450 volts was reached. It was found that 65 percent of the "teachers" punished the "learners" to the maximum 450 volts, clearly demonstrating the influence of peer pressure and the power of authority.

Milgram's research suggests that three factors influence obedience: physical proximity (the less distance between the "teacher" and the "learner," the less likelihood of shocks being administered), the need to place personal responsibility for actions at the feet of a third party, and a lack of influences likely to incite defiance/rebellion (usually from individuals independent from the group).

It can be argued that all three of these factors also have an influence on cyberstalking. First, in terms of proximity, there are several ways in which an individual involved in stalking-by-proxy for another person or group can maintain a distance from his victim. For example, it has already been argued that emotional detachment can be achieved by maintaining anonymity. Second, an individual might avoid personal responsibility by making the other person or group responsible for his actions, rather than considering his own beliefs as a reason for his behavior. For example, a person might claim that the members of a newsgroup pressured him to take part in cyberstalking, effectively avoiding blame for any harm caused to others. Finally, a person who frequents newsgroups or chat rooms where extreme views are regarded as being normal has limited opportunities to hear more reasonable and independent viewpoints. In many cases, an individual may actively avoid such opportunities since they may result in cognitive dissonance (a condition that occurs when a person is forced to choose between two contradictory beliefs or actions).[13]

Formation of Strategic Identities

Italian researchers Talamo and Ligorio (2001) have studied how identity is perceived and constructed in cyberspace. Their work contends that individuals may create numerous "cyber-identities" based on strategic goals. They argue that "Identity is not a static characteristic. . . . Rather, it is negotiated through discourse in interaction, based on the context features and the roles assumed by the participants within the context" (p. 119). From this, it is reasonable to suggest that an Internet user might develop several cyber-identities for different purposes. For instance, a person working from home might develop a sober, pragmatic cyber-identity for dealing with business matters and a more relaxed, friendly cyber-identity for conversing with friends and family. It might also be possible for an individual to develop deviant cyber-identities so that he can take part in criminal or antisocial activities. For instance, a person might create a racist cyber-identity to be used in chat rooms occupied by other racists.

This concept is an attractive one because it can be used to explain how a person can become involved in deviant behavior while online, but refuse to take part in similar acts when offline. The formation of a deviant cyber-identity enables a person to place a great deal of emotional distance between himself and his actions while online. Any deviant acts carried out while online can be blamed on the cyber-identity, essentially absolving the person of any responsibility for the harm caused to others. As an aside, if some people can form deviant cyber-identities that allow them to harass others, we might also consider the possibility that some people may form "victim" cyber-identities that somehow identify them as being particularly vulnerable or attractive targets.

Lack of Policing

The difficulties involved in policing the Internet may encourage some people to carry out deviant or criminal acts.[14] For instance, with little fear of arrest or prosecution, a person who might never use child pornography in the offline world might not hesitate to download pictures and movies from Usenet or web sites. Similarly, an individual who would never take part in offline stalking may be willing to become a cyberstalker. It can be argued that such acts might take place simply because there is no one there to stop them from happening.

Noted American criminologist Marcus Felson (2002) argues that criminal acts have three "almost-always elements": a likely offender, a suitable target, and the absence of a capable guardian against the offense. According to Felson, there are also three "often-important elements" that may feature in a crime: props (such as tools), camouflage (to help the criminal avoid notice), and an audience whom the criminal wishes to impress or intimidate. It does not take a great deal of effort to identify all of these elements in a typical cyberstalking incident. In fact, many of these elements have already been discussed within this chapter, albeit using different terms. For example, the discussion has already dealt with props (in the form of computer equipment, software, and services) and camouflage (in the form of anonymous e-mail, encryption, and other techniques).

However, it is Felson's (2002) concept of a "capable guardian" that is of particular importance here. For Felson, the guardian need not be a police officer and can be any person capable of preventing the crime. Furthermore, it is the *absence* of the guardian that allows the crime to happen. The example of chat rooms can be used to show how Felson's argument can be applied to cyberstalking. Most parents are likely to prefer that their children use moderated rather than unmoderated chat rooms. This is because the presence of the guardian (the moderator) helps to safeguard children in various ways, for example, by acting as a deterrent to pedophiles or by discouraging bullying.

Formation of Deviant Groups

There is some evidence that those who commit deviant acts via the Internet often seek out like-minded individuals. Small groups sometimes form, allowing members to encourage each other and share resources. For instance, in my own work dealing with online predators such as pedophiles, I have noted that "the Internet enables paedophiles to locate one another and form alliances that can span several different countries. Once organised, the members of such groups can encourage each other to commit more serious crimes" (Bocij and McFarlane, 2002b). According to writers such as Berg (2001), pedophiles in the offline world are constrained by social norms and are wary of the risk involved in making contact with like-minded people. However, he argues that "the Internet has made it possible for predators to find entire online fraternities of pedophiles with which to share experiences, to transmit child pornography instantly and anonymously to one another and [to] experience the comfort of a reassuring support group" (2001, p. 15). Berg extends his argument to include all of those who take part in deviant acts. He cites the formation of online communities populated by those who share norms considered deviant by our offline society:

> A central advantage the Internet offers to those disposed to sociopathic behaviors is that it creates the possibility for the first time for such individuals to find one another, to congregate in online communities, to share ideas and to provide one another with the potent benefit of group reinforcement for their antisocial attitudes. (Berg, 2001, p. 15)

There is some evidence that organized groups of cyberstalkers already exist. Chapter 8, for example, describes several forms of corporate cyberstalking that involve organized groups. In addition, there are a number of discussion groups and web sites devoted to stalking and cyberstalking. One discussion group, for instance, allows users to post questions asking for advice on stalking various people, such as an ex-wife or former employer.[15]

CONCLUSION

Computer technology is cheaper, more accessible, and easier to use than ever before. In addition, people have become more computer literate, largely due to increased access to education and training. It is therefore not surprising that more people have begun to use technology to help them carry out deviant acts, such as harassment. This is because technology can help them to remain anonymous, disguise their activities, and destroy incriminating evidence.

The anonymous nature of the Internet may also encourage people to harass others through mechanisms such as disinhibition and deindividuation. In addition, research has shown that it becomes easier to harm others if they can be dehumanized and seen as objects rather than people.

An interesting idea that deserves to be investigated more thoroughly involves the idea that some people may form several cyber-identities to meet different purposes. This may mean that some people form deviant cyber-identities that allow them to harass others.

As has been shown, there is some evidence that those who commit deviant or antisocial acts often seek out others like them and form small groups for mutual support and encouragement. The next chapter develops this theme further by looking at how organized groups can pose a threat to the safety of young people.

7

Threats to Young People

THE LINDSAY SHAMROCK STORY

In early 2000, Stephanie Lavoie bought a computer for her fifteen-year-old daughter, Lindsay Shamrock. Shamrock soon became addicted to the Internet and would spend hours online each day.

One day, Shamrock's mother, Lavoie, found love letters stored on the computer from a thirty-five-year-old man in Greece named Kon. The letters described how Kon wanted Shamrock to marry him and be the mother of his children. Although Kon lived thousands of miles away, Lavoie remained concerned enough to demand that Shamrock cease contact with him. By that time, however, Shamrock was convinced that she loved Kon and that he loved her (CBSNews.com, 2002b).

Despite being told to leave Shamrock alone, Kon continued to send letters and e-mails and soon began calling her in the middle of the night. At one point, Kon told Lavoie that he knew where they lived and was planning to buy a house nearby. Lavoie tried to prevent contact between Shamrock and Kon in a number of ways; for example, she began taking the computer keyboard with her to work so that Shamrock could not use the computer unsupervised. She even sent copies of Kon's letters and e-mails to the FBI, but they told her there was little they could do.

One day in August 2000, Lavoie returned from work to find that Shamrock had disappeared from their home near Tampa, Florida.

When Lavoie reported Shamrock as a missing person, the case was passed to Sgt. Gary Klinger, head of the local missing persons unit. Klinger analyzed the messages on Shamrock's computer and learned that Kon was actually Franz Konstantin Baehring, a German citizen. Baehring was in regular contact with Lavoie and usually sent messages expressing his concern for Shamrock. Klinger encouraged Lavoie to remain in contact with Baehring so that he could gather more information and try to find Shamrock.

Klinger had been convinced that Shamrock was still in the country but started to change his mind when Baehring began hinting that she was with him. A major breakthrough came when Shamrock's instant messaging nickname was traced to Thessaloniki, Greece. Greek police used the media to circulate pictures of Baehring and Shamrock and soon received a call from someone who had seen Shamrock in Thessaloniki. Shamrock was found near the town center and taken into custody. Baehring was arrested a day later at his home, where police found a large collection of pornography and evidence that he had not acted alone (CBSNews.com, 2002b).

Two other people had helped Baehring arrange for Shamrock to leave the country. The first, Martina Crivaro, worked at a cell phone company and helped Baehring set up a prepaid account for Shamrock. Baehring was able to enlist Crivaro's help by convincing her that Shamrock was being physically and sexually abused. Crivaro agreed to help "rescue" Shamrock by collecting her, taking her to the airport, and putting her on a plane. After her arrest, Crivaro pleaded guilty to interfering with parental custody and was placed under house arrest for two years.

Baehring had met his second associate, Robert Arnder, online and had promised him $2,000 for his help. Baehring hoped that Shamrock would be able to impersonate Arnder's eighteen-year-old daughter, Dawn, so that she could use her passport to leave the country. Arnder helped Shamrock to change her appearance by cutting her hair and dyeing it dark brown. He also gave her a pair of glasses and colored contact lenses. Police traced Arnder from e-mail that Dawn had sent to Shamrock. When investigators searched Arnder's home, they found numerous homemade sex videos, many of which featured children. They also found a collection of child pornography, some of which had been sent by Baehring and featured Shamrock. Arnder was eventually sentenced to eighty-five years in prison for other crimes. Dawn was placed in protective custody after it was learned that she had been a victim of sexual abuse.

Following Baehring's arrest, investigators came to believe that Shamrock may not have been his first victim and that he may have been involved with a child pornography ring (McAuliffe, 2001c). One investigator said that Baehring may have intended to force Shamrock to work as a prostitute and take part in pornographic films. Evidence later emerged that Baehring had attempted to seduce or harass many teenage girls from around the world.

Surprisingly, during Baehring's trial Shamrock claimed to still love him, despite the sexual abuse she suffered (BBC News, 2001a). Baehring was sentenced to eight years in prison but Shamrock's family was told he was likely to serve only three years if he received parole and time off for good behavior. In February 2002, Stephanie Lavoie told the press that Baehring had continued to harass her family from his Greek prison by sending threatening letters and e-mails. The situation became serious enough that the U.S. Postal Inspection Office was asked to intervene (*The News Herald*, 2002).

INTRODUCTION

What is the threat posed to young people[1] by child pornography?[2] What is the threat posed to young people by pedophiles[3] and other predators? How do the activities of young people expose them to cyberstalkers? The threats discussed within this chapter can be divided into two broad categories. The first group is made up of behaviors that are already well known but that are now being carried out on a larger scale than ever before. The distribution of child pornography is a good example of such a behavior. The second group is made up of entirely new threats that are made possible by new technology. Many of these new threats can be seen as a natural extension of an existing crime. For example, I will show later on how a massive surge in demand for child pornography has resulted in the creation of commercial services that create pornographic materials to order.

One of the arguments I make within this chapter is that there is a link between pornography and cyberstalking. Many people believe that child pornography encourages pedophiles to abuse young people. The Internet provides greater access to child pornography and allows pedophiles to approach young people from relative safety.

Although young people are at risk from individuals, there are also organized groups that exploit teenagers in a variety of ways. Many of the examples given in this chapter show that such exploitation can take place on a massive scale once people combine their resources or turn sexual abuse into a business activity.

It is also noted that young people may themselves be responsible for some of the risks they face. It is known, for example, that many young people make use of adult web sites and even subject other teenagers to threatening behavior. In addition, some young people deliberately encourage the attention of pedophiles in order to solicit money or gifts.

INTERNET USE BY YOUNG PEOPLE

A number of studies have found that the majority of young people in the United States, Canada, Europe, and Australia make regular use of the Internet. In the United States, for instance, a study by the Department of Commerce found that 75 percent of young people ages fourteen to seventeen, and 65 percent of teens between ten and thirteen years old, regularly use the Internet (National Telecommunications and Information Administration, 2002).

Similar figures have been reported for other technologically advanced countries. In the United Kingdom, a National Opinion Poll survey reported that 75 percent of all children between seven and sixteen years old were regular Internet users (Cyberspace Research Unit, 2002). In Canada, a national survey of 6,000 young people was conducted by the Media Awareness Network in 2001.[4] The survey found that 99 percent of young people aged nine to seventeen had used the Internet at some time, and 79 percent said they had Internet access at home. The *Year Book Australia 2003*, published by the Australian Bureau of Statistics,[5] reported that 55 percent of all children between nine and eleven, and 72 percent of children ages twelve to fourteen, had accessed the Internet at some point during 2000.

As more young people have begun to use the Internet, they have attracted the unwelcome attention of child pornographers, pedophiles, and other deviants. For instance, in December 2000, the Pew Internet and American Life Project surveyed twelve to seventeen year olds and found that nearly 60 percent of those online had received messages from strangers (Livingstone, 2001).

A survey conducted on behalf of the National Center for Missing and Exploited Children reported a number of more disturbing figures (Finkelhor, Mitchell, and Wolak, 2000). The survey involved telephone interviews with 1,501 children ages ten to seventeen. In brief, some of the main findings were:

- One in four had an unwanted exposure to some kind of image of naked people or people having sex in the last year.

- Roughly one in five children had received a sexual solicitation or approach.
- One in thirty-three children had received an aggressive solicitation, meaning that someone asked to meet them somewhere, called them on the telephone, sent them regular mail, money, or gifts.
- Approximately one-quarter of young people who reported these incidents were distressed by them.
- Less than 10 percent of sexual solicitations and only 3 percent of unwanted exposure episodes were ever reported to authorities, such as a law enforcement agency, an Internet Service Provider, or a hot line.

Similar figures have been reported in other countries, such as the United Kingdom. For instance, a report by the UK Internet Crime Forum (ICF) found that approximately 20 percent of children who use chat rooms have been approached by pedophiles and other deviants while online (ChildNet International, 2001).

Lack of parental supervision may be partly to blame for the experiences of some young people. A survey by the National School Boards Foundation in the United States contacted 1,735 families to explore how they use the Internet.[6] The survey found that 78 percent of young people aged thirteen to seventeen said they used the Internet when they were alone. In addition, a study by the Cyberspace Research Unit (2002) found that one in two children reported that their parents never supervise their online activities. These figures suggest that some parents may use the Internet as a sophisticated baby-sitting device, essentially placing the responsibility for their children's safety in the hands of complete strangers.

Harassment and Young People

The National Center for Missing and Exploited Children survey found that one in seventeen respondents had been threatened or harassed (Finkelhor, Mitchell, and Wolak, 2000). The majority of incidents (65 percent) took place in chat rooms, and another 24 percent through instant messaging. Similar figures were reported in a survey conducted by National Children's Homes (NCH), a British charity, which found that one in four children were victims of online bullying (National Children's Homes, 2002). When the figures are broken down, they show that 7 percent of respondents received threatening messages in chat rooms and an additional 4 percent by e-mail.

It is worth noting that some studies have reported much larger values when describing levels of harassment experienced by young people. For instance, a relatively recent study carried out by the Girl Scout Research Institute found that 30 percent of girls had experienced sexual harassment while using chat rooms (Au, 2002). Some of the differences noted between countries or between males and females might be explained in several ways. Donna Hughes is an academic and a prolific writer with a special interest in the trafficking and sexual exploitation of women and children. She notes that "there are country and cultural differences in use of new information technologies. For example, in contrast to the United Kingdom trend where more girls use chat, in the United States and Canada, 60 percent of chat users are male" (2001, p. 16). In addition, there is evidence to suggest that teenage girls are at most risk from stalkers and pedophiles because of the way in which they use the Internet (Hughes, 2003; Finkelhor, Mitchell, and Wolak, 2000). For instance, females tend to use the Internet primarily as a communication tool, whereas males tend to view it more as an information source (Internet Crime Forum, 2001).

Those most at risk from any form of harassment or solicitation are young people considered "vulnerable," perhaps through disability, poor judgment, or a need for attention, understanding, and friendship (Finkelhor, Mitchell, and Wolak, 2000; ChildNet International, 2001). The work of Kenneth Lanning, a former FBI agent, is often cited in papers and discussions dealing with the identification of pedophiles. According to Lanning (1992), some of the traits associated with pedophiles include being skilled at identifying vulnerable victims, being able to identify with children (better than with adults), and being skilled at manipulating children. Pedophiles are often able to gain the confidence of vulnerable teenagers, for example, by appearing sensitive to their problems, perhaps by offering support, advice, and encouragement. Lanning states: "They literally seduce the children by befriending them, talking to them, listening to them, paying attention to them, spending time with them, and buying gifts for them" (1992, p. 19). This kind of approach can be compared to a technique called *love bombing* that is sometimes used by religious movements to gain the loyalty and obedience of converts (Giddens, 2001). The relationship between some stalkers and their victims has also been described as being similar to a "cult dynamic" (Gross, 2000, p. 85). Once a relationship has been established, it can be exploited in various ways, for example by asking the teenager for a physical meeting (Hughes, 2001).

There is evidence to suggest that young people themselves may be responsible for some of the sexual harassment and threatening behavior experienced by their peers. For instance, it has been reported that young people perpetrate nearly half of all online solicitation cases in the United States and almost half of all aggressive solicitations (Finkelhor, Mitchell, and Wolak, 2000). In addition, research by the UK

Home Office suggests that up to a third of all sex crimes are carried out by young people (Internet Crime Forum, 2001).

Pornography and Young People

Young people may also be partly responsible for the creation and distribution of pornography, including child pornography. As consumers, teenagers may inadvertently be helping to stimulate a sector of the industry that profits from the exploitation of young people. A 1998 survey found that almost a third of American households with Internet access visited online sex industry sites at least once per month (Hughes, 1999). It is reasonable to suggest that many of those using adult web sites were likely to have been young people. In fact, the Children's Online Privacy Protection Act (COPPA) Commission was told in July 2000 that 19 percent of visitors to top adult-oriented web sites were under fifteen (Livingstone, 2001). In addition, it has been suggested that a quarter of young Internet users in the United Kingdom visit gambling and pornography web sites (Livingstone, 2001).

The National Coalition for the Protection of Families (NCPCF) web site cites a number of statistics drawn from various sources that can be used to illustrate the size of the adult industry in the United States.[7] For instance, the adult industry produces some 11,000 movies each year, an output twenty times greater than that of Hollywood. In addition, rentals and sales of adult videos and DVDs are worth more than $4 billion annually. However, according to some, as well as being the world's largest producer of adult entertainment, the United States is also the largest producer of child pornography distributed via the Internet (Hughes, 2001). Again, the NCPCF web site helps to indicate the size of the child pornography industry by reporting that "an estimated 325,000 US children aged 17 or younger are prostitutes, performers in pornographic videos or have otherwise fallen victim to 'commercial sexual exploitation.'" However, some sources, such as *The Glasgow Herald*, offer much larger estimates, reporting that the producers of child pornography in the United States "are said to have filmed, and criminally exploited, more than 1,000,000 children" (*The Glasgow Herald*, 2002).

There appears to be a direct link between the use of child pornography and the sexual abuse of children. For example, Julie Posey, founder of PedoWatch,[8] claims that more than 80 percent of those who purchase child pornography are active child molesters. In many cases, the Internet appears to play an extremely important role as a means

of distributing materials and contacting children. As an example, the
Internet Crime Forum reports:

> The USPIS [U.S. Postal Inspection Service] reports that the Internet is
> increasingly used as a tool in exploiting children, particularly in the con-
> text of child pornography: during 1997 just 33% of cases involved the use
> of computers, whereas this figure had risen to 77% by the year 2000. The
> available data also indicates that since 1997 36% of offenders caught by
> the USPIS were identified as having committed actual sexual abuse of
> children. (Internet Crime Forum, 2001, p. 15)

The number of FBI cases provides a further example of the rapid
growth of Internet use by pornographers and pedophiles:

> In fiscal year 1998, the FBI opened up roughly 700 cases dealing with
> online pedophilia, most of them for posting child pornography, and
> about a quarter dealing with online predators trying to get children un-
> der 18 to meet with them. By 2000 that figure had quadrupled to 2,856
> cases. (Nordland, Bartholet, and Johnson, 2001)

Child pornography represented a serious problem even at the very
beginning of the Internet's rise to popularity in 1996 and 1997. For
instance, in 1997 New York attorney general Dennis Vacco announced
that an eighteen-month police operation called Operation Rip-Cord
had identified more than 1,500 suspected child pornographers who
were using the Internet to exchange materials (CNN Interactive, 1997).

It is imperative that the harm caused by child pornography not be
underestimated. Academic Donna Hughes echoes the feelings of many
who campaign against pornography by stating that "women and children are harmed physically, sexually, and emotionally in the making
of pornography" (Hughes, 2002a). It must be remembered that child
pornography, by its very nature, is the record of the sexual abuse of a
child.

The National Coalition for the Protection of Families web site describes a number of other ways in which pornography can harm individuals, families, and communities. According to the site, pornography
can shape attitudes and encourage behavior that harms users and their
families, for example by encouraging promiscuity. It can also become
addictive, leading to several other effects, including encouraging a
desire for more extreme materials, desensitizing the user so that what
is first seen as deviant eventually becomes acceptable, and encouraging a tendency to act out the behaviors seen. In terms of the Internet,
the NCPCF says, "A recent study by researchers at Stanford and

Duquesne universities claims at least 200,000 Americans are hopelessly addicted to E-porn." One of the most disturbing statements made on the NCPCF web site is the claim that pornography "serves as a how-to for sex crimes, primarily the molestation of children."

The demand for child pornography is such that specialized services have now started to appear. In Russia, for example, a commercial service enables people to specify the exact kind of child pornography they want to receive. If the required material does not already exist in the company's library, it can be created to order (Groves, 2001). The Russian pornography-on-demand service also highlights a significant problem: the difficulty involved in locating and prosecuting those who create and sell child pornography. In the example described here, it is a U.S. web site that promotes the service and processes payments. The content itself is stored on Russian and Indonesian servers. By separating the different parts of the business in this way, it becomes difficult—if not impossible—to arrest and prosecute the owners.

Another example involved a web site operated by Thomas and Janice Reedy, a couple from Fort Worth, Texas, who provided an adult verification service for adult industry sites (Hughes, 2001; U.S. Attorney, 2001; Coman, 2003; Savino, 2001). After verifying a user's age by checking credit card details, they issued passwords that allowed access to other adult web sites, including sites that contained child pornography. Subscribers were also given access to bulletin board systems in which pedophiles traded passwords for access to other child pornography sites where people offered or sought children for purposes of sexual abuse (Hughes, 2001). The company operated by the couple, Landslide Productions, Inc., gave more than 350,000 users from sixty countries access to 5,700 adult sites. At one point, it was estimated that the company was earning a profit of more than $1.3 million each month (Coman, 2003). Approximately 30 to 40 percent of the company's income came from sites containing child pornography.

Landslide acted as a gatekeeper for one Russian and two Indonesian webmasters (Burke, 2000). This configuration effectively divided the business into two parts: the company handled the processing of payments within the United States, but the pornographic content was stored on foreign servers. Following a lengthy investigation, the Reedys were arrested and prosecuted on over eighty charges. Although warrants were issued for their arrest, the Indonesians and Russian were not extradited. A number of other webmasters also avoided arrest. The Reedys, however, received lengthy sentences: Thomas Reedy was sentenced to 1,335 years in prison and Janice Reedy was sentenced to fourteen years (Savino, 2001).

These examples should emphasize the fact that the activities of pedophiles are no longer restricted to a relatively small geographical area. Previously, pedophile activity across international boundaries was limited to a relatively small number of "sex tourists," who travel from the United States, Canada, and Europe to countries where they are unlikely to be prosecuted for engaging in sexual activity with children. Often, such visits are disguised as business trips or vacations. Undoubtedly, one of the attractions is that there is little likelihood of exposure in the abuser's own country. However, widespread Internet access now means that almost any pedophile can become a *virtual sex tourist*, a person who causes the sexual abuse of a young person from a distance without being physically present. For instance, UNICEF now estimates that 80 percent of pedophile-related investigations involve more than one country, and 90 percent involve the Internet (Whittle, 2002).

Assessing Risk

As some of the conflicting estimates given within this chapter show, it can be difficult to gain an accurate view of the level of danger faced by young people. Limited knowledge of how cyberstalkers and other predators use the Internet means that, whereas there are only a few things that are certain, there are many uncertainties. For instance, it is certain that young people are at risk from pedophiles and others who have adopted the Internet as a means of locating potential victims. However, it is not known with any real certainty how many young people are at high risk, the mechanics of how online pedophiles select victims, what factors increase or decrease risk, and so on.

Care must be taken to separate media speculation and hysteria from genuine fact. If the risk to young people is underestimated, it may encourage a sense of complacency that places them in danger. However, exaggerating the risk to young people may also result in harm, for example by causing unnecessary anxiety and distress to them, their parents, and others.

The Tina Bell diaries provide a good example of where exaggeration resulted in a great deal of public anxiety. Richard Barry, a reporter working for the British arm of ZDNet, posed as a twelve-year-old girl named Tina Bell in order to demonstrate how pedophiles might be using the Internet to locate victims (Barry, 2001a, 2001b, 2001c; McAuliffe, 2001a, 2001b; Vorderman, 2001). Over a period of four weeks, Barry used Yahoo!'s Instant Messenger application in order to explore the chat rooms operated and maintained by Yahoo! The results of Barry's investigation were recorded in a crude diary of events. The conversations that took place in various chat rooms were also recorded, and Barry reproduced some of these in the articles he published after the investigation.

The results of Barry's investigation caused a great deal of concern when they were interpreted as suggesting that almost every child who uses the Internet regularly will come into contact with pedophiles. Barry himself stated: "I have no doubt that if Tina had existed, she would be in danger of being raped . . . just like any other vulnerable child who wanders into the Crying Rooms operated and maintained by Yahoo!" (Barry, 2001a).

Public anxiety further increased when celebrities and others made a series of dramatic statements. As an example, a ZDNet UK article stated: "An investigation carried out by ZDNet News UK reveals that it takes less than a minute for a predator to approach a child in some Yahoo! Messenger chatrooms" (McAuliffe, 2001b). In another article, a well-known British celebrity stated: "We can now prove that our children are just two clicks of the computer mouse away from a paedophile" (Vorderman, 2001). Yet more publicity arose when details of the investigation appeared on national television and when various celebrities issued strongly worded public statements demanding action from the government and Internet Service Providers.

It can be argued that, in this case, the benefit gained by bringing the danger posed by online pedophiles to the attention of the public was offset by the anxiety and distress caused to young people and their families. It should be remembered that the Tina Bell diaries did not represent a genuine scientific experiment, so the results reported may not have been typical. Furthermore, it could be suggested that it was somewhat irresponsible to report the investigation in such a dramatic way.

ONLINE PREDATION

Chapter 1 reported that a number of people have suggested a clear link between cyberstalking and the sexual abuse of children. *Cyberstalking: A New Challenge for Law Enforcement and Industry*, a 1999 report published by the U.S. attorney general, supports the existence of this connection. As mentioned earlier, the report explains how pedophiles use the Internet to locate victims and establish relationships with them (Reno, 1999).

The view of the U.S. attorney general is shared by others, including Donna Hughes. In a report prepared for the Council of Europe,

Hughes describes the activities of online pedophiles in terms of stalking:

> Traffickers and stalkers use the Internet in a number of ways to contact and recruit victims. There are many sites and forums on the Internet for adults to engage in sex talk, but child stalkers seek out children for the purpose of engaging in age inappropriate graphic sex talk to provide sexual satisfaction for the perpetrator. Often the child stalkers will escalate by enticing the child to engage in more sexual activity, sometimes resulting in the perpetrator meeting the child. (Hughes, 2001, p. 15)

Others support this stance; for instance, one writer argues that

> the most direct threat to children is online predation. Adults with a sexual interest in children can identify, contact and groom potential victims via the Internet. . . . The danger is growing as more children, and more adults with a sexual interest in children, go online. (Blom, 1998)

The threat posed by pedophiles is a significant one, especially since it has been estimated that there are one dozen pedophile groups around the world with thousands of members (Ko, 2001). In terms of online pedophile networks, a good example is the first phase of the FBI's Operation Candyman, which took place in early 2002. Investigators were able to find the e-mail addresses of some 7,000 members of pedophile groups, including 2,400 overseas members (*The Scotsman*, 2002).

The belief that pedophiles use the Internet as a way of grooming victims is a common one. ChildNet International describes the grooming process in this way:

> The sexual abuse of children is usually carefully planned and stage-managed. In the process of grooming, the perpetrator creates the conditions which will allow him to abuse the children while remaining undetected by others, and the child is prepared gradually for the time when the offender first engages in sexual molestation. (ChildNet International, 2001, p. 2)

The process of grooming young people via the Internet can be extremely subtle and it may take months before a pedophile carries out an illegal act. Donna Hughes describes how some pedophiles use pornography as a way of preparing young people to accept more serious behavior:

In chat rooms, perpetrators engage children in sexual conversation or expose them to sexual material, including adult and child pornography. Predators sexually exploit children online through this sexual talk. Perpetrators ask children to send them pictures or sexual images of themselves or their friends. They may encourage the children to perform sex acts on themselves or friends for the stalker's sexual satisfaction. Stalkers use these activities as part of a grooming process to entice children into more direct contact, such as telephone conversations and eventual physical meetings. (Hughes, 2002a, p. 17)

Other researchers also support this view. For example, one writer states that "research has indicated that child pornography is regularly used by paedophiles in cyberspace as a means of de-sensitising children and normalising sexual activity between adults and children" (Feather, 1999).

It is worth remembering that pedophiles use pornographic images for a wide variety of reasons, not just for grooming children. For example, it has been argued that they may be used as a means of justifying the behavior of those who abuse children, as a way of making children compliant by blackmailing them, as trophies, or even as a form of currency for exchange with other pedophiles (Quayle and Taylor, 2002).

Another threat posed by pedophiles is the formation of organized groups capable of sharing resources and acting on a larger scale than isolated individuals would be able to. Reporter Eric Blom explains that "direct contact between adult predators and children is not the only danger posed by online computer networks. Children also are threatened by the online communities that sexual predators are building on the Internet" (1998). He goes on to suggest that "in many . . . corners of the Internet, child molesters find advice and support that was not available to them prior to the growth of online computing." This view is shared by others, who argue that "prior to the Internet, paedophiles remained a relatively isolated group, but through this new technology they have been able to form much larger social networks that have been referred to as 'virtual communities'" (Quayle and Taylor, 2002, p. 867). A similar sentiment is echoed by Mahoney and Faulkner, authors of a report for the Child Advocacy Task Force that deals with pedophiles and the Internet. In the report, they explain how pedophiles can help each other to abuse young people:

The advancement of Internet technology allows pedophiles to exchange information about children in an organized forum. They are able to meet in "online chat rooms" and educate each other. These online discussions include sharing schemes about how to meet, attract, and exploit children—and how to lure the parents of their victims into a false sense of security about their presence within the sanctity of the family structure. It has become an online "How To" seminar in pedophilia activities. (Mahoney and Faulkner, 1997, p. 2)

A good example of an organized pedophile group involves a police operation known as Operation Cathedral, which took place in 2001. Operation Cathedral was an international investigation that began after U.S. Customs officers exposed a pedophile gang called The Orchid Club in 1996, and found three British citizens associated with its activities. Although the investigation was coordinated by UK police officers, a total of twelve countries were involved in the operation, including the United States, Australia, Austria, Belgium, Finland, France, Germany, Italy, Norway, Portugal, and Sweden. The operation was responsible for uncovering the activities of a notorious pedophile ring known as The Wonderland Club (Nichols, 2001). Membership of the club was open only to "serious players" who owned personal collections of more than 10,000 images of children. It is possible to gain some idea of the scale of the group's activities by considering the fact that more than 750,000 indecent images of children were exchanged via the Internet. However, it is far more disturbing to note that police forces were able to identify 1,236 separate children as victims (Nichols, 2001). In November 2001, it was reported that only seventeen of these children had been identified (*The Glasgow Herald*, 18 November 2001). There is also some evidence to suggest that some of the children who were sexually assaulted may have been killed.

It seems clear that the Internet supported the activities of The Wonderland Club by allowing members to exchange materials quickly, easily, and with relatively little danger of discovery. It is known that members were making use of the Internet as far back as 1996, when a U.S. citizen, Ronald Riva, broadcast the abuse of his daughter's ten-year-old friend. Similarly, there were reports that some "images showed babies being sexually assaulted and at times the abuse of children was relayed live online" (*The Glasgow Herald*, 18 November 2001).

The use of web cams, video conferencing, and other real-time services has not been restricted to The Wonderland Club. For instance, Donna Hughes has suggested that pedophile groups

sometimes transmit and view live broadcasts of the sexual abuse of children. . . . Using the new technology of live videoconferencing, sex predators from around the world can witness the live sexual abuse of a child and record the broadcast for future use. (Hughes, 1999)

Hughes also reports cases in which pedophiles sent digital cameras to contacts they thought were boys for them to broadcast live sex acts to the men (2001). The men planned to use video-capture equipment to record movies that could be distributed later on.

There is evidence that some pedophiles groups have been quick to adopt new technology in order to support their activities. It has been reported, for example, that pedophiles may already be using some of the techniques that have been adopted by terrorists and drug dealers, such as steganography (Starrs, 2001). Steganography involves hiding information inside other types of information, such as images or music. In this way, an innocuous picture or music file might contain a concealed message accessible only to someone with the correct software and, of course, a passphrase.

An example of a highly organized pedophile group that made of use of technology to conceal their activities is The Round Table. In March 2002, a police investigation coordinated across a number of countries resulted in the arrests of members of a relatively large pedophile group (Allen, 2002). In addition to the United Kingdom, the countries involved in the investigation were Canada, Finland, France, Germany, Japan, the Netherlands, Spain, Sweden, Switzerland, and the United States. The group is alleged to have created a password-protected chat room so that members could trade photographs and pictures of child pornography. In addition, they are also said to have used sophisticated encryption methods to conceal their activities.

The adoption of sophisticated technology and methods such as steganography and encryption makes it difficult to locate pedophiles and gather evidence against them. Perhaps the single biggest problem is that it becomes extremely time consuming and expensive to glean even the most basic pieces of information. As an example, police officers may need to spend hundreds of hours in order to trace the sender and recipient of a single e-mail message. It must also be recognized that not every country is willing or able to combat crimes such as cyberstalking. According to some sources, only twenty or so countries are technologically sophisticated enough to deal with problems such as the distribution of child pornography via the Internet (*The Glasgow Herald*, 2002).

Pedophile Web Sites

The speed with which pedophiles have come to embrace the Internet and associated technology can be shown by looking at how quickly the number of child pornography web sites has grown. For instance, the Irish government's Department of Justice, Equality and Law Reform reported that

> the results of a systematic review of sites revealed 238 that have appeared between 18 June and 8 November 1997 offering access to girl-related child pornography or erotica. Boy-related sites are greater in number. (1998, p. 34)

Such growth is significant given that it took place in the early days of the Internet's popularity boom.

The scale of pedophile activity on the Internet can also be understood by examining the growing number of pedophilia-related web sites. Typically, these sites are used to provide information and advice to those engaged in the abuse of young people: "Web pages exist on which paedophiles disseminate information to other 'travelling' colleagues about where to go to find the best or easiest victims" (Quayle and Taylor, 2002, p. 867). The exact number of pedophile web sites is not known, but there are likely to be many thousands. For example, writing in 1998, one reporter stated: "More than 8,000 sites on the World Wide Web encourage adults to have sex with children" (Blom, 1998). However, some writers have estimated that the number of sites offering support, advice, and pornographic materials may be much larger. In 2001, for instance, it was reported that "there are at least 23,000 pedophile Web sites that provide essays, pedophile stories and photo galleries of young children and adolescents, most often boys" (Ko, 2001, p. 35).

The popularity of pedophilia-related web sites also helps to illustrate the scale of the problem. Hughes (1999) has suggested that some pedophilia sites average 170,000 visits per month, equivalent to more than 225 visitors per hour. An example of how a single site can attract huge amounts of traffic is as follows:

> An investigation of a child-porn Web site by U.S. Customs agents in the summer of 1999 . . . recorded 4,107 hits from different Internet user addresses in the first month, as well as 95,450 downloads of images. In its third month, the site recorded an astounding 147,776 hits from individual users, and the download of 3.2 million images. (Nordland, Bartholet, and Johnson, 2001)

Apart from allowing them to share resources, the web sites created by organized groups of pedophiles present four other major risks. First, as mentioned earlier, pedophiles can use web sites to exchange information and advice. For instance, an Australian National Crime Authority Report "found substantial evidence that child sex abusers net-worked through the Internet, exchanged child pornography, and, in a few cases, used the Internet to locate potential victims" (Hughes, 1999, p. 21). As a further example, it has been reported how some web sites offer advice to pedophiles on how to use the Internet to locate schools or playgrounds before going on vacation (Blom, 1998).

The second problem involves pedophile web sites being used to misinform young people, perhaps by providing them with misleading advice or false information. For example, there have been reports that some web sites advise young people that they should never reveal their "secret" relationship with an adult (Blom, 1998). In addition, the existence of publicly accessible web sites containing information that advocates or promotes pedophilia may in itself be a problem. For instance, the presence of an attractive, official-looking web site may help to legitimize the behavior of pedophiles in the mind of a young person. After all, a young person might reasonably expect that a site that blatantly promotes illegal or deviant behavior would be prevented from being published.

The third risk posed by pedophile web sites is that they can help some people to believe that their behavior is perfectly normal and legitimate. Hughes, for example, describes pedophilia-related web sites as "havens for men who sexually abuse children. They can access these sites and read articles that defend pedophilia as a 'sexual preference,' and engage in discussions with each other that enable them to defend and rationalize their behavior" (Hughes, 1999, p. 19). Higher levels of child abuse may be one of the results of such behavior since some experts believe that materials advocating sex with children can actually increase the abuse of children (Blom, 1998).

A good example of a web site that describes pedophilia as a legitimate sexual preference is operated by the North American Man/Boy Love Association (NAMBLA).[9] NAMBLA describes itself as an organization that supports "the rights of youth as well as adults to choose the partners with whom they wish to share and enjoy their bodies." As early as 1995, NAMBLA published an article entitled "Man/Boy Love on the Internet," which gave details on how to use the Internet to contact children (Hughes, 2001).

The NAMBLA web site contains a variety of information that it claims supports its views, including essays, links to scientific papers, poetry (for example by Walt Whitman), and interviews with academics, writers, and poets (such as Allen Ginsberg). However, the NAMBLA web site also advertises a book entitled *Boys Speak Out on Man/Boy Love*, which contains letters and articles written by young boys, such as "It Shouldn't Be a Crime to Make Love" by Bryan, age twelve, "Sex Is Really Beautiful with My Friend" by Dennis, age thirteen, and "Thank God for Boy-Lovers" by Victor, age fourteen.

Another risk posed by pedophile web sites arises from their widespread availability. Before the Internet became widely accessible, young people were relatively shielded from threats such as child pornography and the approaches of pedophiles. For example, a pedophile seeking access to a given child would need to infiltrate the home or find another way of making direct contact. It can be argued that the Internet has now allowed pedophiles to enter the home, providing direct access to young people with relatively little risk of discovery. Furthermore, pedophiles face minimal risk of exposure since they no longer need to leave their homes in order to locate information, advice, support, and pornography. For instance, Hughes states: "Unlike the brothels and strip clubs in distant places, these sites can be easily brought into the average home, and users can access every type of sexual exploitation and abuse imaginable in minutes" (Hughes, 2001, p. 4).

Many pedophiles are willing to travel long distances in order to meet in person with the young people they have contacted via the Internet. For instance, it has been noted that many of these "travelers" are even willing to travel to other countries to meet children (Hughes, 1999). In one case, children from Sri Lanka as young as five were being offered for sale via the Internet (Hughes, 1999). In another case, in 1999 a convicted pedophile from the United Kingdom was arrested after arriving in the United States to find a fifteen-year-old girl he had arranged to meet with over the Internet (Hughes, 2003).

In order to give some idea of the scale of the problem, Hughes (1999) reports that from 1996 to 1998, the National Center for Missing and Exploited Children in the United States was involved in sixty traveler cases. She offers a further example by describing a three-year Internet law enforcement project conducted by the Keene Police Department in New Hampshire that resulted in the arrests of 200 offenders who targeted male children (2001). Forty-eight of those arrested were travelers. Four travelers had come from Canada, Holland, and Norway, and the others came from ten different states in the United States.

There may be many reasons why travelers choose to abuse young people in other countries or states. Obviously, the main motivation for a pedophile becoming a traveler is the desire to avoid exposure in his own community as a criminal or deviant. However, some travelers may also be motivated by the possibility of gaining easier access to victims or by a reduced likelihood of arrest. For instance, sex tourists frequently travel to countries such as Thailand, where sex with under-age prostitutes is easily available and tolerated by the authorities. It has even been suggested that some American travelers may choose to pursue children in Canada because they are likely to be treated more leniently if apprehended and convicted (Ko, 2001).

Occasionally, a victim may travel to meet a cyberstalker or other predator. As an example, the story of Lindsay Shamrock describes how Franz Konstantin Baehring persuaded Shamrock to run away from home to live with him. Shamrock left her family and traveled 5,000 miles—from Florida to Greece—in order to be with Baehring because she was convinced she was in love.

Usenet and Newsgroups

Usenet is an online discussion forum where people can read messages posted by others, reply to them, or post their own comments.[10] Each discussion group is called a newsgroup, and there are as many as 40,000 newsgroups available (Department of Justice, Equality and Law Reform, 1998). The messages posted to a newsgroup can contain file attachments, allowing pictures, sound, video, and other data to be disseminated to other users. Since some newsgroups are used to distribute pornography or copyrighted materials (such as music), some Internet Service Providers refuse to provide access to them, or they censor the messages available.

Pedophiles tend to use newsgroups for two main purposes: sharing information and distributing pornography. In terms of sharing information, Hughes argues that "Usenet newsgroups are still popular sites for the exchange of information on how to find women and children for sexual exploitation" (Hughes, 2002a, p. 135). Hughes provides a specific example of this in one of her earlier papers, where she claims that "men use the Usenet newsgroups, such as alt.sex.prostitution, to communicate with each other about where to go to find children for prostitution" (Hughes, 2001, p. 22).

With regard to the distribution of child pornography, Ireland's Combating Paedophile Information Networks in Europe (COPINE) Project estimates that over 1,000 photographs featuring the sexual abuse of children are posted to Usenet each week (Quayle and Taylor, 2002; Hughes, 2002a). Even as early as 1998, researchers found that

> there were in total 40,000 newsgroups, 0.07% of which contained major elements of child erotica and child pornographic pictures. These pictures amounted to 6,058 in total, two thirds of which depicted child erotica and

one third could be described as pornographic. (Department of Justice, Equality and Law Reform, 1998)

Similar figures have also been quoted more recently by the Internet Watch Foundation (IWF),[11] which estimates that there are 30,000 newsgroups currently in existence, of which twenty-eight regularly contain child pornography (Groves, 2001). Over 70 percent of the illegal material reported to the IWF originates from these newsgroups.

Some have suggested that there are more than sixty newsgroups known to contain child pornography (Taylor, Quayle, and Holland, 2001). In addition, there is evidence that pictures posted to Usenet feature an average of two new children per month (Taylor, Quayle, and Holland, 2001). In the United Kingdom, the National Crime Squad took part in an international police operation called Operation Landmark in late 2001. During the operation, officers "monitored activity in 33 Internet newsgroups used by pedophiles over a 16-day period. They found 105,000 illegal images had been posted, featuring thousands of different children, and there were nearly 10,000 'hits' by online paedophiles" (Groves, 2001).

Chat Rooms and Instant Messaging

Internet Relay Chat (IRC) allows people to take part in live discussions via the Internet. A client program is needed in order to use IRC. The client runs on the user's machine and allows messages to be sent and received from a server. The server coordinates communications by ensuring that everyone taking part in the discussion receives every message. Users can choose to join an existing discussion—called a channel—or start a brand new one. It is difficult to estimate the number of channels available because users can create new ones at will and there are many private channels that can only be accessed with a password. Estimates of the number of publicly accessible channels available range from 100,000 (Hughes, 2002a) to more than 580,000.[12]

Chat rooms are similar to IRC in that they enable groups of users to take part in discussions and exchange files. It is worth mentioning that some chat rooms and discussion groups are supervised by moderators who make sure that users follow the rules governing acceptable behavior.[13] However, most groups are unmoderated, and individual behavior tends to be regulated informally, usually by consensus among the most senior or influential members of the group.

Instant messaging packages, such as ICQ, AOL Instant Messenger, and MSN Messenger allow users to communicate with people listed in a personal e-mail directory called a buddy list or contact list.[14] Whenever the user's computer connects to the Internet, a client program checks to see if any of the people in the contact list are also online. The client program displays the name and status of each person in the contact list (e.g., online, offline, etc.). Using the client program, a user can send and receive messages to and from any contacts currently online. Messages are sent and received in real time, with none of the delays normally associated with e-mail, newsgroups, and bulletin board systems.

One of the problems with instant messaging is that once a connection has been established between two or more users, a server is no longer required and all communication is direct between the client programs. This makes it difficult for law enforcement agencies and others to monitor the activities of suspected pedophiles. In addition, several writers have pointed out that it is also difficult to gather evidence of illegal or deviant activities because most instant messaging and chat room software does not provide the facility to record and archive messages. For these reasons, chat rooms and instant messaging are attractive to pedophiles and those involved in the distribution of child pornography. As an example, with regard to chat rooms and stalking, Hughes states: "No messages are archived or stored and no log files are maintained, as is done with e-mails or web accesses, so stalkers use them to look for victims without the danger of being traced by law enforcement authorities" (Hughes, 2002a, p. 140). The same point is also made by the United Kingdom's Department of Health, which reports:

> As well as abusing the Internet to distribute child pornography, a number of adults are also misusing chat rooms on the Internet to try and establish contact with children. Cases have been reported of adults posing as children in an attempt to establish contact with children in Internet chat rooms in order to "groom" them for inappropriate or abusive relationships. Chat rooms create a particular problem because they occur in real time and there is no record of the material held. (Department of Health, 2001, p. 12)

Some idea of the scale of pedophile activity in chat rooms can be obtained by considering some simple examples. First, the Irish Department of Justice, Equality and Law Reform (1998) reported on a survey of IRC networks done in late 1997. Activity on the Dalnet network included thirty-one channels with names related to child sex and a total of 281 participants, and activity on the Undernet network included twenty-four channels with 237 participants. Naturally, the number of channels and participants could not take into account an unknown number of hidden or password-protected chat rooms. Second, in 1997, the U.S. nonprofit organization PedoWatch reported that 1,500 people each day joined the preteen erotica trading channels on IRC (Hughes, 1999). Finally, also in 1997, an investigative reporter found nine Internet chat rooms that dealt with child pornography using names such as "preteen sex pics" and "preteen boy sex" (Hughes, 1999). These rooms had approximately 250 users, all with pornographic images of young boys to exchange.

As mentioned earlier, chat rooms and instant messaging tend to be used to distribute child pornography or locate victims. For instance, the report by the Irish Department of Justice, Equality and Law Reform states: "All IRC networks continue to have channels devoted to both the exchange of child pornographic pictures, and to 'chat' related to fantasy and alleged sexual assaults on children" (1998, p. 3). The report goes on to say that "there have been a number of reported instances of known paedophiles using such interactive sessions with children to gain their confidence before attempting to arrange meetings." Hughes links cyberstalking, sexual assaults on children, and real-time communications by suggesting that "there have also been numerous cases of online stalking of adults that began with conversations in chat rooms, which led to physical meetings that turned into sexual assaults" (Hughes, 2002a, p. 10).

There have also been a number of cases in which pedophiles and others have used stalking-by-proxy as a method of victimization. For instance, it has been reported that "offenders have precipitated the victimization of adults and children by third parties by posting messages, supposedly from the victims, asking for men to come and rape them or use them for prostitution" (Hughes, 2001, p. 15). Examples of this type of behavior appear in a number of the stories in this book, including the accounts dealing with Jayne Hitchcock and Cynthia Armistead (chapter 1), David Cruz (chapter 4), and the Boehle family (chapter 6).

One of the reasons pedophiles use chat rooms and web sites may be related to the ease with which they can gather information about potential victims. The Annenberg Public Policy Center conducted a study that examined the attitudes of parents and their children about releasing personal information on the Internet (Turow and Nir, 2000). The study found that it was surprisingly easy to obtain information from young people, such as their names and addresses. For example, 22 percent of young people were willing to trade information about themselves or their parents in exchange for a gift of any kind. When the value of the gift was taken into account, 45 percent of young people said they would trade information in exchange for a gift worth $100 or more.

Peer to Peer (P2P) Networking

Peer to peer (P2P) file sharing enables computer users to connect their systems together directly so that they can communicate with each other and share files.[15] Modern P2P systems are based on the Gnutella network, which does not rely on a central server. As with instant messaging and chat rooms, this makes it difficult to monitor the behavior of users and gather evidence against those engaged in illegal activities. Some of the client programs used to access the Gnutella network include LimeWire, BearShare, Morpheus, and WinMX.

Although P2P services originally focused on allowing users to exchange music files, they rapidly expanded to include other types of data, such as graphic and video material. Some users were quick to exploit these new features in order to exchange software, movies, and pornography. A monitoring feature of the Gnutella network allows users to see what searches are being done by others. According to the U.S. Customs Cyber Smuggling Center, most searches are for adult and child pornography (Hughes, 2002a).

Perhaps one of the reasons P2P has become popular as a means of distributing child pornography is because both P2P services and client programs have evolved in response to demands for increased security. The Freenet network,[16] for instance, allows anonymous communications and file sharing, and Kazaa[17] and Filetopia[18] are examples of client programs that make use of encryption to provide higher levels of security. However, it is worth remembering that there are many perfectly legitimate reasons for some users to remain anonymous or choose to encrypt their communications. For instance, many companies use encryption to safeguard sensitive commercial information.

CAMGIRLS AND WEB LOGS

A recent trend has been for many teenagers to publish their diaries via the Internet, complete with photographs and even video sequences. Some of the web sites produced by these teenagers are very sophisticated, containing features such as guest books, user polls, and even instant messaging facilities. Some sites even feature live video feeds from webcams. The teenagers who create sites containing video are usually known as camgirls or camboys.

Under normal circumstances, a great deal of effort would be needed to produce an online journal consisting of many brief entries organized in date order and then consolidated within a single page. However, many sites are created using specialized software that simplifies the task of publishing a web diary. One of the most popular programs in use is called Blogger[19] and is available free of charge. The program has become so popular that creating web journals is now often referred to as "blogging." The program's web site describes a "blog" as follows:

What is a weblog/blog?
A blog is a web page made up of usually short, frequently updated posts that are arranged chronologically—like a what's new page or a journal. The content and purposes of blogs varies greatly—from links and commentary about other web sites, to news about a company/person/idea, to diaries, photos, poetry, mini-essays, project updates, even fiction.

There may be many millions of camgirls, camboys, and bloggers across the United States and Europe. For instance, one report states that "in America, about one in every five children aged 12 to 17—more than 4 million of them—now has a personal web page. . . . The sites are filled with regularly updated logs, stories, poems, pictures and even real-time video images" (Preston, 2001). The existence of a large number of teenage diarists is also supported by the fact that a number of dedicated hosting services have recently become available, such as Teen Open Diary and Deardiary.net.[20] These sites provide various facilities for creating online diaries but also provide features for those interested in reading diary entries, such as a search facility.

At face value, publishing an online dairy seems innocent enough and does not appear to pose any danger to the writer. However, many people have pointed out that web diaries expose a great deal of information about their authors, enabling pedophiles and other predators to select potential targets more easily. Some people have noted that many teenagers do not realize that information such as their full/real name and address is often available in the public domain (Valetk, 2003; Frauenfelder, 2002). For instance, when a domain name is registered, the details of the owner—including address and telephone number—can be looked up with a "WhoIs" query, a relatively simple process that can be done via the Internet.[21]

Although some teenagers may be inadvertently exposing themselves to risk, it is more disturbing to find that some teenagers *deliberately* set out to attract the attention of older men. Many teenagers, mainly females, produce web sites that solicit gifts from visitors who are usually complete strangers. Often, a web site will contain a link to a "wish list" hosted by a company such as Amazon.com. Many companies offer this service as a way to let friends and relatives know which gifts would be most appreciated for a special occasion, such as a birthday. A person reading the wish list follows a simple series of steps in order to select the gift, pay for it, and then have it sent directly to the list's owner.

Although many teenagers offer nothing in exchange for the gifts they want, some offer to send photographs or other items to a person who sends a gift. The following describes how some teenagers exploit their sexuality in order to encourage gifts:

> But some young girls are taking these most public of diaries a stage further, and posing in their bedrooms for prurient webcam photographs that they use to persuade strangers to buy them gifts. Although many children simply point visitors to their "wish lists" on shopping sites such as Amazon . . . a number are actively soliciting gifts with the promise of more revealing photographs in return. (Rowan, 2002a)

In addition to money, camgirls often receive gifts such as digital cameras, DVD players, webcams, DVDs, books, videocassettes, cordless telephones, lingerie, and even pets (Anderssen, 2002; Cha, 2001; Frauenfelder, 2002; Rowan, 2002a). One camboy, for instance, claims to have received a DVD player, sixty-two CDs, and eighteen movies within the space of a few months (Cha, 2001). However, the motivation behind becoming a camgirl or camboy is not solely a desire for material gain. As one writer has noted, "The truth is most cam girls are as interested in garnering attention as they are in gathering Wish List merchandise or PayPal 'donations'" (Frauenfelder, 2002).

Although the majority of camgirl sites receive only a handful of visitors, others have become extremely popular. One reporter has said that the most popular sites can receive up to 5,000 visitors each day and can generate up to 200 e-mail messages a day (Cha, 2001, p. A01). Another has described a camgirl site that receives more than 1,000 visits each day (Anderssen, 2002), and a third has told of a single site that receives 6,000 visitors each month (Frauenfelder, 2002). The owner of this last site enjoys such popularity that she operates a fan club on Yahoo! that has 1,000 registered members.

It seems apparent that the more popular the web site, the greater the likelihood of receiving money or expensive gifts. As mentioned earlier, one way in which camgirls attempt to attract more visitors to their sites is by publishing more revealing photographs. For instance, some camgirls promise nude photographs or other materials in exchange for gifts (Anderssen, 2002). However, many camgirls also form links with adult web sites in order to generate an income. Although some money can be made by advertising pornography sites, much more can be made from the commission earned by convincing people to sign up with adult sites. In the United States, camgirls can earn $10 for each person who signs up for a given service (Anderssen, 2002). For many, this provides enough money to pay for a web connection, but others can earn even more. For instance, *The Observer* describes the case of a UK camgirl who received a commission of £100 (approximately $160) from advertising adult web sites (Rowan, 2002a). The newspaper also describes the case of a fourteen-year-old camgirl named Kerry:

> But what sets Kerry's site apart from the typical schoolgirl's are the links she trails from her front page to adult sites that pay her for referring new subscribers. And not only does she trail other sites but last week, she says, she received a cheque for $80 from Cam Girls Gone Wild, where paying visitors can see her "bikini photographs."

For many people, the reason men buy gifts for camgirls is very clear: "For adult admirers, the hope is often that their gifts will buy more than just photos. For example, a predator may eventually ask for sexually explicit photos or try to persuade the minor to meet offline" (Valetk, 2003). Although some people have claimed innocent motives for sending gifts to camgirls, many of their reasons seem dubious. For instance, some people have claimed that web journal entries have literary merit and can be compared to works such as *Anne Frank: The Diary of a Young Girl*[22] or even *The Adventures of Huckleberry Finn*.

Camgirls face a number of dangers. For example, pictures of camgirls have been stolen by pornographers who have used them on their own sites (Cha, 2001). In addition to the distress caused to the teenagers, such a development also raises the possibility that pedophiles or stalkers might target them. Even the relatively innocent act of posting web journal entries and photographs to a personal web site may be enough to bring a camgirl to the attention of pedophiles. Whatever the risk, it is almost certain to increase when camgirls link their sites to adult content hosted elsewhere.

In the United Kingdom, the National Hi-Tech Crime Unit believes that pedophiles are already targeting some camgirl sites (Rowan, 2002b). This observation is supported by a growing number of personal accounts describing stalking incidents that can be easily found via search engines. Ironically, many of these accounts are held within web logs created by camgirls and camboys. The danger posed by stalkers has been raised by several writers (for example, Anderssen, 2002; Valetk, 2003), including one who states:

> For parents and law enforcement, the overwhelming concern is that any interaction between minors and total strangers could lead to stalking and other unhealthy obsessions. Internet safety experts . . . warn that pedophiles use camgirl sites to interact with teens, meet them in chat rooms, and ultimately persuade them to meet in person. (Valetk, 2003)

Many camgirls and camboys operate their sites without their parents' knowledge (Cha, 2001; Frauenfelder, 2002; Rowan, 2002a). Some deliberately mislead their parents concerning the content of their sites, but others simply exploit the fact that they have limited parental supervision. If a problem arises, there is a natural reluctance to involve parents, making it easy for the situation to spiral out of control.

Some camgirls admit to meeting with people they have met on the Internet. Although many take precautions—by bringing a friend along, for example—others seem to have little concern for their safety. The case of Christina Long, a thirteen-year-old girl murdered by a man she met via the Internet, provides a tragic example of the dangers involved in Internet dating (Long's story is described at the end of this chapter).

In Japan, teenagers have started to engage in a practice called *enjo kosai* (compensated dating), which involves offering an escort service in exchange for money or gifts: "In exchange for escorting wealthy, middle-aged patrons to cafes and restaurants (and often providing them with sexual favors), the girls receive financial compensation, which they use to buy consumer electronics, cosmetics, and clothes" (Frauenfelder, 2002). Many Japanese teenagers join Internet dating services and promote themselves in much the same way as camgirls. However, as the number of dating services has increased, so too has the number of crimes related to Internet dating. For instance, in the first six months of 2002, the number of crimes more than doubled, growing from 302 to 793. More than 70 percent of these crimes involved girls between the ages of thirteen and eighteen (Ninemsn, 2002). Among the offenses recorded were a murder, twenty-three rapes, and six cases of robbery. It seems only a matter of time before compensated dating begins to appear in the United States and Europe.

It can be argued that adults seeking to exploit camgirls and camboys bear much of the responsibility for placing them at risk. For instance, there are many web sites that provide reviews of camgirl sites, including detailed comments on the physical appearance of the teenagers. Some sites even provide directories of camgirl pages, allowing users to search for sites by the camgirl's age, her location, and whether or not the site contains nudity and/or pornography.[23] It is worth noting that the listings provided by these sites are often accompanied by prominent advertisements for web sites offering pornography or adult dating services.

To attract more visitors to their sites, many teenagers join cam portals. These are special web sites that show previews from a number of web cams simultaneously. Since previews are usually shown in order of popularity, camgirls need to find ways of attracting attention to themselves, for example, by behaving outrageously or by showing nudity. The more visitors to a camgirl's site, the more prominently the site is advertised, resulting in yet more visitors to the camgirl's site, and so on. Many cam portals are subscription-based and attract subscribers by promising access to pornographic images and video feeds featuring teenagers. In many cases, the relationship between a camgirl and the owner of a cam portal is symbiotic. The camgirl receives a commission for each person who subscribes to the service, generating a profit for the cam portal and helping to increase traffic, some of which is directed back to the camgirl's web site. The greater the number of people attracted to the cam portal, the more the owner and the camgirl profit.

The camgirls and camboys situation seems to have come about as part of the natural evolution of the Internet. There are several factors that may have been an influence:

> The cam girls phenomenon could not have happened before this moment in history. It's the result of a combination of specific ingredients: inexpensive yet powerful technology to send and receive video images over the Net; a culture that places a higher value on fame than on the skills and talent that make people famous; teen celebrities who happily flaunt their bodies on the covers of national magazines; and the timeless rite of passage that is a teenage girl's search for identity and blossoming awareness of her own sexual power. (Frauenfelder, 2002)

CONCLUSION

With increased levels of access to the Internet comes an increased risk of contact with pedophiles and other predators, especially since most young people are unsupervised when they use the Internet. In fact, some studies have reported that roughly one in five young people have received a sexual solicitation or approach, and that up to one in seventeen young people have been threatened or harassed.

Those most at risk from any form of harassment or solicitation are young people who are considered especially vulnerable, perhaps through disability or a need for attention. This is because many pedophiles and other predators are skilled at identifying the most vulnerable young people.

It has been shown that there appears to be a direct link between the use of child pornography and the sexual abuse of children. Some organizations claim that child pornography encourages the abuse of children. It is also known that some commercial suppliers of child pornography operate on a massive scale. In addition, the demand for child pornography is so high that specialized services exist that are able to create materials to order.

Pedophiles may use child pornography for a number of purposes, including as a way of justifying their behavior. The Internet has allowed pedophiles to form organized groups that support the widespread distribution of child pornography and allow resources to be shared. These groups can also provide members with advice, information, and support. There is also evidence that some pedophiles are willing to travel long distances—even abroad—in order to meet young people contacted via the Internet. The emergence of camgirls and camboys is very disturbing since it suggests that some teenagers may be deliberately attracting the attention of pedophiles in order to solicit money and gifts.

The material presented so far has focused on individuals and small groups. The next chapter widens the discussion by looking at new forms of cyberstalking that involve organizations and government departments. In addition, the material looks at different motives behind cyberstalking, such as fraud and terrorism.

THE CHRISTINA LONG STORY

Christina Long was thirteen years old and attended a Catholic school. A popular student, she got good grades, led the cheerleading squad, and was also an altar girl. However, Long was said to have a troubled home life and had been sent to stay with an aunt because her parents had substance abuse problems (CBSNews.com, 2002a).

Long made regular use of Internet chat rooms and instant messaging, telling her guardian that she was talking to friends from school. However, in reality, she was using provocative screen names to contact strangers in chat rooms and routinely engaged in sex with people she met there (*USA Today*, 2002b).

In May 2002, Long failed to return from a local mall, so her aunt, Shelly Riling, contacted the security staff. Unable to find Long, the security staff eventually contacted the police. Police officers checked Long's computer and found e-mail messages suggesting that she had arranged to meet a married restaurant worker that evening named Saul Dos Reis. According to the police, Long had first met Dos Reis in an Internet chat room, where he used the screen name "Hot es300," apparently referring to a Lexus car model (*USA Today*, 2002a). The police also said that Long had met Dos Reis for sex several times before.

When questioned, Dos Reis admitted to accidentally strangling Long while they were having sex in his car in the mall parking lot. He also claimed not to have known that Long was a minor and even suggested that her death might have been caused by an undiagnosed heart condition (Arce, 2003). Dos Reis eventually led police officers to Long's body, which was found lying face down in a shallow ravine around twenty-five miles from her home (ABCNews, 2003). Dos Reis had also tried to create an alibi for himself by sending an e-mail to Long after her death. The e-mail asked how her date had gone and asked her to write back.

Dos Reis was convicted on a charge of manslaughter and three charges of sexual assault. He received a sentence of thirty years.

8

Cyberstalking and Organizations

THE AMANA MONA STORY

In January 2001, a twenty-five-year-old Palestinian woman was arrested for luring a young Israeli man to his death. Amana Mona was
arrested after the body of sixteen-year-old Ofir Rahum was found
outside of the West Bank town of Ramallah (Weisman, 2001b).

After a month of interrogation, Mona admitted to planning to kidnap the Israeli teenager as an act of protest against the murder of
Palestinian children. As part of her plan, Mona had established relationships with a number of Israeli teenagers via the Internet. She eventually chose Rahum as her victim, a young man described as shy,
studious, and a "computer freak" (Weisman, 2001a). While preparing
for the kidnapping, Mona received advice from another Palestinian on
how best to carry out her plan.

Mona eventually arranged to meet Rahum and took him to the Palestinian town of Ramallah. Once there, two senior activists in Yasser
Arafat's Fatah faction, Hassan Khadi and Abdel Dula, tried to pull
Rahum from the car. When Rahum struggled, one of the men opened
fire with a Kalashnikov rifle, killing him. The two men buried the body,
but it was eventually found and reported to the Israeli authorities.
During their investigation, Shin Bet (the Israeli internal security
agency) operatives found information on Rahum's computer that allowed them to locate Mona. Although Mona's brother claimed that she

did not know how to access the Internet and did not own a home computer, it was reported that some of Rahum's communications were traced to the computer she used at her job as an administrator with the Ramallah-based monthly magazine *Snawbar* (Weisman, 2001c).

When interrogated, Mona claimed that she only wanted to kidnap Rahum and had never intended for him to be killed. However, she confessed to luring Rahum to the meeting at which he was killed (BBC News, 2001b).

INTRODUCTION

What forms of cyberstalking involve organizations, such as companies and government departments? What harm does corporate cyberstalking cause? Chapter 1 offered a definition of cyberstalking that suggested an organization could become a victim of cyberstalking or might even use cyberstalking as a means of dealing with competitors. The term *corporate cyberstalking* is often used to describe incidents that involve organizations, such as companies.

In this chapter, I use a number of examples to put forward a typology of corporate cyberstalking. I suggest that incidents involving corporate cyberstalking can be divided into two broad groups, depending on whether the organization acts as a stalker or as a victim. In addition, examining the motivations behind corporate cyberstalking allows these groups to be subdivided further. As shown by the examples given later, the motives behind corporate cyberstalking can be very different from those commonly associated with offline stalking and cyberstalking. These motives can range from a desire for revenge against an employer to cyberterrorism.

WHAT IS CORPORATE CYBERSTALKING?

Many people associate corporate cyberstalking with the notion of a company—usually represented by a single employee or manager—setting out to harass an individual. Indeed, the first cyberstalking case to make international headlines was that of Jayne Hitchcock, a writer who claimed to have been stalked by the Woodside Literary Agency for several years. It is important to note, however, that this kind of incident normally involves a senior figure in the organization making a conscious decision to divert company resources toward a campaign of harassment. What distinguishes this kind of cyberstalking from other types of corporate cyberstalking is that the manager's actions are almost always based on personal reasons, such as a grudge against a former intimate.

Occasionally, an organization may be an unwitting accomplice to a cyberstalker rather than an active and willing participant. There have been many cases in which employees have used company e-mail to harass other staff members. In one case, for instance, a network administrator was dismissed for harassing a clerk. Undeterred, the administrator broke into the company's systems and continued his campaign of harassment. In addition to sending embarrassing e-mail messages about the clerk around the firm, he stole sensitive company information and even gave the clerk a $130,000 pay raise (MSNBC, 2001).

Another example of a company becoming an unwilling accomplice to a cyberstalker (Bocij, Bocij, and McFarlane, 2003) involved a company employee, "Mr. Smith,"[1] who used his employer's resources to harass a number of women via e-mail and Internet chat rooms. Victims would be selected by searching the personal profiles that many people submit to various services, such as ICQ. Smith appeared to select victims who were single and lived relatively close to him.

Smith adopted several distinct identities when communicating with his victims. He used these identities to minimize the possibility of being caught once he began to conduct a sustained campaign of harassment against his victims. This harassment would take a number of different forms, including sending abusive e-mail messages, placing surveillance software on the victim's computer, following the victim, and making threats that implied he would assault the victim in her own home.

Smith was eventually caught when he deviated from his usual pattern of behavior and selected a married woman as a victim. The woman's husband was a computer consultant with expertise in computer security. This man was able to trace Smith's name, address, and place of employment. It was found that Smith was a network administrator for a relatively large local company and had been using his employer's facilities in order to stalk his victims. His stalking behavior included making use of company software packages, such as route planning software and a database containing a register of electors, to find personal information about victims; establishing numerous false e-mail accounts; and intercepting e-mail messages meant for senior management, deleting them, and then impersonating managers in replies.

Once notified of Smith's activities, senior management was quick to offer a guarantee that the matter would be dealt with. However, it does not appear that the police were informed of Smith's actions, and it does not appear that he was fired from his job.

Although most of the examples given here involve companies, it is worth pointing out that the resources of charities, local government, and other not-for-profit organizations are also open to abuse. For instance, it is alleged that a research student at Glasgow University in Scotland abused Internet and e-mail facilities when he began to correspond with pedophiles under the guise of a research project (Martin, 2001; Major, 2001).

It is also important to point out that organizations may sometimes hold some of the responsibility for incidents in which company resources are used to harass others. It can be argued that organizations have a duty to ensure that resources are used appropriately. Even when legislation does not impose such a duty, it is difficult to claim that companies have no professional or moral responsibility to protect the public. Of course, there are also very sound business reasons for ensuring that organizational resources are not abused in the ways described here. For instance, the Electrohippies case (discussed later in this chapter) describes some of the costs that can arise from a denial of service (DoS) attack.

Some organizations use cyberstalking as a way to control information about them that is posted to the Internet. As an example, recent years have seen many companies use Strategic Lawsuits Against Public Participation (SLAPPs) to prevent individuals from publishing various kinds of information on the Internet, such as complaints. The Civil Liberties Monitoring Project suggests that SLAPPs can be used "to intimidate activists into silence by filing meritless lawsuits against them . . . for such torts as slander or intentional interference with business advantage" (Kirk, 1998). Some well-known SLAPP cases include the Electronic Frontier Foundation (EFF)[2] and its support of a parody of a favorite children's character named Barney, Carla Virga and Terminix,[3] and some of the numerous disputes concerning Scientology.[4]

Although the use of SLAPPs is perfectly legal in many countries, there may be circumstances in which their use exposes an organization to civil or criminal legal action. For instance, many companies "follow" their critics around the Internet, keeping a close watch on web sites, bulletin boards, and chat rooms for any material that criticizes the company. Sometimes, especially in the case of web sites, a company may wish to act against a particularly vocal critic, and an unusual cat-and-mouse situation may ensue. In such a scenario, an individual establishes a web site containing criticisms of a company. When the company becomes aware of the web site, a complaint or legal threat is made to the Internet Service Provider and the critic's web site is taken down. The owner is then forced to move to another ISP and the cycle begins again. If the complaints made to ISPs are unfounded, the company might face civil action (e.g., for libel) or even criminal charges (e.g., harassment).

A good example of this kind of cat-and-mouse game involves the case of Mark Zeman and GeoCities.[5] Zeman alleges that GeoCities, a free web-space provider, actively pursues those who criticize the company on their web sites. His personal web site states: "GeoCities has followed critics around the Web, tracked them down, threatened, and otherwise harassed them and their ISPs and Web hosts. GeoCities has in the past threatened legal action against those that dare host any critic."

Zeman's allegations against GeoCities are three-fold. First, he argues GeoCities follows its critics around the Internet and issues legal threats against any ISP unwise enough to host a web site containing criticisms of the company. Second, although no explicit accusation is made, Zeman appears to suggest that his web site has been deliberately banned by several software packages that are used to filter web content (sometimes known as censorware). Finally, Zeman claims to have received various legal threats from GeoCities based on copyright and trademark infringement. According to Zeman, all of these actions make it difficult for people to exercise the right to free speech because they are effectively being censored by GeoCities.

Zeman claims that there are many web sites that contain criticisms of other free web-space providers, but very few that criticize GeoCities. This, he says, is evidence that shows GeoCities has adopted a policy of (legal) harassment against its critics. He also claims that he is not the only one to have been censored by GeoCities. His web site lists a number of web rings (groups of related web sites) and individual web sites devoted to those claimed to have been censored by GeoCities.

Each of the examples given so far has described an incident in which an organization has become involved in harassing an individual. There are, however, many occasions when an organization can become a *victim* of harassment.

As noted in chapter 1, cyberstalking results in "emotional distress" to the victims. It is necessary to expand upon the notion of distress here in order to be able to apply the definition to corporate cyberstalking. In terms of an organization, it is suggested that distress means any form of harm to the organization, its employees, or its resources.[6] In general, it is possible to measure the damage caused by corporate cyberstalking in financial terms. For instance, one of the cases described later in this chapter concerns Jonathan Lebed and the way in which he manipulated share prices in order to make a profit of $285,000. However, companies can suffer other forms of damage that are not quite so easy to measure. For example, it is difficult to measure a loss in public confidence caused by rumors and misinformation disseminated via the Internet.

A typical example of corporate cyberstalking in which an organization becomes the victim usually involves one or more individuals targeting a specific company for financial gain or in order to exact revenge against a former employer. Often, these cases involve individuals posting false or defamatory information to various sites on the Internet, such as chat rooms. This is sometimes known as bashing or cyber-smearing (Smith, 2000). This kind of behavior can be directly compared to a type of offline stalker known as the resentful stalker. According to researchers (Mullen, Pathé, and Purcell, 2000, pp. 76–77), the behavior of such people involves "responding to a perceived insult or injury by actions aimed not just at revenge but at vindication." In outlining a tentative typology of cyberstalkers, a colleague and I have also proposed a category known as the "vindictive stalker," which is similar to the resentful stalker (McFarlane and Bocij, 2003).

Cyber-smearing is a serious matter since the damage it causes is often more serious than if the information were contained in a letter or even a newspaper article. In the case of a letter, the potential audience for the information is very limited. In the case of a newspaper article, a retraction can be printed quickly and easily and is likely to reach the same audience who saw the original article. However, it is almost impossible to retract a message posted to a chat room or discussion board. Usually, the information contained within the message becomes persistent, meaning that it remains easily accessible for the foreseeable future and hence increases the harm done to the company over time. It is also worth noting that the potential audience for a message posted on the Internet is far larger than the circulation of any newspaper in the world. For instance, in 2000, a young lawyer working in the United Kingdom received a message from a former girlfriend that recalled a sexual encounter they had shared in the past. The lawyer forwarded the message to a small group of his friends who decided to circulate it further without his knowledge. Within days, the message had been read by an estimated 10 million people (Topham, 2000; King, 2001).

False or defamatory information is often posted to financial chat rooms and message boards in order to perpetrate online stock fraud. The most common method, known as "pump and dump," usually involves the perpetrator buying large quantities of a given company's stock and then artificially increasing the value of the stock by posting rumors such as "news" of a potential takeover. As soon as the value of the stock rises, the perpetrator sells his or her shares at a large profit. Occasionally, the perpetrator may artificially decrease the value of a stock so that shares can be bought at a bargain price to be resold once the stock recovers.

The harm caused by this form of cyberstalking must not be under-estimated. As explained earlier, the damage caused to an organization's public image is often severe and long lasting. However, the financial losses that accompany online stock fraud can sometimes harm an en-tire industry. For instance, in August 2000, Mark Jakob, a twenty-three-year-old former student, released a body of false information concerning Emulex. Within an hour the company's stock had fallen in value by $2.5 billion, but Jakob had realized a personal profit of $240,000 (Berensen, 2000). Fearful that Emulex indicated a problem within the sector, panicked investors began selling shares in other com-panies, causing shares in Brocade and Qlogic to fall in value too (Grice and Ard, 2000).

Occasionally, an organization may use cyberstalking as a competi-tive strategy. One incident, for example, involved a legal action started by Amway against Procter & Gamble (Lopez, 1999). In this case, it was alleged that Procter & Gamble had sponsored a web site that encour-aged complaints against Amway. It is alleged that the site featured negative news stories, personal testimonials, and even confidential documents belonging to Amway. This kind of behavior can be consid-ered corporate stalking-by-proxy since it involved a company using a third party to harass a competitor. In another case, a Washington law firm, Steptoe and Johnson, was accused of launching a "cyber-war" against DigDirt.com, a firm that provides information from public records to private investigators, lawyers, and law enforcement agen-cies. According to DigDirt.com's owner, Michael Moore, the employ-ees of Steptoe and Johnson carried out a number of attacks on the company, including breaking into company web sites on some 750 occasions, launching denial of service attacks, and posting defamatory messages to Usenet (Bicknell, 1999).

Individuals may sometimes pursue an organization in order to further a social or political goal. At one level, a person might use the Internet as a means of making a peaceful protest against a government's policy. At another, more direct action may be taken in order to *force* compliance from a company or government. For instance, a report by Michael Vatis of the Institute for Security Technology

Studies provides several detailed examples of recent cyberterrorism incidents, including clashes involving India and Pakistan, Israel and the Palestinians, and NATO and Serbia in Kosovo (Vatis, 2001). In addition, the story of Amana Mona also shows how technology can be used for political purposes.

Although most cyberterrorism is aimed at government agencies, it is worth remembering that businesses and noncommercial organizations may also make tempting targets for cyberterrorists. For instance, a company might be attacked because it has links to the defense industry. As an example, *Information Week* reported that AT&T and Lucent Technologies were threatened by pro-Palestinian hackers in November 2001 (Hulme and Garvey, 2001). Public services, such as hospitals, are also vulnerable because of the wide-scale disruption and public alarm that an attack might cause.

CATEGORIES OF CORPORATE CYBERSTALKING

Cases involving corporate cyberstalking can be divided into two broad categories: incidents in which an organization acts as a stalker and incidents in which an organization becomes a victim of stalking. It is also possible to group corporate cyberstalking incidents together by examining the motives behind the harassment. As discussed in the previous section, the motives behind corporate cyberstalking can range from a desire for revenge against an employer to cyberterrorism.

Keeping all of this in mind, it is now possible to suggest a typology of corporate cyberstalking, summarized by Table 8.1.

The upper part of the table represents categories of corporate cyberstalking in which an organization becomes a victim, and the lower part shows the categories in which the organization becomes the stalker. Category names have been used as a simple way of identifying and describing a given category. These names also help to make clear the differences between categories.

CORPORATE CYBERSTALKING EXAMPLES

Examples have already been provided to support the points made so far. However, some additional examples will help to clarify and illustrate each of the categories described within the typology. The following six case studies have been selected to highlight the seriousness and diversity of corporate cyberstalking incidents.

Table 8.1
Proposed Typology of Corporate Cyberstalking Incidents

Stalker/victim	Category name	Description
Individual/organization	Vengeful	The individual wishes to exact some form of revenge against the organization (e.g., cyber-smearing).
Individual/organization	Individual gain	The individual is seeking some form of benefit (e.g., financial gain obtained via stock fraud).
Individual/organization	Ideological	The individual acts in support of beliefs (e.g., cyberterrorism and hacktivism).
Organization/individual	Unwitting	The organization is unaware of the actions of an employee and is an unknowing accomplice.
Organization/individual	For profit	The organization seeks to realize some form of (business) benefit by its actions (e.g., silencing critics using SLAPP). The victim is normally an individual.
Organization/individual	Competitive	The organization seeks to improve its competitive position. The victim is another organization.

Example One: Vengeful (Gibson Research Corporation)

Gibson Research Corporation (GRC) is a leading Internet security research organization based in the United States. In May 2001, GRC experienced a series of denial of service attacks over a three-week period.[7] These attacks effectively prevented access to GRC's web site by flooding the company with fake Internet traffic.

The first attack lasted for seventeen hours until Steve Gibson, GRC's owner, found a way to deal with the massive flood of data inundating the company's web site. During this period, the company's web site was unavailable to customers, resulting in disruption to sales, technical support, and other services. Eventually, it was found that the data being sent to the company's web site could be filtered, enabling the company to identify which traffic was genuine and which was not. This meant that the routes being used to send fake traffic could be closed down and the web site could begin operating again. However, even though customers could now access the company's services, the web site remained under attack for several hours.

Over the next few weeks, the company was attacked five more times, each time more serious than the last. The final attack saw GRC's systems filter out nearly 2.4 billion packets of data, representing approximately 55 million attempts to connect to GRC's web site.

Determined to identify the attacker and prevent any further disruption to his company's web site, Gibson attempted to trace the origin of the attacks. His investigation revealed that a total of 474 computers had been used to attack the company's web site and that each of these computers had been infected with a zombie program. Using the computer's Internet connection, the zombie program was used to generate fake Internet traffic directed toward GRC's web site. Each zombie was programmed to connect to a specific IRC server at regular intervals in order to receive orders from the owner. When the owner wanted to begin an attack, a single instruction sent to the IRC server activated every zombie program simultaneously. The attacker also infected each computer with a Trojan called Sub7Server. Once activated, the Trojan could be used to carry out various actions, such as transmitting passwords, copies of e-mail messages, and other sensitive data to its owner. The Trojan provided almost complete control over the infected computer, prompting Gibson to suggest that "any user with Sub7 in their machine might as well have the hacker standing right next to them watching every move they make while using the computer" (2002).

Shortly after one of the attacks on the company's web site, Gibson noted a newsgroup message claiming responsibility—and credit—for the attacks on the company's server. The message was from someone called "Wicked" who claimed to be a thirteen-year-old boy. Gibson immediately began a dialogue with Wicked in an attempt to understand what had prompted the attacks against GRC and to see if further attacks could be avoided. It appeared that Wicked believed that Gibson had insulted him and his friends in a newsgroup posting. Wicked claimed that Gibson had referred to him and his friends as "script kiddies," a derogatory term used to describe aspiring hackers with poor technical skills. However, Wicked's only knowledge of the alleged insult came secondhand—he had not seen the posting himself, nor did he seem to know where it had appeared. Although Gibson explained that he had never made such a comment, Wicked continued to attack the GRC web site. Gibson described Wicked's attitude as follows:

> From my dialog with "Wicked," I saw that these repeated attacks were "fun" for him. He was like a child pulling the legs off a spider to see what it would do, watching it flail and attempt to get away from its tormentor. And, as we have seen, he experiences absolutely no remorse and has no regard for any damage being done as a consequence. He believes that he can not and will not be caught. Hiding behind the anonymity created by the Internet's trusting technology, he exhibits no social conscience. (2002)

After a great deal of effort, Gibson was able to determine that much of the bogus traffic being directed toward the company web site originated from a particular Internet Service Provider. He contacted the ISP and asked for assistance but, despite assurances, received no help. Gibson's view of this is highly critical: "Our industry's leading consumer ISP's are worse than useless when asked for any form of help relating to Internet security or the welfare of the paying customers" (2002). Gibson also contacted the FBI but was told that, for various reasons, they were unlikely to investigate the case, causing him to comment: "There are just too many large problems for the smaller ones— which may be destined to grow larger—to receive help or attention" (2002).

Gibson decided that his only option was to locate the source of the zombie programs being used to attack the company. In order to do this, he decided to create his own zombie program by reverse-engineering a copy of the program being used against the company. Gibson's modified zombie collected information about other zombie programs and their users. Eventually, Gibson learned that the program being used against his company appeared to have been created by someone called

"^b0ss^." Wicked had simply modified an existing program and launched it against GRC. Following an IRC conversation with ^b0ss^, who promised to contact Wicked and ask him to stop harassing the company, the attacks against GRC ceased.

GRC's experience highlights a number of important points. To start with, although the reason behind the attacks on the company might seem trivial to the outside observer, Wicked clearly perceived the comments supposedly made by Gibson as a gross insult. Since there is no evidence that Gibson made the statement attributed to him, it seems that Wicked began his campaign of harassment based on nothing more than a rumor. Those responsible for the rumor effectively attacked the company using stalking-by-proxy.

Since GRC received little or no help from ISPs and law enforcement agencies, the company was faced with the choice of dealing with matters itself or simply putting up with the attacks on its web site. In putting up with DoS attacks, a company would be resigning itself to accepting any losses incurred as a result. Companies with a limited Internet presence might suffer only small losses, but those that rely more heavily on the Internet might suffer more significant harm. Furthermore, losses can be direct or indirect. Lost sales are an example of a direct loss, and reduced customer satisfaction is an example of an indirect loss.

Some simple figures may give some perspective regarding the level of risk and potential losses companies face. A survey by the Computer Security Institute found that more than one-third of respondents had experienced a DoS attack (Kaplan, 2001). Given companies' tendency to underreport attacks to avoid bad publicity, the actual incidence may have been much higher. In terms of costs, it has been estimated that direct losses from DoS attacks on companies like Yahoo!, eBay, and others in February 2000 amounted to $1.2 billion (Kaplan, 2001).

Only large companies or those that specialize in Internet services are likely to have the expertise needed to deal with DoS attacks and locate those responsible. Smaller companies will be unwilling to invest precious resources in a cat-and-mouse game aimed at preventing further attacks, especially when the prospects of success are limited. As GRC's case shows, a tremendous level of technical expertise may be needed to identify those responsible for a DoS attack. Furthermore, even when such expertise is available, it does not guarantee that the attacker will be caught. It is also worth making the point that any company or individual is susceptible to a DoS attack. GRC has an international reputation as a leading developer of Internet security products but was still unable to prevent a number of attacks on its web site.

Although those seeking to prevent DoS attacks may need a great deal of technical expertise, comparatively little knowledge is needed to initiate an attack against a company or individual. For instance, in GRC's case, Gibson explains that Wicked and his friends simply modified an existing program that he had obtained from the Internet:

> They did this, not using any tool they had written, and not possessing the ability to create such a tool themselves, but using a powerful "IRC Bot" that had been passed around extensively. Neither Wicked nor his friends know who wrote it or even where it came from. (2002)

Example Two: Individual Gain (Jonathan Lebed)

In September 2000, the Securities and Exchange Commission (SEC) settled a civil law suit against Jonathan Lebed,[8] who was just fourteen when he allegedly used the Internet for a major "pump and dump" scheme (Raphael, 2000a).

According to the SEC, Lebed bought inexpensive shares from little-known companies and then used financial message boards in order to promote the shares before selling them at a profit. Using a number of aliases, Lebed sometimes flooded message boards with up to 600 messages intended to manipulate the value of his shares. Among the stocks traded were Manchester Equipment Co., Inc.; Just Toys, Inc.; Yes Entertainment, Inc.; Fotoball USA, Inc.; West Coast Entertainment, Inc.; Havana Republic, Inc.; Classica Group, Inc.; and Firetector, Inc. Lebed allegedly targeted Man Sang Holdings twice, posting messages claiming that it was "the most undervalued stock in history," that its price would rise from $2 a share to reach $20 "very soon" (McNamee, 2000), and that it would be the "next stock to gain 1,000 percent" (Ames, 2001).

Between August 1999 and February 2000, Lebed made at least eleven trades, earning profits of between $11,000 and $74,000 each time. The SEC also claimed that Lebed even set triggers that would automatically sell shares when they reached a certain price so that he would not miss a price increase while at school (Ames, 2001). In total, Lebed was reported to have made a profit of $273,000 from these trades.

Lebed settled the case with the SEC by agreeing to follow a cease-and-desist order and paying back the profits he made. Including interest, Lebed repaid a total of $285,000. However, some sources claim that Lebed's overall profit was closer to $800,000 over the six months or so he traded (Lewis, 2001). If so, then Lebed was allowed to retain almost half a million dollars. It is also worth noting that Lebed settled his case without admitting or denying the SEC's charges.

Lebed's case shows that it is relatively easy to manipulate stock values through chat rooms and web sites. Although today's investors seem less trusting of the financial information they come across via the Internet, it is not difficult to take advantage of some Internet users. As an example, in 1994 The Motley Fool created a fake stock called Zeigletics as an April Fool's prank.[9] According to one writer, people quickly came to believe that a huge profit could be made:

> Even though the company, its product, and the exchange were complete fabrications, financial message boards on America Online and Prodigy were filled with lively discussions about the company. People actually tried to purchase Zeigletics stock based solely on what they read on the message boards! (Perlman, 2000).

Example Three: Ideological (Electrohippies)

In December 1999, a British group called the Electrohippies organized what they described as a "virtual sit-in" at the World Trade Organization's (WTO) web site (Cassel, 2000). It is estimated that more than 450,000 participants took part in a massive denial of service attack that overloaded the WTO's web site for hours at a time on several occasions (Cassel, 2000).

The group's protest was organized via its web site,[10] where participants were given instructions on when, where, and how to act. In addition to DoS attacks, the group also attacked the WTO's e-mail system. A message on the group's web site stated: "So far we've demonstrated that the WTO's public information system is not immune from public pressure. Now we move to their private information system—their email."

In early 2003, Electrohippies organized a protest against the war in Iraq. Part of the protest involved distributing a web page containing information such as the reasons for the protest, how members of the public could take part, and details of related protests. The web page was provided under the GNU Free Documentation License, meaning that it could be copied freely and hosted on other web sites.[11] The page was adopted by many individuals and organizations around the world, achieving widespread distribution within a matter of days.

According to the web page, the reasons for the protest were as follows:

> As we see it, this is not just an argument over whether Saddam is a nasty dictator. It's also about the way governments can ignore overwhelming public opinion, and how countries like the USA can defy global opin-

ion and unilaterally attack and kill the innocent civilians of another state without any restriction or sanction. In short, this whole issue is symptomatic of the divide between a world dominated by corporate-influenced political power, and by the free will of the people of the globe.

The aim of the virtual sit-in (sometimes called a cyber sit-in) was to bring attention to the protestors' cause. Electrohippies described their aim like this: "For this protest, the electrohippies will be seeking to 'degrade the service' of Tony Blair's web site, and George W. Bush's web site. We believe that this is valid because these sites are and will be used to propagate the misleading justifications for war in Iraq."[12] The attempt to "degrade the service" of the web sites involved a distributed denial of service attack to be carried out by ordinary members of the public.

Those wanting to take part in the protest could do so in two ways.[13] The first was to load a special protest web page and keep it open on the user's desktop while he or she used his or her computer as usual. The web page contained a special script that accessed the target web sites at regular intervals, effectively generating a small volume of dummy traffic directed toward the target web site. The more people who took part, the greater the volume of traffic. In order to ensure that the action would be as effective as possible, all traffic was initially directed to Tony Blair's web site. As more people joined the action, some of the extra traffic generated would be sent to George Bush's site.

The second way of taking part in the protest was by downloading a small Java program that performed the same function as the script contained on the protest web page. Although this option was for more experienced computer users, it had the advantage of being more powerful in terms of the traffic it could generate.

It is difficult to assess what impact the protest action had on the Electrohippies' targeted sites, especially since thousands of U.S. and UK web sites came under attack during the conflict. For example, it was estimated that 20,000 web sites were attacked in the first week of the war (ZDNet UK, 2003). However, it is likely that a significant number of people took part in the action and that this resulted in some disruption to the target sites. For instance, it was reported that the British prime minister's web site was briefly shut down by a DoS attack during the time of the protest (Law, 2003; Hines, 2003). However, only one incident was reported in the media, and this suggests that the protest action was only partly successful. No similar incidents were reported concerning the White House and other U.S. government web sites.

Some people have described the activities of the Electrohippies as hacktivism, which is often described as political activism carried out via the Internet or, more simply, as hacking in order to spread socially conscious messages (Kirby, 2002). However, some groups have challenged the behavior of the Electrohippies and similar groups, calling it nothing more than cyberterrorism.

An interesting point made by the Electrohippies is that online protests have an "internal democratic threshold." Put simply, since it takes thousands of computer users to generate the volume of Internet traffic needed to shut down a web site, an online protest can only be successful if it has a great deal of public support. It can also be argued that the support of thousands of computer users worldwide adds legitimacy to a protest, helping to justify it on moral and ethical grounds.

However, critics of the Electrohippies have argued that online protests act against democracy since they effectively censor certain points of view. For instance, the Cult of the Dead Cow (cDc), a well-known hacking group, has argued that a distributed denial of service attack is nothing more than attempt to shout down an opponent.[14] They also question the argument that the support of thousands of computer users can justify an attack on a given opponent: "If numbers lend legitimacy—as the Electrohippies propose—then the lone bomber who tried to assassinate Hitler in his bunker was wrong and the millions who supported the dictator were right." It can be argued that using the Internet to make a political protest is nothing more than an expression of free speech. However, in supporting a denial of service attack, protestors may be committing a criminal act. In the United Kingdom, for instance, defacing a web site or launching a denial of service attack might be seen as an act of terrorism—or cyberterrorism—under some circumstances (Knight, 2001). A person convicted under the United Kingdom's Terrorism Act (2000) is likely to face much more severe punishment than under laws dealing with hacking and other activities. This leads to an important point about the damage that defacements and DoS attacks cause to web sites. At present, it can be argued that online protests cause relatively little harm and that any damage can usually be repaired quickly and easily. However, the line between hacktivist and cyberterrorist can become blurred very easily (Denning, 2001), and the damage caused by online protests can escalate very quickly. For instance, during the Iraq war, thousands of U.S. web sites—including the U.S. Navy and U.S. Air Force web sites—were attacked by antiwar hackers (BBC News Interactive, 21 March 2003), undoubtedly causing a great deal of damage. At a time when the United States and the United Kingdom were at war with Iraq, the behavior of American and British antiwar hackers might have been interpreted as hacktivism, cyberterrorism, or even treason.

Taking part in a denial of service attack might also be seen as an attempt to deny others the right to free speech. In the United States, this might be seen as a violation of the First Amendment, and in Europe, it might be viewed as a violation of individual human rights as defined by the Universal Declaration of Human Rights.[15]

It should also be remembered that any attack on a web site is likely to result in a financial cost to the site's owner or operator. With this in mind, the organizers of online protests may become subject to civil action designed to recover damages from them. In some cases, the damages claimed might amount to millions of dollars. For instance, it has been estimated that interruptions to web services can cost companies as much as $125,000 per hour (Duffy, 2000). The losses incurred by very large companies, such as Amazon.com, might be even greater since most of the company's revenues are generated by online sales.

Web site owners might face further losses and become subject to legal action if it can be shown that they did not take precautions against hackers and denial of service attacks. For instance, insurance companies are unlikely to cover losses resulting from denial of service attacks if security was inadequate or if business continuity planning[16] was poor. In addition, a web site defacement that contains slanderous statements might allow the owner of the site to be sued for libel (Evers, 2000). Furthermore, if a company's web site is used to launch a denial of service attack, the company might face a compensation claim based on the view that they were negligent by not taking proper precautions (Gardiner, 2000). For instance, in 2000, Nike was sued for £25,000 (approximately $39,000) by an Internet Service Provider, FirstNET, after the Nike web site was hijacked briefly and used to direct visitors to an Australian protest site (Raikow, 2000; Ward, 2000). According to FirstNET, Nike was negligent because it failed to implement any security measures at all in order to protect the web site from "i-jacking." The result was a huge amount of traffic that caused disruption and prevented many of FirstNET's clients from accessing services.

Example Four: Unwitting (MassMutual)

An information technology (IT) auditor working for MassMutual noticed that a particular computer belonging to a senior executive kept getting infected by computer viruses (Messmer, 2003). Puzzled by this, he investigated further and found that the machine kept getting infected because it was being used to download pornography, including pictures and video files with names like "teengirl.jpg." After additional investigation, he found that the machine had been used to access chat rooms with titles such as "daddyanddaughter." The machine had also been used to visit web sites dealing with incest fantasies.

Most networks automatically create logs that provide a record of network activity. This information serves many purposes, from helping to diagnose technical problems to identifying possible intrusion. In this case, examining records of Internet activity showed that the executive was spending a great deal of time in chat rooms devoted to incest fantasies. It was also found that he had boasted about molesting his twelve-year-old daughter.

Convinced that the executive's daughter might be in serious danger, the company immediately reported the executive to local law enforcement. The decision was made to contact the family in order to ensure the child's safety. Fortunately, after interviewing the child, investigators felt sure that she had not been molested in any way.

As a consequence of his actions, the executive was dismissed from his position with the company. His behavior also led to divorce.

MassMutual's experience raises an important issue regarding civil and criminal liability. Although the company was unaware of the executive's actions, this might not have provided protection against legal action. In many countries, a company may sometimes be held liable if its resources are used in support of criminal activity. For instance, the United States has particularly strict laws with regard to child pornography. As one writer has commented: "No matter how it gets there, having child pornography on a corporate network causes a litany of legal issues—from creating a hostile work environment to criminal liability" (Gaudin, 2003). By involving law enforcement at an early stage, the company helped to protect itself against legal action while also meeting its moral and ethical responsibilities.

It is also important to remember that the executive's misuse of company resources probably incurred significant costs. For instance, a great deal of staff time was probably needed to deal with virus infections, especially if the executive accidentally infected machines belonging to his colleagues. Furthermore, each virus infection likely had a cost in terms of lost productivity or damage to data files.

The company's reputation might have suffered significant harm had staff failed to discover the executive's activities. It is easy to imagine the damage that might have been caused by the accusation that the company "helped" the executive to abuse a child by providing access to resources. Even more harm might have resulted if the company had not involved law enforcement agencies as it could have been accused of attempting to cover up the executive's actions.

It can be difficult to take action against employees who misuse company facilities if the company does not have an acceptable use policy in place. For instance, some actions—such as discussing incest online—are likely to be protected by the right to free speech and are probably not illegal (Messmer, 2003). However, if these kinds of actions are prohibited by an acceptable use policy, the company will be within its rights to impose sanctions against those who abuse company ICT resources.

Example Five: For Profit (Hank Mishkoff)

In 1999, Hank Mishkoff[17] created a web site called ShopsAt-WillowBend.com as an unofficial fan site for a new shopping mall (Shepardson, 2003). The Taubman Centers company planned to develop the new mall, The Shops at Willow Bend, just three miles from Mishkoff's home. According to Mishkoff, his intention in creating the site was to offer a public service by including features such as interactive maps showing the way to the mall and a discussion group so that people could talk about their experiences there (Donald, 2003). Mishkoff maintains that the web site contained a disclaimer making it clear that his site was unofficial and that he had no intention to confuse or deceive consumers or to make a profit of any kind (Out-Law.com, 2003; Donald, 2003; Gustafson, 2001).

In May 2001, some two years after establishing his web site, Mishkoff was contacted by one of Taubman's attorneys, Julie Greenberg. Greenberg insisted that Mishkoff remove his web site and stop using the domain name, or the company would sue for trademark infringement and cyber-squatting. Cyber-squatting is a way of extorting money from a company by registering its domain name with the intent of selling it back to the company for a profit. Greenberg also insisted that ownership of the domain name should be transferred to the company.

Mishkoff informed Greenberg that he would cooperate with her demands if she could provide some evidence that he was acting illegally. Although Mishkoff and Greenberg exchanged correspondence for several months, Greenberg failed to explain how Mishkoff's web site was breaking the law. Mishkoff's web site[18] contains copies of letters that he claims show his good intentions. In one letter, for example, he stated:

> Ms. Greenberg, if you still believe that my website causes trademark infringements or "cybersquatting" violations, I'd be grateful if you could steer me to the relevant sections of the laws that you believe I'm

violating. Since I have no desire to break any laws, I will surrender the
domain name as soon as you convince me that I'm doing so.

A few months later, in July 2001, he repeated his offer to transfer the
domain to the company: "I urge you to let me know exactly what language in which sections of what laws you believe me to be violating . . .
if my interpretation agrees with yours, I will immediately relinquish
control of my domain name to your client."

In August 2001, just a few weeks after Mishkoff's latest offer to
transfer his domain to Taubman, he was notified that he was to be
sued for infringing trademark rights and violating cyber-squatting
laws. Mishkoff's immediate response was to register a number of
domains that could be used to create protest web sites. The names
registered were WillowBendSucks.com, WillowBendMallSucks.com,
ShopsAtWillowBendSucks.com, TheShopsAtWillowBendSucks.com,
and TaubmanSucks.com. He wrote to Greenberg informing her that
he would create a number of protest web sites if the company
continued with its legal action. Surprisingly, Greenberg contacted
Mishkoff a week later offering to settle the dispute for a payment of
$1,000. In exchange, Mishkoff would turn over ownership of the
domains he had registered and would agree to a number of other
terms, such as not registering any other domain names connected to
the company.

Although it appeared that the dispute had been settled, things went
wrong when Mishkoff received a formal agreement document containing a number of new conditions that had never been discussed.
Mishkoff rejected the new terms but offered to abide by the original
agreement. Taubman's response was to continue with its legal action.
The company applied for an injunction that would force Mishkoff to
take down his original ShopsAtWillowBend.com web site. The injunction was granted and Mishkoff was ordered to remove the web site.
A few months later, the company applied to expand the scope of the
injunction to include all of the protest sites Mishkoff had created. This
modified injunction was also approved, and Mishkoff was ordered to
take down all of the protest sites.

It is worth noting that Mishkoff has accused Taubman's legal representatives of a number of underhanded tactics (Gustafson, 2001).
Among his allegations are that his opponents deliberately made false
statements, that they failed to follow court procedures, and that they
failed to disclose documents and evidence.

Until early 2002, Mishkoff had been representing himself because
of the costs involved in hiring legal help. Although acting alone,

Mishkoff had been receiving help and advice via the Internet, including advice given to him by legal experts he communicated with in chat rooms. However, the injunction against Mishkoff's protest sites meant that his battle with Taubman had started to evolve into a civil liberties case, which brought his situation to the attention of organizations such as the American Civil Liberties Union (ACLU) and Public Citizen, a nonprofit advocacy group.

In February 2002, Paul Levy, a lawyer for Public Citizen, agreed to represent Mishkoff, and this seemed to have an immediate impact on the case (Reporters Committee for Freedom of the Press, 2002). In March 2002, the injunction preventing Mishkoff from operating his protest sites was stayed, allowing him to put the content online again. In May 2002, the ACLU filed a "friend of the court" brief with the Court of Appeals on Mishkoff's behalf (Bonisteel, 2002). Ann Beason, litigation director for the ACLU's Technology and Liberty Program, is said to have stated: "We became interested because this was the first case to reach a federal appeals court where a large corporation was trying to intimidate its online critic" (Donald, 2003). Because this development was reported on the ACLU's web site and in the media, it generated a great deal of publicity for Mishkoff's cause.

In February 2003, the Court of Appeals dissolved the injunctions against Mishkoff, allowing him to reinstate his protest web sites. Taubman agreed to dismiss its entire case and was made to pay Mishkoff $714 in court costs. The Court of Appeals judgment was notable because it ruled that a domain name could be seen as an expression of free speech (*Metro Times*, 2003). The Court of Appeals noted: "We find that a domain name is a type of public expression no different from a billboard or a pulpit, and Mishkoff has a First Amendment right to express his opinion about Taubman" (Donald, 2003).

Mishkoff's lawsuit is a good example of a typical SLAPP case. However, whereas most SLAPP cases involve a company's attempts to silence a particularly vocal critic, it is unclear what Taubman hoped to achieve by targeting Mishkoff. Mishkoff has maintained that he was a "fan" of Taubman even after Greenberg's initial threats of legal action. Although it is possible that Mishkoff's ShopsAtWillowBend.com web site might have drawn some visitors away from the mall's official site, Mishkoff was actually promoting the mall on Taubman's behalf, and his site featured a prominent link to the official web site. Given that Mishkoff was an active supporter of the mall, it seems strange that Taubman failed to consider how Mishkoff's enthusiasm might be channeled more productively, in a way acceptable to both Mishkoff and the company.

In many cases, SLAPPs are used to silence critics by threatening them with the huge legal costs involved in defending against claims that may be completely without merit (Beder, 1995). In an article that describes strategies for dealing with complaint sites, Lopez notes that "in many cases . . . the mere threat of legal action is enough to scare a Web site operator into submission" (1999). However, there are likely to be occasions when people are not intimidated by the threat of legal action and are willing to invest their resources in countering any claims made against them. In these circumstances, companies would do well to consider the potential costs of a drawn-out battle. In Mishkoff's case, it can be argued that the company's legal action undoubtedly cost hundreds of thousands of dollars. However, the company has also had to bear the embarrassment of the negative publicity generated by the case. The damage caused to its public image should not be under-estimated. For instance, Mishkoff's protest web sites are likely to be maintained for the foreseeable future, and news stories about the case will be accessible via search engines for years to come. In addition, the legal precedent established by the case will be quoted in courtrooms and on other protest web sites for many years. For example, one commentator has suggested: "This case is going to get cited a lot by defendants" (Schwimmer, 2003).

Further damage to Taubman's reputation arises from allegations of unfair and dishonest behavior on the part of their legal representatives. Mishkoff's site—especially the documents reproduced there—portrays Taubman in a very poor light. For instance, the documents available on Mishkoff's site seem to show that Mishkoff and Julie Greenberg reached an understanding on how the dispute could be settled but that Greenberg then reneged on the agreement. Mishkoff also alleges that Taubman's legal team made false statements in court, and this appears to be supported by the judgment issued by the Court of Appeals.

Example Six: Competitive (Microsoft)

The Open Source Initiative's web site[19] describes a series of documents produced by Microsoft employees that outline how the company planned to deal with competition from open source software (OSS), such as Linux (an operating system) and Mozilla (a web browser). The first document was named "Halloween" because of the date it was leaked. Over a period of a year, six Halloween documents were leaked, each containing information that was embarrassing to Microsoft.

A Microsoft engineer produced the first memorandum, which suggested that Microsoft could deal with competition from OSS by subverting common standards. The engineer, Vinod Valloppillil, stated in his report: "By extending these protocols and developing new protocols, we can deny OSS projects entry into the market" (Ricciuti, 1998). The memo also stated that Microsoft's usual fear, uncertainty, and doubt (FUD) tactic would be unlikely to work for products like Linux.

The last of the Halloween documents dragged the highly respected Gartner group into the argument. According to the Open Source Initiative, Gartner published a series of five articles that criticized Linux and predicted that its popularity would decline once Windows 2000 became more established. The press responded to these reports by publishing numerous articles suggesting that Linux was doomed to failure. However, Eric Raymond of the Open Source Initiative claims that there is evidence to show that Microsoft wrote and published the articles on Gartner's web site.

If one accepts the allegations made by the Open Source Initiative, then Microsoft was responsible for harassing the developers of Linux and other open source software for more than a year in order to maintain their competitive advantage.

Microsoft has also been accused of using anticompetitive strategies against the producers of rival web browsers, such as Opera, Netscape, and Mozilla (Wilcox and Junnarkar, 2001a; Junnarkar, 2001). In late 2001, it was found that some browsers were unable to access MSN.com, Microsoft's portal. When users tried to access MSN, they received a message telling them that they would not be able to view MSN properly with the browser they were using. Instead, they were invited to download the latest version of Internet Explorer (Junnarkar, 2001).

It was claimed that early versions of Netscape Navigator crashed when attempting to use the site. Later versions seemed to function properly, but problems were reported when trying to access Microsoft's.NET Passport service, a system that allows users to access personalized content and services (Wilcox and Junnarkar, 2001a). In addition, some Mac users claimed that they were unable to access the Hotmail e-mail service (Wilcox and Junnarkar, 2001a).

A particularly serious allegation was made by Opera Software, who claimed that MSN was deliberately preventing users of the Opera browser from using the site (Wilcox and Junnarkar, 2001a). When a browser connects to a server, it sends a string of data that identifies which browser is being used and its version. This is called the user-agent string. According to Opera Software, when MSN identified that visitors were using Opera, they were shut out of the site and shown a message encouraging them to download Internet Explorer. Opera Software's chief executive, Jon von Tetzchner, claimed that if the string that identified the browser was modified by even a single character, the browser could access the site. Microsoft admitted that MSN checked for the Opera browser, but only because it wanted to encourage people to use browsers that were compliant with Internet standards. However, some writers have not been convinced by Microsoft's explanation and support Opera's view that Microsoft deliberately targeted their product. For example, one reporter commented: "This is a staggering thought: somewhere in the headquarters of the world's largest computer company sits a team whose specific job it is to decimate a little company in Oslo who dared to create an alternative product" (Lee, 2002).

Although all of the problems preventing rival browsers from accessing MSN were dealt with quickly, some people felt that Microsoft had acted deliberately in an attempt to convince users to switch to Internet Explorer (Wilcox and Junnarkar, 2001a) At the time, ZDNet noted that "a move to favoring Internet Explorer over other browsers would give Microsoft a considerable advantage as it prepares to jump into the world of Web services" (Wilcox and Junnarkar, 2001b). ZDNet also noted that the problems some people experienced in accessing MSN came only a few months after a court ruling on an antitrust action against Microsoft. The court found that "commingling of Internet Explorer and Windows 95 and 98 software code hampered competition from Netscape Communications" (Wilcox and Junnarkar, 2001a).

Whether or not Microsoft acted deliberately in preventing rival browsers from accessing MSN, the incident resulted in a controversy that gained international publicity for several weeks. One consequence of this publicity was a backlash against Microsoft that resulted in a "torrent of new customers" for competing browsers such as Opera and Amaya (Konrad and Junnarkar, 2001).

Microsoft courted controversy again in 2003 when Opera Software claimed that the MSN home page had been deliberately engineered to make the Opera browser appear faulty (Lettice, 2003). According to Opera Software, when different browsers accessed the MSN home page, they were sent different files. Opera received a file bigger than the one sent to Internet Explorer but with less content. Furthermore, the style sheets sent to each browser were also different. Style sheets describe how a browser should display the different parts of a web page and are used to ensure that pages are displayed consistently. For example, they can be used to make sure that all headings are shown using the same typeface. The style sheet sent to Opera instructed it to display content offset to the left, making it appear that the browser was not displaying the page correctly (Lettice, 2003).

Opera Software claims that MSN checked the user-agent string to detect if a visitor to the site was using Opera. If so, they were sent a faulty style sheet. However, when MSN was sent a user-string that identified a nonexistent browser (Opera Software used "Oprah" in their tests), the fully working Internet Explorer style sheet was returned. This was suspicious, argues Opera Software, because there should be no reason to send browsers different style sheets. According to Hakon Lie, Opera Software's chief technology officer, this information supports the accusation that Microsoft deliberately set out to target the Opera browser (Festa, 2003).

Opera's response to Microsoft's "dirty tricks" was the tongue-in-cheek release of a special version of Opera 7, called the Bork edition (Rouse, 2003). The browser worked perfectly well for all sites except MSN, where all the words were turned into the language of the Swedish chef from *The Muppet Show*.

CONCLUSION

This chapter has concentrated on new forms of cyberstalking that involve an organization acting either as a victim or as a stalker. It has been shown that the motives behind corporate cyberstalking incidents can be very different from those commonly associated with offline stalking and cyberstalking. For instance, some organizations use cyberstalking as a way of silencing critics. It has also been shown how some people may turn to corporate cyberstalking in order to further a political, religious, or social belief. For instance, hacktivism can be described as political activism carried out via the Internet.

Any company or individual is susceptible to cyberstalking behaviors such as denial of service attacks. Companies can help to protect against some forms of corporate cyberstalking by implementing an acceptable use policy or taking other precautions.

In the next chapter, attention returns to the individual and the effectiveness of legislation in dealing with cyberstalking.

9

Cyberstalking and the Law

THE "MARY SMITH" STORY

In a highly unusual case, "Mary Smith,"[1] a student from Missouri, became involved in three separate cyberstalking incidents.[2]

The first incident took place in 1993, when Smith went home for winter break. Using her parents' computer, Smith visited a chat room for people interested in outdoor recreation. Over a period of a few days, Smith spoke to a man who shared her interest in river rafting. When Smith returned to college, she found fifteen messages waiting for her from the man. He began to e-mail her constantly and even started to send packages in the mail. Smith eventually decided that she needed to be forceful in dealing with the man, so she contacted him and demanded that he leave her alone. The harassment stopped by the end of the semester.

The second incident took place three years later, after Smith attended a graduate workshop in Montana. After the workshop, Smith moved to Hawaii to continue her education. A student she had spoken with during the workshop sent her a postcard via her parents. Smith replied by sending a single postcard to the man. She then began to receive lengthy typed letters from the student, then daily e-mails. The student even constructed a web page about Smith. The page, titled "Mrs. Right," contained photographs of Smith that had been taken without her knowledge and a 100-page novel based on the graduate workshop and dedicated to Smith. The harassment eventually ended when the student found a girlfriend.

The third incident took place in 1998 and involved a strange coincidence. "Joe Jones" would eventually become Smith's husband, but before they met, he once went out for dinner with the neighbor of one of Smith's friends. When the neighbor asked him out a second time, Jones declined, explaining that he was not interested in a relationship with her. The neighbor became angry and started to make abusive phone calls to Jones, often in the middle of the night. She also began sending him insulting e-mail messages.

Some time later, when the woman learned that Jones and Smith had started to date, she expanded her activities to include Smith. Smith also began to receive e-mails, some of which contained made-up pornographic stories about her or Jones. On one occasion, the woman posted Smith's name and telephone number on an Internet personals site. The material included a physical description of Smith and made various sexual comments. Within a short time, Smith began to receive lewd calls from strangers. The woman also subscribed to *Playboy* in Jones's name and ordered sex aids online. All of these items were delivered to Jones's office in order to embarrass him.

Whenever Smith and Jones threatened to involve the police, the harassment would stop for a short while before starting up again. However, when all patience was lost, Jones and Smith finally decided to get a restraining order against the woman. This seemed to have an immediate effect, and the harassment ceased altogether.

INTRODUCTION

How does the law deal with stalking and cyberstalking? Is cyberstalking regarded as a crime? How effective are antistalking laws? In this chapter I look at the legislation used around the world to deal with stalking and cyberstalking.

It is important to note that the following material is not intended to provide an exhaustive guide to international legislation. Rather, the discussion is meant to compare and contrast legislation used around the world. A particular emphasis is placed on how the countries discussed define harassment and stalking. The material also looks at some of the problems involved in applying antistalking laws to cyberstalking.

STALKING AND THE LAW

Chapter 1 suggested that one way of defining cyberstalking might be to look at how the law can be used to deal with cases of stalking and harassment. In this section, I offer a brief survey of the legislation used by different countries to deal with harassment. As will be shown, there is a great deal of variation in how different countries deal with stalking and harassment in general.

The United States

In the United States, the first laws related to stalking were enacted in 1990, as a result of the murder of the actress Rebecca Schaeffer by Robert Bardo in 1989 (Petherick, 1999). Since that time, U.S. legislation has matured relatively quickly. In 1999, for example, twenty-three states enacted laws dealing with stalking, meaning that every state now has specific antistalking legislation (Miller, 1999; Rosenfeld and Harmon, 2002). Similarly, in 1998 only a small number of states had legislation dealing specifically with harassment conducted via the Internet (Meloy, 1998), but today most state antistalking laws make specific reference to electronic communications.

However, the way in which stalking is treated by the law varies from state to state.[3] For example, in California—the first state to pass stalking-related legislation—harassment is defined as

> a knowing and willful course of conduct directed at a specific person which seriously alarms, annoys, torments, or terrorizes the person, and which serves no legitimate purpose. The course of conduct must be such as would cause a reasonable person to suffer substantial emotional distress, and must actually cause substantial emotional distress to the person.

Michigan is often cited as having the strongest antistalking law in the United States (Mullen, Pathé, and Purcell, 2000, p. 262). Michigan legislation defines harassment as

> conduct directed toward a victim that includes, but is not limited to, repeated or continuing unconsented contact, that would cause a reasonable individual to suffer emotional distress, and that actually causes the victim to suffer emotional distress. (Mullen, Pathé, and Purcell, 2000, p. 262)

In most states, harassment is seen as a deliberate act intended to cause the victim "substantial emotional distress." In this way, legislation across the United States can be seen as being largely in keeping with legislation found elsewhere in the world, such as the United Kingdom. However, it can be argued that harassment does not always involve an intention to cause fear or distress. As an example, in discussing a category of stalkers called intimacy seekers and incompetent suitors, Mullen, Pathé, and Purcell write:

> There is considerable merit in the notion that some stalking behaviours are the product of the insensitive, inept and grossly overconfident actions of individuals who cannot conceive that their approaches would generate anything less than reciprocal interest. (2000, p. 116)

This point highlights an interesting and important issue that is probably best explained using a simple example. Imagine the case of a young man who wishes to strike up a relationship with a woman he works with or goes to college with. The young man asks the woman out a number of times and is rejected each time. At what point does the man's attempt to begin a relationship with the woman move from an innocent request for a date to a case of stalking? Furthermore, since the man only wants to go on a date with the woman, there is clearly no intention to cause her any distress. In fact, the man might be horrified to learn that the woman is fearful of him or that he has caused her any worry. When there is clearly no intention to cause the woman "substantial emotional distress," could this be considered a genuine stalking case?

These problems become a little clearer by considering the definitions of stalking used by California and Michigan. In California, harassment must involve "a knowing and willful course of conduct . . . which serves no legitimate purpose." The young man would probably be able to defend himself against a charge of stalking by arguing that he had not intended to cause the woman any distress. He might also argue that asking a woman for a date is perfectly innocent and serves a legitimate purpose. Since both California and Michigan propose a test of reasonableness, the young man might also be able to defend himself in Michigan by arguing that the woman was unreasonable in becoming distressed over being asked out for a date.

Another interesting point arises from Michigan's definition of harassment and the notion that contact between a victim and her harasser may occur without the victim's consent. In many cases of harassment, it is presumed that both parties are known to each other and that a prior consensual relationship existed before the harassment started. As an example, it is often suggested that the most common victim of stalking is likely to be a woman who has shared an intimate relationship with her (usually male) stalker (Mullen, Pathé, and Purcell, 2000, p. 45). However, this assumption can be dangerous as it could result in the harassment being treated less seriously than if a stranger were involved. In addition, such a view would tend to be dismissive of the very real fear, anxiety, and distress suffered by victims.

Raising the issue of consent within legislation offers a means of improving the protection offered to harassment victims. For example, the receipt of abusive e-mail messages from an anonymous source or a person unknown to the victim would clearly constitute unconsented contact. Similarly, even in cases in which the victim knew the harasser, it would be the harasser's responsibility to show that the victim's consent to make contact in this way had been obtained. For instance, a male harasser might need to show that a female victim consented to him sending sexually explicit messages by letter or e-mail. Given the ability of modern software to maintain easily verified records of all incoming and outgoing communications, it becomes simpler to demonstrate that the harasser's attentions are not invited.

Although individual states have developed robust laws that can be used to deal with cyberstalking, effective federal legislation is lacking. For instance, the WiredPatrol web site (WiredPatrol, 2002) comments: "US Federal Laws against stalking have to date been of little help to stalking victims." This sentiment is shared by others; for example, legal writer Harry Valetk comments: "Ironically, despite the elusive, multi-jurisdictional nature of cyberstalking, no uniform federal law exists to protect victims or define ISP liabilities" (2002).

For Valetk, federal legislation is needed to eliminate inconsistencies and ensure that people receive the same level of protection throughout the United States. For instance, it has already been shown that definitions of stalking can vary from state to state, leading to inconsistencies in how stalking is treated. Valetk illustrates his point with a suitable example:

> Consider that Arizona's stalking statute only prohibits credible threats of violence against the victim, whereas California and South Carolina prohibit threats against the victim's immediate family. In Maine, a stalker's course of conduct can constitute an implied threat. But what legal standard applies to a cyberstalker from Maine, terrorizing an Arizona resident, using a California ISP? (2002)

It is worth pointing out that some federal legislation may be of use when dealing with cases of offline stalking. This may be helpful under certain circumstances, for example, when cyberstalking begins to move offline. An example of such legislation is The Communications Act, which makes it an offense to make obscene or threatening telephone calls (WiredPatrol, 2002).

The United Kingdom

The United Kingdom has no legislation that deals specifically with harassment perpetrated via the Internet. However, existing legislation has sometimes been extended to deal with issues such as the transmission of threatening messages via e-mail. Two pieces of legislation with relevance to online harassment are the Malicious Communications Act (1988) and the Protection from Harassment Act (1997).

The full title of the Malicious Communications Act is:[4] "An Act to make provision for the punishment of persons who send or deliver letters or other articles for the purpose of causing distress or anxiety." Section 1 of the act describes an offense as follows:

Any person who sends to another person—
(a) a letter or other article which conveys—
    (i) a message which is indecent or grossly offensive;
    (ii) a threat; or
    (iii) information which is false and known or believed to be false by the sender; or
(b) any other article which is, in whole or part, of an indecent or grossly offensive nature, is guilty of an offence if his purpose, or one of his purposes, in sending it is that it should, so far as falling within paragraph (a) or (b) above, cause distress or anxiety to the recipient or to any other person to whom he intends that it or its contents or nature should be communicated.

However, the act allows for defenses based on the notion that the perpetrator must know or believe that his or her actions were unreasonable:

A person is not guilty of an offence by virtue of subsection (1)(a)(ii) above if he shows—
(a) that the threat was used to reinforce a demand which he believed he had reasonable grounds for making; and
(b) that he believed that the use of the threat was a proper means of reinforcing the demand.

As can be seen, this act provides only limited protection against harassment in that it deals exclusively with communications that are considered indecent, offensive, or threatening. Note the similarity with U.S. law in that the harasser must have the intention to cause distress in order to be guilty of a crime. Returning to the example of the young man repeatedly asking a woman for a date, it seems unlikely that this legislation could be used to deal with such a situation. For instance, in some cases it would be difficult to establish that repeated requests for a date could be considered threatening, especially if these requests were phrased without the use of offensive language or threats.

Despite this limitation, the Malicious Communications Act provides a measure of protection against some activities commonly associated with online harassment, such as identity theft. As mentioned earlier, identity theft involves impersonating a computer user in e-mail messages, instant messaging conversations, or posts made to bulletin boards. In many cases, identity theft is used to damage the victim's reputation, either as an act of revenge or as a way to force the victim into meeting the perpetrator's demands. However, two important points must be made here. First, the protection offered by the act is duplicated within other legislation, such as that dealing with libel. Second, the punishment for those found guilty of an offense is a fine rather than other penalties, such as imprisonment, thus raising the question of whether the act is an adequate deterrent. It must also be asked whether the act can offer a means of helping to protect victims against further acts of harassment. As an example, there have been many cases in which harassment has eventually evolved into a physical attack against the victim.

The Protection from Harassment Act (1997) is potentially more useful than the Malicious Communications Act since it covers a broader range of activities. It describes harassment as follows:[5]

A person must not pursue a course of conduct—
(a) which amounts to harassment of another, and
(b) which he knows or ought to know amounts to harassment of the other.

Interestingly, the act does not set out in detail what is meant by harassment, preferring to define it in terms of how a reasonable person might construe a given course of action:

For the purposes of this section, the person whose course of conduct is in question ought to know that it amounts to harassment of another if a reasonable person in possession of the same information would think the course of conduct amounted to harassment of the other.

As mentioned earlier, the idea of a test of reasonableness is very important because it provides an effective way of identifying genuine stalking cases. Unlike legislation enacted elsewhere, and unlike many existing definitions of stalking and cyberstalking, the Protection from Harassment Act does not set out to describe the frequency, severity, and form of action required to constitute harassment. It is worth remembering, for example, that the laws of some countries and U.S. states actually specify a certain number of incidents that must take place before an offense can be considered to have occurred. For instance, Illinois requires harassment to have taken place on at least two occasions before stalking is said to have occurred (Mullen, Pathé, and Purcell, 2000, p. 260).

The test of reasonableness allows the act to take into account a wide range of acts, including many that might not be treated seriously under other legislation. It was suggested earlier that the behavior of a young man who persistently attempts to establish a relationship with a woman might not be regarded as an offense under the Malicious Communications Act. It was also suggested that the sanctions available under the Malicious Communications Act were limited to financial penalties. The Protection from Harassment Act, however, might offer individuals a greater measure of protection since it can view behavior such as frequent, unwanted communications as an act of harassment. Furthermore, the penalties allowed under this act are more severe and include imprisonment.

Canada

Although Canadian legislation does not deal directly with cyberstalking, the Canadian Criminal Code can be used to deal with harassment conducted via the Internet. The offense of Criminal Harassment is defined as:[6]

(a) repeatedly following from place to place the other person or anyone known to them;
(b) repeatedly communicating with, either directly or indirectly, the other person or anyone known to them;
(c) besetting or watching the dwelling-house, or place where the other person, or anyone known to them, resides, works, carries on business or happens to be; or
(d) engaging in threatening conduct directed at the other person or any member of their family.

Each of the clauses listed here might easily be extended to deal with the Internet:

- The first clause might deal with cases in which a harasser follows a user into different chat rooms or bulletin boards.
- The second clause might deal with instances of identity theft, where the harasser poses as the victim and contacts colleagues, friends, or relatives of the victim. In addition, this clause might also deal with acts such as posting abusive or untrue messages to chat rooms and bulletin boards.
- The third clause might deal with electronic surveillance, such as the interception of e-mail messages or the use of Trojan horse software to monitor the victim's activities.

An offense under Canadian law carries a sentence of not more than five years.

Australia

In general, Australian stalking-related legislation is in keeping with the United Kingdom, the United States, and Canada.

Although all Australian states have stalking legislation, it varies from state to state (Ogilvie, 2000a). Victoria, for instance, allows for a prison sentence of up to ten years whereas the maximum prison sentence in Western Australia is eighteen months. It is worth noting, however, that the state of Victoria's legislation makes explicit mention of e-mail and electronic communications (Mullen, Pathé, and Purcell, 2000, p. 270).

OBSERVATIONS ON STALKING LEGISLATION

It is worth making some general observations about the legislation described so far. First, all of the legislation considered deals with acts related to harassment and offline stalking. Although some of the legislation mentions areas related to cyberstalking, such as sending offensive e-mail messages, only a few laws deal specifically with cyberstalking. As noted in earlier chapters, it is worth bearing in mind that some people make a distinction between harassment and stalking by suggesting that harassment deals with a broader range of behaviors. This distinction can be seen within some of the legislation that has been described. The United Kingdom's Protection from Harassment Act, for example, can be applied to disputes between neighbors, racial harassment, or even bullying at school.

Second, the protection the law offers to victims depends heavily on the ability of the lawyers, law enforcement officials, and courts to extend existing legislation to cover acts of harassment involving technology. None of the legislation described here, for example, explicitly mentions modern forms of electronic communications, such as instant messaging or Multimedia Messaging Services (MMS).

Third, by their nature, the laws enacted by any given country only extend to the citizens of that country. This means that it would be difficult—if not impossible—to prosecute a harasser whose victims were located in a foreign country. In some countries, including the United States, it may sometimes be just as difficult to prosecute a harasser from another state as it is to prosecute someone from another country.

However, it may be more relevant to highlight the fact that different countries will use different legal definitions of terms such as *harassment* and *stalking*. It was shown earlier, for example, that the relatively small difference in wording between California's definition of harassment and Michigan's might have a significant impact on how cyberstalking is viewed and dealt with.

Fourth, much of the legislation described here focuses on behavior that is considered threatening. Canada's legislation, for example, mentions "threatening conduct," and California's uses the word *terrorizes*, raising the question of what is usually called a "credible threat"—a threat that is believable because there is a good chance that it can actually be carried out (Brewster, 2001). The key issue is whether a credible threat is likely to cause more fear and anxiety than a threat that is unlikely to be carried out. In turn, this suggests the possibility that threats made via the Internet might be viewed less seriously than threats made in other ways, such as by telephone, because they are considered less likely to be carried out. As an example, a threat made to a U.S. citizen by an Australian citizen might be seen as unrealistic and would therefore be unlikely to cause a great deal of fear and anxiety. However, this view is based on the underlying assumption that the threats made by a harasser will involve violence toward the victim or her family. Furthermore, by placing an emphasis on issuing threats, other damage that might be caused by harassers is marginalized. This becomes important in the context of cyberstalking. For example, some harassers attempt to embarrass their victims by circulating rumors to friends, colleagues, and relatives, and, as explained in chapter 8, when conventional methods are used, such as telephone calls and letters, the extent of the harm caused may be relatively limited. The Internet, on the other hand, provides an opportunity to distribute information worldwide to an almost unlimited number of people. Furthermore, electronic communications may be indexed and archived, allowing them to remain accessible for many years.

Finally, all of the legislation described in this section contains an implicit assumption that harassers are lone individuals. However, as seen in chapter 8, there is some evidence that harassment carried out via the Internet sometimes involves small groups of people working together and sometimes involves business organizations.

Is Cyberstalking a Crime?

Throughout this book I have often referred to cyberstalking in terms of deviancy, rather than criminal behavior. This is because cyberstalking is not considered a criminal act in many countries around the world. Even in countries with legislation that deals with stalking or harassment, some of the behaviors associated with cyberstalking may be perfectly legal. It is certainly possible, for example, to instill fear in someone without making any explicit threats that might be punishable in law. This was the situation in a case I worked on involving a serial cyberstalker (Bocij, Bocij, and McFarlane, 2003). In one incident, the cyberstalker talked about "visiting" his victim at her home when her husband was away on business. Although the victim found this extremely frightening, no explicit threat was made. If challenged, the cyberstalker could easily have claimed that he was simply trying to be friendly and had no intention of causing any distress.

The idea that some behaviors may be perfectly legal when looked at in isolation is not new. The U.S. Department of Justice, for example, says this about stalking:

> Stalking is a distinctive form of criminal activity composed of a series of actions (rather than a single act) that taken individually might constitute legal behavior. For example, sending flowers, writing love notes, and waiting for someone outside her place of work are actions that, on their own, are not criminal. When these actions are coupled with an intent to instill fear or injury, however, they may constitute a pattern of behavior that is illegal. (Travis, 1996)

As can be seen, some actions are perfectly legal until they form an overall campaign of harassment or it can be shown that there is an intention to cause distress.

In the United States, most state antistalking laws now deal with harassment conducted over the Internet, which means that cyberstalking is likely to be seen as a criminal act in most parts of the country. In some parts of the United States, however, cyberstalking is likely to be seen as a crime only if it forms part of an overall campaign of harassment. A similar situation exists in a number of other countries, including the United Kingdom, Canada, and Australia. In these countries, existing harassment laws can be extended to deal with cyberstalking but may not cover every case or every form of cyberstalking behavior.

EFFECTIVENESS OF THE LEGAL SYSTEM

It can be argued that people rely on the law to protect them from stalkers in two main ways. First, there are various mechanisms—such as restraining orders—that attempt to keep the stalker away from his victim or to restrict stalking behaviors, such as following the victim. Second, if the stalker persists in harassing his victim, the law can be used to punish his behavior by imposing a fine, a prison sentence, or some other sanction. Furthermore, selected cases are publicized in the hope that they will act as a deterrent to would-be stalkers.

There is evidence to suggest that police intervention, restraining orders, and other methods often fail to prevent stalkers from pursuing their victims. Regarding restraining orders, for example, a National Violence Against Women Survey reported that

> about a quarter of female stalking victims and about a tenth of male stalking victims obtain restraining orders against their stalkers. Of all victims with restraining orders, 69 percent of the women and 81 percent of the men said their stalkers violated the order. (Tjaden and Thoennes, 1998, p. 2)

Other studies on the legal responses to stalking have reported similar results. For example, in order to gain an insight into how the legal system helped them to handle their situations, Brewster (2001) interviewed 187 women who had been stalked by a former intimate partner. Just over half of victims (51 percent) filed for protection from abuse orders (PFAs), but in 62 percent of these cases, the PFA either had no effect or worsened the stalker's behavior. Of those who turned to the police for help, 77 percent felt that police involvement either had no effect or made the stalker's behavior worse. Only four of the victims whose stalkers went to trial felt that such action was effective. Brewster's study concludes by stating that "overall, more than half of the legal attempts to discourage the stalker had no effect according to the victim, and another 17% of the attempts was followed by a worsening of the stalking behavior" (2001, p. 105).

Although restraining orders and other legal tools do not appear to act as a deterrent to many stalkers in the United States, they are sometimes highly effective against cyberstalkers. For example, in the "Mary Smith" story, a restraining order effectively ended the harassment.

Although restraining orders may sometimes fail to deter stalkers in the United States, the situation is entirely different in some other counties. For example, Dussuyer (2000) conducted a survey of magistrates and police officers in Australia in order to assess the effectiveness of stalking legislation. When police officers were asked about the status of the stalking cases they had worked on, almost three-quarters (74.5 percent) reported that the stalking had ceased as a result of "formal judicial processes," cautioning, or for other reasons, such as the stalker receiving counseling. Similar findings were made in a 1997 study by the Australian Bureau of Crime Statistics and Research on the effectiveness of Apprehended Violence Orders (AVOs) (Gouda, 2000). AVOs can be thought of as equivalent to a restraining order or court injunction. The study found that the majority (82.7 percent) of those who had been stalked before applying for the AVO were not stalked by the defendant in the month after the AVO was granted. Additional research found that this reduction in stalking was sustained over time, suggesting that AVOs provide an effective tool against stalkers.

There also seems to be a common perception that stalkers are often treated leniently by the court system. A recent U.S. study looked at the cases of 390 men charged with the offense of stalking (Jordan et al., 2003). The study found that most cases resulted in dismissal, including more than half (54 percent) of felony charges and 62.2 percent of misdemeanor charges. In many cases, charges of stalking were reduced to lesser offenses, most often the misdemeanor level of stalking or another threat-related crime. Overall, the study found that the charges filed resulted in a conviction rate of only 28.5 percent. It was noted, however, that this rate was comparable to other felony offenses, such as rape and aggravated assault.

One reason stalkers and cyberstalkers may be treated leniently is because their crimes are not seen as being extremely serious. For instance, Baker (1999) has provided several examples of cases in which cyberstalkers received relatively light prison sentences. She suggests that many cyberstalking cases are brought to trial as a result of sting operations mounted by police departments and the FBI. As a result, those charged with offenses such as traveling interstate with the intent to have sex with a minor can claim that their crime was victimless and deserves a lighter sentence. Part of this argument involves the suggestion that an undercover agent might continue a sexual conversation in a chat room or via e-mail when a real child might end it. In this way, the agent might encourage a person who would not act on his desires otherwise. Baker also suggests that sentencing guidelines allow reduced sentences for those who admit responsibility for their actions and have no prior criminal record.

The problem of stalkers and cyberstalkers sometimes receiving light sentences is not restricted to the United States. For instance, regarding the Canadian justice system, the Ontario Women's Justice Network[7] has commented that "sentencing is minimal: first offence stalkers will most likely receive probation and even repeat offenders receive only minimal jail terms." A similar situation exists in other countries, such as the United Kingdom and Australia, and it is relatively easy to find examples of cases in which stalkers received sentences that seem lenient considering their actions. For instance, in 1999, women's groups in the United Kingdom were angered when a stalker, Anthony Burstow, received a prison sentence of only four months for stalking Tracey Morgan, despite having been jailed three times previously for harassing her (Fleet, 1999). The case of the Boehle family, described in chapter 6, provides another example in which a cyberstalker appeared to receive a light sentence.

CONCLUSION

As this chapter has shown, the United States has the most well-developed antistalking laws in the world: all states have antistalking legislation, and the laws enacted by most also deal with cyberstalking. In the United Kingdom, Canada, and Australia, existing legislation can be extended to deal with cyberstalking cases. However, cyberstalking may not be seen as a crime in some countries. In addition, some of the behaviors associated with cyberstalking may be legal in some countries.

In the United States, restraining orders and other methods often fail to prevent stalkers and cyberstalkers from harassing their victims. However, research from other countries shows that these methods can be very effective.

There seems to be a common perception that stalkers and cyberstalkers are treated leniently by the legal system. In the United States, research suggests that the majority of stalking cases result in dismissal. There is also concern that those convicted of stalking tend to receive relatively light sentences.

Having examined legal responses to cyberstalking, the next chapter provides practical guidance on how to avoid becoming a cyberstalking victim and how to deal with online harassment.

10

Dealing with Cyberstalking

THE PAMELA GILBERT STORY

Pamela Gilbert, a university lecturer, has written an essay (2002) on her experience of cyberstalking. In it, she raises several interesting points about power and how individuals can use the Internet to shape the way others are seen.

In the early 1990s, Gilbert had a casual dating relationship with a colleague, "Tim," that lasted for just two weekends. Gilbert felt that the relationship was not working and told Tim that she no longer wanted to date him. Angered, Tim began to send Gilbert angry e-mail messages until she stopped responding. He then began to shadow Gilbert's movements on the Internet by joining the listservs[1] that she used. Understandably, the feeling of being placed under surveillance disturbed Gilbert, but the situation worsened when Tim began using other people to remind her of his presence. For example, on one occasion he responded to a message posted by another professor at Gilbert's university and asked the professor to say hello for him— which the professor did in a committee meeting.

On another occasion, Gilbert received a message from a student asking for help with a project on pornography. Tim had seen the student's request for help and passed on Gilbert's contact details, telling her that Gilbert was an expert on the subject. Some years earlier, Gilbert had worked as a nude model, and she later learned that Tim (wrongly) believed her to be terrified that her past might be exposed to her employers. However, rather than taking any form of direct action, Tim had chosen to play a kind of cat-and-mouse game, relying on Gilbert to make sense of his actions. Another example of this behavior involved Tim telling Gilbert that his lungs were in poor health because he was a heavy smoker. Tim later told his friends that he had invented this story to make Gilbert think that he had AIDS.

In 1995, Tim contacted Gilbert and told her that he wished to renew their professional relationship. Gilbert agreed and they corresponded from time to time. Occasionally, Tim would mention that he was working on a major research project and ask if Gilbert's computer had graphics capabilities because she would find parts of his work very interesting. In August 1995, one of Tim's colleagues, Naomi, contacted Gilbert and told her that Tim had been looking for some of Gilbert's nude photographs so that he could use them against her. Tim planned to send copies of the pictures to Gilbert's colleagues and students in order to damage her reputation and career.

According to Naomi, Tim had become obsessed with Gilbert and was spending a great deal of time gathering information about her. He followed Gilbert's online movements through a utility program called finger,[2] making assumptions about her whereabouts and sleeping patterns from the information returned. For instance, when Gilbert did not use her computer one weekend, he told Naomi that she was taking part in an orgy at a hotel somewhere. Following are some of his other behaviors:

- Tim asked one of his students to follow Gilbert and report on her movements.
- He ordered a copy of Gilbert's thesis and did a textual analysis of it and all of her e-mail. According to Gilbert, Tim was able to quote much of her e-mail verbatim.
- He researched Gilbert's life and studied abnormal psychology, claiming that it might provide insights into her personality; Tim even taught a course on paranoia based on the results of his research.
- Much of Tim's time was spent researching the porn industry in an attempt to find people who might be able to provide information on Gilbert's life. This included visiting adult stores and interviewing people who worked in the porn industry.
- He described Gilbert to some of his colleagues as a nymphomaniac with Mafia connections, possibly a satanist, who "slept with big Hollywood lawyers" (Gilbert, 2002).
- He posted a picture of Gilbert's face to adult newsgroups, offering a $200 reward for information or pictures related to her past.

- Naomi reported that Tim had mentioned buying a gun and was planning to confront Gilbert.

Gilbert's employer and the police were supportive but were unable to prevent Tim's harassment. When confronted with his activities, Tim attempted to reinterpret his behavior in various ways. This included claiming that he was researching a book and that Gilbert was stalking him. Shortly after Tim claimed that Gilbert was harassing him, he stopped posting to the Internet.

In seeking help with Tim's behavior, Gilbert spoke to a lawyer who advised her to make her situation known to as many people as possible since this would help keep her safe. Gilbert chose to make her version of events known through the Internet and by publishing the essay described here. Although the harassment carried out via the Internet seems to have stopped, Gilbert remains concerned about her physical safety: "On the Internet, our physical power is equal, depending in part on technical ability, which can be acquired. Our social power is neither equal, nor imbalanced in clearly defined or constant ways. In the parking lot, the stakes are different" (2002).

INTRODUCTION

What measures can individuals take to protect against cyber-stalkers? What additional measures are needed to protect children? How can companies protect themselves against cyberstalking? What should you do if you become a victim of cyberstalking? This chapter looks at two broad areas: how computer users can help to avoid becoming victims of cyberstalking and what they should do if they experience harassment.

One of the first issues this chapter deals with is the need for users to exercise strict control over the personal information they share over the Internet. It will be shown that the more information available, the more easily a cyberstalker can pursue his victim. This theme runs throughout the chapter and encompasses topics such as encryption, anonymous remailers, and hackers.

Another large part of remaining safe when using the Internet is relying on common sense, and this is reflected within many of the guidelines provided here. For instance, one of the guidelines given in a later section suggests never meeting someone in person unless accompanied by a friend. This advice is similar to that given to someone going on a blind date and helps to ensure that what is supposed to be a pleasant experience stays as safe as possible.

It should be noted that the guidelines presented within this chapter do not represent a general guide to computer security. The advice given focuses on dealing with the activities of cyberstalkers and does not attempt to address any other areas. It should also be noted that some of the explanations provided have been deliberately simplified in order to aid understanding. Similarly, some of the guidelines are brief since providing more comprehensive information would depart from the central topic of cyberstalking. The material presented here has been provided with the expectation that readers will seek out more detailed information if needed.

CYBERSTALKING PREVENTION

In order to improve clarity, this section has been broken down into several parts. The first part shows how easily cyberstalkers can gain access to information about their victims and emphasizes a need to keep tight control over personal information. The next parts provide safety guidelines, covering areas such as e-mail use, chat rooms, hacking, and computer viruses. Finally, there are separate sections that offer some additional safety guidelines specific to young people and to business organizations.

Controlling Information

One of the ways in which people can protect themselves against cyberstalkers and other predators is by controlling their personal information to ensure that it does not become accessible to others. Many computer users are shocked to learn that a great deal of information about them is available via the Internet. Much of this information can be gathered free of charge by anyone with a little time and patience. The more active a person has been as an Internet user, for example by using newsgroups and chat rooms, the more information that is likely to be available.

I recall an incident several years ago in which a young woman posted a message to a hacking newsgroup asking for advice on how to protect her computer. One of the replies she received contained a complete profile of her, including her address, telephone number, place of work, names of friends and relatives, and even the name of her dog. The person who replied to her explained that he had created the profile to demonstrate to her—and others—how vulnerable she had made herself simply by posting to Usenet. He further explained that the profile he had created had used information sources that were free of charge and easily available to all Internet users. In finding the name of the woman's dog, for example, he had simply used DejaNews,[3] a service that allows newsgroup posts to be searched, to locate any posts made using her e-mail address. One post had been to a group for dog lovers, when the woman had asked for advice on her dog's illness.

There are numerous free services that allow information to be gathered on a given Internet user. Even search engines, such as Google, can be used to locate personal web pages, newsgroup postings, chat-room profiles, guest-book entries, and other materials that can provide useful pieces of data. For instance, starting with a person's name and location, it is often very easy to locate additional data, such as an address and telephone number. Paying a relatively small fee provides access to more sophisticated programs and services, such as NetDetective,[4] with which it may be possible to find an individual's social security number, criminal record, car registration, and financial information.

As a further example, the free AnyWho service[5] allows users to locate information on virtually anyone living in the United States. The minimum amount of information needed to perform a search is a person's last name and the state he or she lives in. Providing a little more information, such as the person's first name, easily narrows the search down. Once the right person has been located, the service provides a full address, telephone number, and even a map with directions to the person's home. There is also the option of paying a small fee in order to access real estate records, which provides further information, such as the price the person's house was last sold at and the number of rooms it contains.

As a cyberstalker or other predator gains access to more information, he is able to carry out a wider range of activities. With only a person's e-mail address, he can post inflammatory messages to newsgroups in order to start a flame war. With the victim's address and telephone number, he can attempt stalking-by-proxy, or he might turn to offline stalking. With a few personal details or a credit card number, he might use identity theft to make fraudulent purchases or alienate the victim's friends and relatives.

In some cases, a cyberstalker may use the information he has to establish a relationship with his victim. For instance, knowing a child's tastes in music, movies, and fashion might allow a pedophile to establish a firm friendship that can be exploited later on. Similarly, a cyberstalker might form a relationship with his victim in order to monitor her or gather further information.

As this section shows, a key principle of cyberstalking prevention is this: controlling access to personal information reduces the danger posed by cyberstalkers. This principle is reflected in a great deal of the safety advice offered by groups such as WHOA and CyberAngels and can be seen within many of the guidelines contained in this chapter. If we take Sir Francis Bacon's view that knowledge is power, we should also recognize that a cyberstalker without information about his victim becomes effectively powerless.

Chat Rooms, Instant Messaging, and Usenet

Many cyberstalking cases begin from arguments that take place in chat rooms or newsgroups.

Cyberstalking may also begin when an online relationship breaks up or a person attempts to form an online relationship and is rejected. It is also important to remember that many cyberstalkers, pedophiles, and other predators use chat rooms to locate potential victims who may be particularly vulnerable.

Before joining in a chat room conversation or posting to a newsgroup, it is a good idea to watch for a while, so that you can learn how the group functions. Since an established chat room community or newsgroup may have developed an informal set of rules or customs, it can be easy to offend users without meaning to. The practice of watching a newsgroup or chat room without taking part is often called lurking.[6] Although some people dislike lurkers, explaining that you are trying to learn how the group functions before joining in usually averts any hostility.

Some people deliberately enter chat rooms, post inflammatory or offensive messages, and then wait for an argument to develop. Once satisfied with the trouble they have caused, they move on to another chat room and repeat the process. A similar thing can happen within newsgroups, but with one major difference: offensive messages are often posted using an anonymous remailer so that the sender cannot be identified easily. People who behave in this way are often called trolls.[7] One of the dangers in responding to trolls is that it may identify someone as a potential victim for harassment since a cyberstalker can be fairly certain that such a person will react to his behavior.

In general, there are three main ways in which all computer users can help to protect themselves against cyberstalkers when using chat rooms and newsgroups. First, users should learn how to behave appropriately when posting to newsgroups or taking part in chat room conversations. The "rules" that describe how to behave correctly when using chat rooms, newsgroups, and other services are often called netiquette.[8] Learning netiquette serves several purposes and may help to protect against those who become aggressive or abusive toward you. For instance, in the event that you become harassed by another user, you are likely to receive support from other people because they will have seen that you acted properly at all times.

Second, you should avoid becoming involved in arguments of any kind. As soon as a discussion begins to involve personal attacks, you should withdraw. Becoming involved in a flame war can quickly build up a lot of resentment that may eventually turn into harassment.

Finally, it has already been pointed out that keeping your personal information private makes it difficult for a cyberstalker to harass you. Although chat rooms encourage users to disclose information about themselves, there are many ways in which sensitive information can be disguised or held back. For instance, when asked where they live, some people name a city near to them. This allows them to talk about their locality while making it a little harder for a potential cyberstalker to locate them.

The following guidelines are derived from a number of sources, including the U.S. Department of Justice (Reno, 1999), National Center for Victims of Crime (Gregorie, 2001), WHOA, WiredPatrol, Cyber-Angels, TheGuardianAngel.com, and others.

1. Use a gender-neutral nickname. Do not use a nickname that might be considered provocative in any way.
2. Consider opening a new e-mail account that can be used for posting to newsgroups or visiting chat rooms.
3. Consider using an anonymous remailer for posting to newsgroups.[9] If you use your normal e-mail address, consider configuring your newsreader program so that your messages are not archived. This will prevent people from locating your old messages via services such as Google Groups.[10] If you have posted to newsgroups before and are concerned your messages may contain information a cyberstalker might use, you can sometimes delete your old messages. Google Groups, for example, provides an automatic removal tool that is quick and simple to use.[11]
4. Never complete personal profiles on services such as ICQ, MSN, and Yahoo! This is likely to be one of the first places a cyberstalker will look for information.
5. Do not give out personal information, such as your real name or telephone number. As has already been seen, this could provide a cyberstalker with a starting point for gathering more detailed information.
6. Never send out pictures of yourself since these could be modified and posted on web sites or in newsgroups.
7. Never respond to offensive or inflammatory comments made in a chat room or posted to a newsgroup. If an argument starts, withdraw from it immediately.

8. Do not flirt with other users. According to organizations such as Wired-Patrol, this is how many cyberstalkers first come into contact with their victims.

9. Never agree to meet someone in person unless you are completely comfortable in doing so. If you do choose to meet someone, arrange the first few meetings so that they are short and take place in a public location. In addition, make sure that a friend accompanies you and that other people know where you are and when you are expected to return.

E-mail

There are four main ways in which cyberstalkers can make use of a victim's personal e-mail. First, a person's e-mail address may reveal information about her that a cyberstalker can make use of. For instance, many people use their full name or where they live as part of their e-mail address. As shown earlier in this chapter, this might provide a cyberstalker with a starting point for gathering more detailed information.

Second, every outgoing e-mail may have a signature that contains information about the sender. A signature is a standard block of text that is automatically added to the end of an e-mail message by the e-mail program. This text usually contains extra contact information, such as a telephone or fax number. A good way of checking what information is being included with outgoing e-mail messages is to send a blank message to yourself.

Third, many people send messages out to multiple recipients without disguising their e-mail addresses. For instance, a person may pass on jokes to all of the people in her address book without hiding the addresses used. A cyberstalker accessing such a message can use the addresses for a number of purposes, ranging from information gathering to identity theft. An easy way to prevent this is by using the blind carbon copy (BCC) feature found within most e-mail packages to send messages to multiple recipients instead of the carbon copy (CC) feature. When a message is sent using BCC, each recipient sees only his or her e-mail address.

Finally, old e-mail messages may provide a cyberstalker with a valuable source of information if he is able to gain access to the victim's computer. However, this danger can be avoided easily by simply deleting or encrypting old messages.

The following guidelines are derived from a number of sources, including various writers (Taylor, 2001; Grossman, 1997), the Florida Computer Crime Center,[12] WHOA, CyberAngels, and others.

1. Never send rude or offensive e-mail. In general, never say something in an e-mail message that you are not prepared to say face-to-face.[13] If you are angry with another person, wait until you have calmed down before sending your message. As many of the examples given throughout this book show, it can take very little to provoke a cyberstalker.
2. Check to make sure that your e-mail signature does not contain information that you do not want made public. The help files that accompany your e-mail program will provide information on how to edit or delete a signature.
3. Consider opening a second e-mail account that can be used for personal and leisure activities. This way, you can make sure that your primary e-mail address is given only to trusted friends, colleagues, and relatives. Many organizations offer free e-mail accounts, including Hotmail, Yahoo!, and Lycos. If you create a new e-mail account, make sure that the address is gender neutral and does not reveal any information about you.
4. Consider getting a personal e-mail certificate (sometimes called a digital signature) so that other people can verify that messages actually came from you. You can also encrypt messages so that only the intended recipients can read them. Personal certificates can be obtained free of charge or at low cost from a number of companies. For instance, Thawte provides a personal certificate free of charge for personal use.[14]
5. Consider encrypting personal messages or those containing sensitive information. If your messages are somehow intercepted, there is less chance of anyone being able to read them. In addition, encryption can sometimes help you to verify the identity of a person who has sent you a message, as well as allow you to prove your own identity. There are numerous free and commercial encryption packages available via the Internet, each offering different features and functionality. Examples include PGP (Pretty Good Privacy), A-Lock, Crypto Kong, and Cryptext.[15]

Trojans and Computer Viruses

In many cases, a cyberstalker may attempt to damage his victim's computer system by transmitting a computer virus,[16] Trojan,[17] worm, or other destructive program. Sometimes, a Trojan may be used in an attempt to gather information about the victim, usually by monitoring activity such as web sites visited, e-mail sent, and so on.

A computer virus or Trojan is usually transmitted by disguising it in some way. In most cases, the victim is responsible for infecting her own machine by running an executable program or loading a data file received from another computer user. For instance, a typical method of sending a virus or Trojan involves sending the victim an electronic greeting card attached to an e-mail message. When the victim views the greetings card, the virus or Trojan is activated and infects her machine.

Another danger arises from the scripting facilities found in programs such as Word, Outlook, and Excel. Many applications have a built-in programming language and allow programs to be stored within data files, such as word processing documents. When the data file is opened, the program runs automatically. This feature can be used to create simple macro viruses that can cause a great deal of harm. For instance, the Love Bug virus alone affected more than 45 million users (BBC News, 2000). In addition, major virus attacks, such as Melissa and Explore.zip, caused damage estimated at more than $12 billion (Raymond, 2000).

Most of the dangers posed by viruses and Trojans can be avoided by following a number of relatively simple guidelines. The following guidelines are derived from a number of sources, including various writers (Bocij et al., 2002, p. 628; Stewart, 2001), Symantec, IRCBeginner.Com, TeamAnti-Virus.org, and others.

1. Install a virus scanner and ensure that virus definitions are kept up to date. Conduct regular scans of your system. Many antivirus programs are available at low cost and some can even be obtained free of charge. Examples of free antivirus programs include AVG and AntiVir.[18] There are also online virus scanners that can be accessed free of charge, such as those available from Trend Micro and Symantec.[19]
2. Do not accept file attachments from people you do not know. In addition, do not accept unexpected file attachments from people you know. This is because some viruses will send e-mail to every person listed in a person's address book in an attempt to infect as many machines as possible. If you receive an unexpected file by e-mail or other means, you should delete it without opening it. If you believe that the file is important and choose to open it, be sure to scan it for viruses first. If you inform your friends and colleagues that they should always give notice if they intend to send any files, there will be little or no danger of you deleting any important data. If you are uncertain about a particular file attachment, you can always e-mail the sender for confirmation that he or she sent it.
3. Make regular backups of important files. In the event of a virus infection or other problem, you will be less likely to lose important data. Most modern computer systems have a CD-writer, enabling users to back up large quantities of data easily. Suitable backup software may have been supplied as part of the operating system being used or may have been bundled with the CD-writer. In addition, there are many backup programs available free of charge that can be downloaded via the Internet.[20]
4. Disable macros and scripting in your web browser, e-mail package, and office applications to prevent macro viruses from infecting your computer. You should be able to find information on how to disable scripting in the help files that accompany the programs you use. Alternatively, the

developer's web site may contain useful information. For instance, Microsoft's web site provides information, software updates, and other resources for all of its products.

In the event of an infection by a virus or Trojan, it is usually possible to repair the computer by using an online service, such as Trend Micro's HouseCall (see Internet Resources in Further Readings). Although most virus scanners will also remove Trojans, it may sometimes be necessary to install a specialized Trojan scanner. A good example is The Cleaner, which can be used free for thirty days.[21]

Hacking and Intrusion

With a few exceptions, the risk posed by a cyberstalker hacking into a victim's machine can be considered very low.

A typical hacker might use an automated tool to scan for computers on the Internet. This method is known as port scanning, which uses automated tools and scripts to check thousands of computers each hour. When a computer is found, it is probed to see if it is vulnerable in some way. If it is, the hacker may then attempt to access files or take some other action. It should be obvious that this kind of approach is very hit-or-miss and makes it almost impossible to target a specific individual or computer. In general, a cyberstalker attempting to gain access to a victim's computer will need some additional information, such as the computer's IP address.[22] However, even with this extra information, the cyberstalker may still not be able to access the victim's computer.

It is important to remember that a great deal of technical knowledge is needed in order to infiltrate a computer system in the way described here. Most cyberstalkers do not have such detailed knowledge, so they often turn to other ways of accessing a victim's computer, for example, by planting Trojan horse programs.

Some cyberstalkers use a false identity in an attempt to establish a relationship with the victim via instant messaging or a chat room. Some instant messaging programs have contained security vulnerabilities that might allow a hacker or cyberstalker to gain access to a victim's computer (for examples, see Delio, 2001; Hansen, 2000). For instance, it has been claimed that several utilities exist for a popular instant messaging program that can be used to retrieve any file from the user's computer. Other utilities can be used to upload files, execute programs, and extract sensitive information (such as passwords). If the cyberstalker can convince the victim to accept file downloads, he may be able to transmit a Trojan horse program disguised as a greeting card or other innocuous file. Peer-to-peer (P2P) applications, such as Kazaa, may also allow a cyberstalker to access files on a victim's computer, perhaps because the program has been configured incorrectly or has a security vulnerability.

If a cyberstalker is able to gain physical access to the victim's computer, he may be able to install surveillance software[23] in order to monitor all activity on the computer. This type of software can be thought as being somewhere in between a key logger and a Trojan. Like a key logger, the program records every keystroke on the computer system, including passwords, outgoing e-mail messages, documents, and so on. Like a Trojan, the program records other information, such as web sites visited, and then secretly transmits a report at regular intervals. Although surveillance software can be installed remotely, this is often difficult to do.

Companies that want to monitor their employees sometimes use surveillance software. A study by the American Management Association found that "more than three-quarters of major U.S. companies record and review employee communications and activities on the job, including e-mail, Internet connections and computer files" (Hirsh, 2001). In some cases, use of surveillance software in the workplace may be illegal.[24] In Europe, for example, this kind of surveillance may breach the right to privacy granted by the European Convention on Human Rights. Although there have been no reported cases of cyberstalkers making use of data gathered through surveillance software used in the workplace, it remains a possibility.

The following guidelines are derived from a number of sources, including writers (Bocij et al., 2002), Symantec, Gibson Research Corporation, WindowSecurity.com, and others.

1. Unless you are connected to a network, disable Windows file and print sharing facilities.[25] This will prevent other people from viewing or accessing your files. If you are connected to a network, you may not be able to disable these facilities or may need help from technical support staff.
2. Test how vulnerable your computer is and take any action necessary to improve security. There are a number of free online services that will test a computer system for vulnerabilities and provide advice on how to deal with problems found. Examples of such services include Shields Up! by Gibson Research Corporation and Hack Yourself from HackerWhacker. com.[26]
3. Install a firewall and keep it up to date. This is one of the most effective ways of protecting a personal computer against hackers and other intruders. A firewall is a program that monitors and controls all incoming and

outgoing Internet traffic on a computer. Any unauthorized traffic is stopped automatically and the user is alerted. This is important since it can allow users to detect any unusual activity, such as the traffic generated by Trojans. Some firewalls also have a "stealth" function that masks the computer, effectively making it invisible to the tools used by hackers. There are many personal firewall packages that are available free of charge. For instance, Zone Alarm is widely regarded as being powerful but very simple to use.[27]

4. Check for updates to your operating system and applications at regular intervals. Install all major updates as these often address any recently found security issues.

Guidelines for Young People

In general, young people face the same risks as adults, but they are also vulnerable to other predators, such as pedophiles. Although it may be a cliché, education and awareness remain a young person's best defense against cyberstalkers of all kinds.

Some young people may also gain a measure of protection from the sense of community that can develop within certain chat rooms and newsgroups. Just as neighbors sometimes band together to improve or protect their neighborhood, Internet users sometimes collaborate in creating an environment that is suitable for themselves and their children. For instance, in some chat rooms, I have seen predators attempt to make contact with young people only to be chased away by an adult. In others, I have seen adults warn a young person when he or she has done something that is potentially dangerous, such as telling someone his or her address or telephone number. However, this kind of protection cannot be relied on. Not every chat room or newsgroup is moderated or inhabited by responsible, civic-minded adults. Furthermore, parents must accept responsibility for the safety of their own children, not rely on strangers to police the Internet. It is also crucial to remember that the Internet should never be used as an electronic babysitter and that parents need to become involved in their children's online activities.

The following guidelines are derived from a number of sources, including the FBI,[28] SafetyEd International, ProtectYourKids.Info, BytesCanada, CyberAngels, NetScams, WiredKids, and others. These guidelines are offered *in addition* to the advice given in other parts of this chapter.

1. Have open discussions with your children about online risks.
2. Spend time with your children when they use the Internet. This will

make you familiar with how your child uses the Internet and provides opportunities for you to teach them about online safety.

3. Keep the computer in a room that is used by the entire family; do not put the computer in your child's bedroom. It becomes more difficult for predators to communicate secretly with your child if the computer screen is visible to other members of the family.
4. Use any parental controls provided by your Internet Service Provider. Some ISPs provide online tools, and others offer software you can download (often called an Internet or web filter). Although parental control programs are never entirely effective, they can help ensure that your children do not access inappropriate web sites or chat rooms.
5. Maintain access to your children's e-mail and check their messages from time to time. This will help you to make sure that they are not in contact with an online predator. You can also check the history on your children's Internet browser to see which web sites they have been visiting.
6. Be aware that your child will be able to access the Internet in a number of places that are out of your direct control, for example, at school or a friend's home.
7. Instruct your child never to give out personal information, such as an address, telephone number, or the name of his or her school. In addition, your child should know never to send out his or her own photograph.
8. Instruct your child never respond to messages that are suggestive, obscene, aggressive, or harassing. Encourage your child to tell you if he or she ever feels uncomfortable about any messages received.
9. Instruct your children never to download files from people or places they do not know. This will help to make sure they do not download pornographic images, viruses, or Trojans.
10. Instruct your children that they must never meet an online friend in real life.
11. Set rules for Internet usage. Try to make sure your child's Internet use takes place at reasonable times and is not excessive.

Guidelines for Business Users

Cyberstalking raises a number of challenges for business managers and sometimes involves dealing with conflicts between duties to shareholders, employees, and the public. In general, it can be argued that managers need to fulfill two main responsibilities. First, there is a general duty to protect the public from any harm caused by company employees or by people using company resources. Chapter 8, for example, described a case in which an employee used his employer's resources in order to harass others.

Second, there is a duty to protect the company itself from any harm resulting from a cyberstalking incident. Such harm might come about in two different ways: being an unwitting accomplice to a cyberstalker, or becoming the victim of cyberstalking. As an example, chapter 8 explained how a company might become exposed to civil or criminal action if its resources are used in support of criminal activities.

Perhaps the simplest and most effective way of controlling company resources is by implementing an acceptable use policy (Bocij et al., 2002, pp. 622–23). An acceptable use policy (AUP) sets out how company ICT resources may be used and, more importantly, what behaviors are forbidden. The AUP also lists the penalties for misuse of company facilities. Using an AUP has two immediate benefits for an organization. First, it provides employees with clear guidance about how to use company resources, making it difficult for anyone caught misusing facilities to claim ignorance. Second, it demonstrates the organization's intent to make sure its resources are used appropriately, which may help to increase public confidence in the company and may also provide a measure of protection against legal action.

Some organizations may find that developing a formal security policy suits their needs better since it is more formal and wide-ranging than an AUP. A formal policy sets out all of the company's security arrangements and often contains detailed procedures for dealing with particular situations, such as backing up data. Information on developing an acceptable use policy or a formal security policy is easily available via the Internet. *The IT Security Cookbook*,[29] for example, provides detailed guidance on a wide range of issues, including how to develop a formal security policy.

I am not aware of any published guidelines that deal with cyberstalking for organizations. The following guidelines are drawn from a wide variety of sources, including the general computer security advice offered by various writers and researchers (Bocij et al., 2002; Blacharksi, 2000; Lee, 2001; Bassett, 2000). Furthermore, these guidelines are of most relevance to small organizations. This is because larger companies will have a team of dedicated security specialists and will have already implemented most of the recommendations given here.

1. Implement an acceptable use policy. Make sure that all employees are aware of the AUP and are familiar with its content. Many companies make compliance with the company's AUP part of the conditions of employment for new employees.
2. Take regular software audits. This involves checking company computer systems to make sure that no illegal content is being stored, such as pornography or pirated software.

3. Try to predict the threats the company is most likely to face. Plan how the company can maintain normal operation in the event of a serious problem, such as a denial of service attack. Business continuity planning is essential since no security measures are ever completely foolproof.

4. Ensure that regular backups are made of important data. Although employees should be encouraged to make backups of their own data, someone should be given overall responsibility for making sure that data stored on a network is backed up at regular intervals.

5. Consider placing controls on the use of company facilities for e-mail and web browsing. There are many different ways to do this. For instance, some companies use specialized software that controls access to certain web sites and maintains a log of user activity. In some companies, personal use of company e-mail and Internet facilities is banned.

6. Consider monitoring the Internet traffic—including e-mail—that passes through the company's systems. Remember that you may need to get legal advice before intercepting and reading employee e-mail messages.

7. Ensure that company systems are protected by a firewall and that antivirus software is installed. Keep antivirus signature files up to date. Make sure that any available updates for operating systems and applications are installed at regular intervals.

DEALING WITH HARASSMENT

As with the previous section, this discussion has been broken down into several parts in order to make it more accessible. The material is presented in a logical order, moving from recognizing cyberstalking to involving the police. Although each part is self-contained, the whole of this section should be used to gain the information needed to deal initially with a cyberstalking case.

Identifying Cyberstalking

Before attempting to take any action, you must first establish whether you have become involved in a genuine case of cyberstalking. An offensive e-mail message or an argument in a chat room may cause a great deal of distress but does not necessarily indicate the start of a campaign of harassment.

It is important to try to remain objective when assessing whether a person's actions constitute harassment. Often, it is a good idea to have a "cooling off" period of a day or so in order to let your emotions settle. During this time, you should avoid using the Internet and try to focus on activities you find relaxing.

When you feel you can be objective, think about your experiences and whether they indicate harassment. In particular, you should consider carefully if any form of threat has been made or if there has been the suggestion that there will be further incidents directed toward you.

If you are not sure whether you are experiencing cyberstalking, you can ask the opinion of someone you trust, such as a spouse or close friend.

When a young person is involved, or if there is any threat of violence, it may be best to err on the side of caution and take appropriate action immediately.

Young people may sometimes avoid telling their parents that they are being harassed or have been approached online by a stranger. For this reason, parents should be alert for signs that a child may need help. A number of organizations have produced lists of warning signs that may indicate a child is being harassed or sexually abused via the Internet. The following list is derived from a number of organizations, including WiredKids, CyberAngels, NetScams, SafetyEd International, AnswerPoint.Org, and the FBI:

- Increased telephone use, especially long distance calls
- Receiving unusual telephone calls, especially from adults
- Receiving gifts through the mail
- Suddenly having a relatively large amount of money
- Signs of Internet addiction, for example, becoming unusually upset when asked to finish using the computer
- Unusual patterns of Internet use, especially late at night or at times when other people are not around
- A desire to be alone when using chat rooms
- Using a headset with the computer in order to make voice conversations more private
- Concealing the screen when another person passes by
- Use of inappropriate vocabulary, especially sexual terms
- Signs of increased aggression or depression
- A decline in schoolwork
- Experiencing nightmares or bed-wetting
- Pornography or other inappropriate materials are downloaded or stored on the computer
- Withdrawal from family or friends
- Using an Internet account belonging to someone else

It should be remembered that the presence of some of these warning signs does not necessarily indicate that a child is at risk. By the same token, a child may not show any sign that he or she is being harassed or is in contact with a pedophile. However, as mentioned earlier, immediate action should be taken in any cases where it is felt that a young person is at risk.

Contacting the Cyberstalker

Some organizations advise cyberstalking victims to contact stalkers and tell them to stop their behavior. CyberAngels, for instance, advises, "Tell the person harassing you in straight forward terms, 'Leave me alone, stop harassing me. Do not contact me again.'"[30] This advice is probably the result of state antistalking laws, which sometimes specify that contact between the cyberstalker and his victim must be "unconsented."

The decision of whether or not to contact the cyberstalker is an important one and must be considered carefully. On the one hand, ignoring the cyberstalker altogether may cause him to lose interest and move on to another victim. On the other, the cyberstalker may decide to step up the harassment in order to get a reaction.

A similar dilemma arises if you try to contact the cyberstalker and tell him to stop his behavior. Any form of contact acknowledges the cyberstalker's actions and may encourage further harassment. Asking the cyberstalker to leave you alone may provide further encouragement since he may see this as a sign of weakness.

It is worth remembering that there is no research that suggests contacting a cyberstalker and asking him to stop his harassment is likely to have any effect. However, studies of offline stalking tend to show that it seldom helps when a victim asks her stalker to leave her alone. For example, Brewster's study (2001, p. 97) of 187 stalking victims found that attempts at discouraging stalkers using methods such as reasoning, pleading, or even arguing were largely ineffective: "Of 408 reported types of discouragement, victims reported behavior improvements following only 37 (9.1%) of these attempts." Even threats may have little effect on a determined cyberstalker. For instance, a study of ninety-five stalking victims found that only one case was resolved through the use of threats made against the stalker (Sheridan, Davies, and Boon, 2001).

As mentioned earlier, it may sometimes be necessary to contact the cyberstalker and ask him to halt his behavior, especially if you need to involve the police or other agencies. Once it has been established that the cyberstalker has ignored your message and continued in his behavior, it often becomes easier to invoke antistalking laws.

All of the organizations that advise contacting the cyberstalker also make it clear that you should do so only once. After you have sent your message, you should not communicate with the stalker again, no matter what the provocation. For instance, the CyberAngels web site states: "Do not reply to anything else the harasser says. No replies to emails, taunts or lies said about you." The WiredPatrol web site[31] also warns that "any additional communication is not only counterproductive, but also extremely dangerous" and explains that "historically, any kind of direct response by a victim has been proven to not only re-enforce [*sic*] the behavior of the stalker, but also irritate an already bad situation."

Many organizations suggest that a cyberstalking case sometimes can be brought to an end by adopting a new online identity. If it is difficult for the cyberstalker to find the new identity, he may become discouraged and simply move on to another victim. Changing online identity is usually straightforward and involves little more than obtaining a new e-mail address and rejoining chat rooms under one or more new user names. However, care must be taken to make sure that the cyberstalker does not obtain the new e-mail address or become aware of any new nicknames used in chat rooms. E-mail sent to the victim's original e-mail address can be ignored completely or screened by creating a set of e-mail filters, a rule that can be used to process incoming e-mail. For instance, a user might create a filter that automatically deletes any messages from a specific e-mail address.

Gathering Evidence

As soon as you believe you are being harassed, you should begin to gather as much evidence as possible against the cyberstalker. An important point to remember is that all electronic data should be copied to floppy disk or CD-ROM. In the event of a virus infection or other disaster, the data will not be lost.

All harassment-related e-mail messages should be saved since these can often be used to find the cyberstalker's identity or location. In the majority of cases, even if it is not possible to identify the cyberstalker, it should still be possible to locate his ISP by tracing his messages back to their point of origin.

Any files sent by the cyberstalker, such as pictures or multimedia, should also be saved. All files should be scanned for viruses since they may have been sent with the intention of transmitting a virus or Trojan.

Whenever possible, any posts made to newsgroups should be recorded. Most newsreaders, such as Outlook Express and Forté Agent, allow messages to be saved to disk. It is important to record messages quickly since they may become unavailable within a matter of days.

If possible, any instant messenger conversations should be recorded as these often provide a great deal of evidence that can be used against a cyberstalker. Some chat programs can be configured so that entire conversations can be recorded and stored on the computer's hard drive. For instance, Yahoo! Messenger, MSN, and AOL Instant Messenger all allow users to store conversations on disk. Instructions on how to use this facility can be found in the help files that accompany each program or by searching the Internet.

If the program being used is not capable of recording a conversation, an alternative is to use a screen capture utility to make a copy of the entire screen at various points in the conversation. As long as the relevant part of the conversation is visible on the screen, it can be captured and saved as a picture on the user's hard disk drive. Although this is a crude and inefficient way of storing parts of a conversation, it has the advantages of being simple and effective. There are many commercial, shareware and freeware screen capture programs available. Examples of free screen capture programs include WinGrab and Screen Grab Pro.[32]

If necessary, screen capture software can also be used to capture parts of conversations that take place in chat rooms. It may also be possible to ask other users to act as witnesses, although many cyberstalkers are careful to avoid acting in front of others.

In general, the software used to create the chat room environment does not allow users to record conversations. However, many providers routinely record all of the activity in the chat rooms they operate so that they can resolve disputes and deal with other problems that arise. In the event of a serious cyberstalking incident, it may be possible to contact the chat room operator and ask him or her to look into the problem or even send copies of records to the police.

Many cyberstalkers use web pages, guest-book entries, web journals (blogs), and even classified advertisements in an attempt to humiliate their victims. All of this data should be recorded so that it can be used as evidence later on. It is often possible to record materials posted on web sites by simply saving the relevant page to disk. However, some types of content may not be saved correctly, making it difficult to gather certain types of information, such as guest-book entries.[33] This problem can often be solved by using an offline web browser, a tool that allows selected pages—or even an entire web site—to be copied to disk for future examination. As with many of the applications mentioned within this chapter, a number of offline browsers are available at low cost or are free. Examples of free or advertising-supported offline browsers include HTTrack, WebStripper, and WebReaper.[34]

Some organizations suggest that harassment victims should begin keeping a diary in order to record the date, time, location, and circumstances of each incident. This is advisable as victims may find the process a good way of dealing with their emotions. In addition, the information they record will supplement that gathered in other ways.

Reporting Harassment

Simply reporting incidents to a relevant organization can sometimes bring harassment to an end quickly and cleanly as many cyberstalkers cease their activities as soon as they become exposed and other people begin to take interest in them. An ISP or other organization will often be able to identify the cyberstalker, forcing him to stop by threatening prosecution. For instance, there have been several cyberstalking cases in which the harassment ended as soon as the identities of the cyberstalkers became known (Karp, 2000). Making sure that other people know that harassment is taking place may also be effective in discouraging a cyberstalker. For example, Pamela Gilbert's story describes how she used the Internet and her writing to protect herself against her stalker.

E-mail

Offensive or threatening e-mail messages can usually be reported both to your own ISP and the ISP where the message originated. However, your own ISP may be reluctant to take any action unless the complaint is very serious. It is usually the responsibility of the cyberstalker's ISP to deal with any complaints (since the messages being complained about originate from its systems).

It is usually easiest to contact your own ISP by e-mail. Contact details can normally be found on the ISP's web site, on the documentation received when your account was opened, or in the telephone directory. Your message should detail your complaint as clearly and concisely as possible. You should also forward copies of the messages you are complaining about since the ISP cannot act without them. Be aware that it may take some time before you receive a response from the ISP. If you do not receive a reply after a few weeks, or if the reply you receive is not helpful, consider sending a follow-up e-mail message or contacting the ISP's customer service department by telephone, fax, or letter.

Contacting the cyberstalker's ISP is often difficult since the cyberstalker may have taken steps to disguise his identity. All e-mail messages are made up of two parts: the headers and the content of the message (the body). Nearly all e-mail packages hide most of the headers from view so that it is easier to read the body of the message. The headers contain a great deal of information, including the name of the e-mail package used to create the message, the date and time the message was sent, and the route taken by the message on its journey to the recipient. If the cyberstalker has used an anonymous remailing service, the headers identifying the origin of the message will have been removed, making it almost impossible to identify the his real e-mail address or ISP. Occasionally, a cyberstalker may attempt to alter or forge the headers of a message to make it appear that it came from another person, including the victim herself. Although this kind of tampering can sometimes be detected, it makes it difficult to identify the cyberstalker's real e-mail address or ISP.

Assuming the message headers are all present and have not been altered, they may contain some basic instructions on what to do if you want to make a complaint. This information will normally be contained in lines marked "X-Info" or "X-Abuse." Typically, the instructions will provide an e-mail address to contact and will ask for copies of the messages being complained about.

Sometimes an e-mail message does not contain the information needed to report an incident. In this case, it is traditional to send complaints to "abuse" at the name of the domain. As an example, if a message came from a Hotmail user and there was no other information about how to report the incident, you might address your complaint to "abuse@hotmail.com."

In some cases, a message sent to an "abuse" e-mail address may be returned as being undeliverable. As all ISPs are supposed to provide an e-mail address called "postmaster," the message could be sent again to an address such as "postmaster@hotmail.com."

Since some cyberstalkers may forge or alter message headers, it is important to remember that much of the information contained within an e-mail message cannot be relied on. From most e-mail packages, the name of the sender, for example, can easily be set to a specific value. If making a complaint, it is important to be sure that the person being complained to is not the cyberstalker himself. Cyberstalkers may sometimes create a "postmaster" e-mail address so that they can intercept complaints. The simplest way to avoid this problem is by using a search engine to research the e-mail address before sending any mail.

If it is not clear whom to direct a complaint to, you may find the name of an ISP to contact by examining the message headers.[35] An e-mail message will normally contain a number of lines that begin with the word *Received* and trace the journey undertaken by the message. These lines are in reverse order, meaning that the first item describes the last stage of the journey—that is, when the message was received at your e-mail account. Examining the very last Received line should identify the sender's system. However, once again, you should take care when deciding whether to rely on this information since it may have been forged.

Newsgroups

In general, newsgroup posts can be treated in the same way as e-mail messages. The headers in a newsgroup post will usually contain a line beginning with "X-Complaints-To" that provides an e-mail address for complaints.

Message Boards

Virtually all message boards (sometimes called forums) have a moderator who makes sure that all users follow the board's rules. Complaints about harassment should be sent to the moderator, together with details of the messages you are concerned about. If you are unable to locate the moderator's e-mail address, you can send a message to the owner or operator of the message board. Most message boards will have one or more frequently asked questions (FAQ) documents available to read online or download to your computer. Before making a complaint, you should read these FAQs in case there is any information about making a complaint.

Chat Rooms

Many chat rooms also have moderators (sometimes called monitors) who make sure that users behave appropriately. Again, complaints about harassment should be sent to the moderator, together with details of the conversations and users you are concerned about. Sometimes moderators can be contacted "live" via the chat room itself, but it is advisable to send a copy of your complaint by e-mail so that there is a record of your concerns. If you are unable to locate the moderator's e-mail address, you can send a message to the owner or operator of the chat room. Once again, there may be FAQ documents available that provide information about making a complaint, and you should refer to these before taking any action.

Web Sites

Complaints about web site content should be directed to the owner or operator of the site. This includes complaints involving guest-book entries, items posted to message boards, web journals (blogs), advertisements, and any other materials. If the web site is being hosted by another company, you should first complain to the owner of the web site and then to the hosting company if you do not receive a satisfactory response. For instance, if a site is hosted using web space provided by Tripod, you might complain to the owner of the web site first and then to Tripod itself.

Most legitimate web sites will provide contact information for members of the public. However, there may be times when it is necessary to identify the registered owner of a given domain. A domain is the name given to the address of a web site, for example, www.msn.com. Web site addresses can also be given in a numeric form called an IP address, for example, 89.177.4.253. When a person buys a domain, it must be registered with an official registrar, such as Nominet or Verisign. The information with which the domain was registered is publicly available and can be accessed by conducting a WhoIs query. If successful, the results of the query will contain contact information for the owner of the domain, such as an address, telephone number, or e-mail address. There are many organizations that allow people to do WhoIs searches free of charge, such as the AllWhoIs service offered by Alldomains.com.[36] It is also possible to find registration information for domains given as IP addresses by using a different kind of WhoIs search. Sam Spade is a well-known service that provides a variety of tools that can be used to locate information about a given domain name or IP address.[37]

Obtaining Advice and Support

Most Internet safety organizations provide a number of services for victims of cyberstalking. First, they provide information and advice on dealing with harassment. Some organizations maintain extensive collections of documents and other resources. Both WHOA and CyberAngels, for instance, maintain comprehensive information on cyberstalking legislation in the United States and other countries.

Second, they provide encouragement and emotional support. This can take a number of different forms, from publishing personal accounts of victims who successfully prosecuted their cyberstalkers to putting victims in contact with each other so they can discuss their experiences.

Third, most organizations provide help with investigating cyberstalking cases. Typically, this involves helping victims identify their cyberstalkers by tracing e-mail messages and newsgroup posts. Organizations like WHOA also work with the police, often helping with specific cases and providing technical support and training.

Finally, certain organizations act as advocates for some cyberstalking victims. For instance, an organization may provide extra support for a victim if she is finding it difficult to get help from her local police.

Although most organizations are based in the United States, many offer support to Internet users from anywhere in the world. All Internet safety organizations can be contacted by e-mail, and many provide quick responses.

Some of the best-known Internet safety organizations include:

Working to Halt Online Abuse (WHOA)
  http://www.haltabuse.org

CyberAngels
  http://www.cyberangels.com

WiredPatrol
  http://www.wiredpatrol.org

Web Police
  http://www.intergov.org

Network for Surviving Stalking (for UK citizens)
  http://www.nss.org.uk

Involving Law Enforcement

In some cyberstalking cases, it may become necessary to involve the police or another law enforcement agency. Most safety organizations recommend involving the police immediately if any of the following conditions apply: you feel that your physical safety is threatened, the cyberstalker has made a threat of violence that you believe may be carried out, or you believe the safety or welfare of a young person is at risk.

Relatively few stalking victims approach the police for help. In the United States, for instance, a National Violence Against Women survey found that only half of victims report their experiences to the police (Tjaden and Thoennes, 1998). Similarly, an Australian study found 57 percent of stalking victims did not report their experiences to the police (Gouda, 2000). The situation seems worse in some countries than in others. In the United Kingdom, the 1998 British Crime Survey found that only a third of stalking victims felt that what had happened to them was a crime, and only half of this group reported their experiences to the police (Budd, Mattinson, and Myhill, 2000).

There may be many reasons why some stalking victims choose not to seek help from the police, but three explanations in particular come up regularly. First, as already mentioned, some people may not feel that what they are experiencing is a crime. This response is almost certainly due to a lack of education regarding individual rights and antistalking legislation. Second, some people may believe that the police will not be sympathetic to them and will not treat their concerns seriously. For instance, a study of 187 stalking victims found that they had very low expectations of the police (Brewster, 2001). Many victims felt that the police would not be understanding and would not do anything to help them. Finally, some people may believe that the police are unlikely to help them for various reasons, such as not being familiar with antistalking laws or because of inadequacies in the law (Abrams and Robinson, 1998). As an example, a study of ninety-five stalking victims in the United Kingdom found that 41 percent of stalking victims were unhappy with the way the police had handled their case for a number of reasons, such as the police being "powerless" to take action against the stalker (Sheridan, Davies, and Boon, 2001).

The research discussed here implies that police involvement is unlikely to be of any real benefit to stalking and cyberstalking victims. This echoes comments made in chapter 9 suggesting that involving the police or taking some form of other legal action may often result in the harassment becoming more serious. However, chapter 9 also quoted research in which police intervention helped to resolve almost three-quarters of stalking cases. In addition, failing to involve the police may limit the effectiveness of any other legal measures that may be available. For instance, in some countries a court may be reluctant to issue a restraining order if the victim has not made a formal complaint to the police. In the absence of any research dealing with the results of police involvement in cyberstalking cases, victims must weigh the risk of making the situation worse against the possibility that the police (and the legal system in general) may bring an end to the harassment.

Approaching the police for help may be more successful if a victim takes time to gather her evidence and plans how to explain her situation as clearly as possible. Complaints are probably best made in person rather than by telephone. It may also be helpful to bring someone to act as a supporter, such as spouse, friend, or relative. Occasionally, it may be possible to ask for a volunteer from an Internet safety organization to act as a representative.

If initial contact with the police is unsatisfactory, it may be necessary to repeat the complaint to a senior officer by letter. Sometimes another organization can be approached to contact the police and ask for action on the victim's behalf. In a case involving a child, for example, it might be helpful if social services backs a request for police assistance. In certain case, it may also be necessary to involve other law enforcement agencies. For instance, many cyberstalking cases are likely to cross state or national boundaries, requiring agencies such as the FBI or Interpol to become involved.

CONCLUSION

A key principle of cyberstalking prevention is that computer users must exercise strict control over their personal information. It should be remembered that cyberstalkers can find information about a potential victim through a wide variety of sources, many of which can be accessed free of charge.

There are some basic precautions that can be taken to reduce the possibility of being harassed. First, it is important to learn how to behave correctly when using chat rooms, newsgroups, and other services since this may help to avoid arguments and other problems. Second, installing a virus scanner and making regular backups of important data help to provide an effective defense against computer viruses and Trojans. Finally, although the risk of a cyberstalker hacking into a victim's computer is relatively low, a firewall should be installed to further reduce the risk of intrusion.

If you become a victim of cyberstalking, it is important to gather as much evidence as possible against the harasser. E-mail messages, newsgroup posts, instant messaging conversations, chat room discussions, and web pages all constitute evidence and can be recorded.

In deciding whether to contact the police, victims should balance the risk of making the situation worse against the possibility of bringing an end to the harassment. However, the police should be involved immediately if a cyberstalker makes a threat of violence that the victim believes may be carried out or if the safety or welfare of a young person is at risk.

Further Readings

SELECTED READING

Chapter 1: What Is Cyberstalking?

Deirmenjian, J. 1999. Stalking in cyberspace. *Journal of the American Academy of Psychiatry and the Law*, 27 (3), 407–13.

Meloy, R. J., ed. 1998. *The psychology of stalking: Clinical and forensic perspectives*. London: Academic Press.

Mullen, P., Pathé, M., and Purcell, R. 2000. *Stalkers and their victims*. Cambridge: Cambridge University Press.

Spitzberg, B., and Cadiz, M. 2002. The media construction of stalking stereotypes. *Journal of Criminal Justice and Popular Culture*, 9 (3), 128–49.

Spitzberg, B., and Hoobler, G. 2002. Cyberstalking and the technologies of interpersonal terrorism. *New Media & Society*, 4 (1), 71–92.

Chapter 2: Stalking or *Cyber*stalking?

Bocij, P., Bocij, H., and McFarlane, L. 2003. Cyberstalking: A case study concerning serial harassment in the UK. *British Journal of Forensic Practice*, 5 (2), 25–32.

Smith, R. 1998. *Criminal exploitation of new technologies*. Canberra: Australian Institute of Criminology (available from http://www.aic.gov.au/publications/tandi/tandi93.html).

Chapter 3: The Incidence and Prevalence of Cyberstalking

Budd, T., and Mattinson, J. 2000. Stalking: Findings from the 1998 British Crime Survey. *Research Findings*, 129, 1–4.

Budd, T., Mattinson, J., and Myhill, A. 2000. *The extent and nature of stalking: Findings from the 1998 British Crime Survey.* London: Home Office Research, Development and Statistics Directorate.

Fremouw, W. J., Westrup, D., and Pennypacker, J. 1997. Stalking on campus: The prevalence and strategies for coping with stalking. *Forensic Science*, 42 (4), 666–69.

Purcell, R., Pathé, M., and Mullen, P. 2002. The prevalence and nature of stalking in the Australian community. *Australian and New Zealand Journal of Psychiatry*, 36, 114–20.

Reno, J., Robinson, L., Brennan, N., et al. 1998. *Stalking and domestic violence: The third annual report to Congress under the Violence Against Women Act.* Washington, DC: Office of Justice Programs.

Tjaden, P. 1998. *Stalking in America: Findings from the National Violence Against Women Survey.* Washington, DC: U.S. Department of Justice (available from http://www.ncjrs.org/pdffiles/169592.pdf).

Chapter 4: Who Are the Cyberstalkers?

Case, D. O. 2000. Stalking, monitoring and profiling: A typology and case studies of harmful uses of caller ID. *New Media & Society*, 2 (1), 67–84.

Harmon, R., Rosner, R., and Owens, H. 1998. Sex and violence in a forensic population of obsessional harassers. *Psychology, Public Policy, and Law*, 4 (1–2), 236–49.

Kienlen, K., Birmingham, D., Solberg, K., et al. 1997. A comparative study of psychotic and nonpsychotic stalking. *Journal of the American Academy of Psychiatry and the Law*, 25 (3), 317–34.

Spitzberg, B., and Hoobler, G. 2002. Cyberstalking and the technologies of interpersonal terrorism. *New Media & Society*, 4 (1), 71–92.

Chapter 5: Who Are the Victims of Cyberstalkers?

Kramarae, C., and Kramer, J. 1995. Legal snarls for women in cyberspace. *Internet Research: Electronic Networking Applications and Policy*, 5 (2), 14–24.

McFarlane, J., Campbell, J., Wilt, S., et al. 1999. Stalking and intimate partner femicide. *Homicide Studies*, 3 (4), 300–316.

Chapter 6: What Motivates Cyberstalkers?

Dworkin, A. 1979. *Pornography: Men possessing women.* New York: Penguin Books.

Joinson, A. 1998. Causes and implications of disinhibited behavior on the Internet. In J. Gackenbach, ed., *Psychology and the Internet: Intrapersonal, interpersonal, and transpersonal implications*. San Diego, CA: Academic Press, pp. 43–60.

McKenna, K., and Green, A. 2002. Virtual group dynamics. *Group Dynamics: Theory, Research, and Practice*, 6 (1), 116–27.

Chapter 7: Threats to Young People

Hughes, D. 1999. Pimps and predators on the Internet: Globalizing sexual exploitation of women and children [online]. Amherst, MA: The Coalition Against Trafficking in Women (available at: http://www.uri.edu/artsci/wms/hughes/pprep.htm).

Feather, M. 1999. Internet and child victimisation. Children and Crime: Victims and Offenders Conference, 17–18 June 1999. Brisbane: Australian Institute of Criminology (available at: http://www.aic.gov.au/conferences/children/feather.pdf).

Lanning, K. 1992. *Child molesters: A behavioral analysis*, 3rd ed. Arlington, VA: National Center for Missing Exploited Children (available at: http://www.skeptictank.org/nc70.pdf).

Mitchell, K., Finkelhor, D., and Wolak, J. 2003. The exposure of youth to unwanted sexual material on the Internet: A national survey of risk, impact, and prevention. *Youth and Society*, 34 (3), 330–58.

Chapter 8: Cyberstalking and Organizations

Burke, E. 2001. *Anti-SLAPP laws and the Internet* [online]. Atlanta, GA: GigaLaw.com (available at: http://www.gigalaw.com/articles/2001/burke-2001-10.html).

Denning, D. 2000. *Cyberterrorism* [online]. Washington, DC: Georgetown University (available at: http://www.cs.georgetown.edu/~denning/infosec/cyberterror-GD.doc).

Denning, D. 2001. Activism, hacktivism, and cyberterrorism: The Internet as a tool for influencing foreign policy. In J. Arquilla and D. Ronfeldt, eds., *Networks and netwars: The future of terror, crime, and militancy*. Santa Monica, CA: RAND, pp. 239–88 (available at: http://www.cs.georgetown.edu/~denning/publications.html).

Naples, G., and Maher, M. 2002. Cybersmearing: A legal conflict between individuals and corporations. *The Journal of Information, Law and Technology*, 2 (available at: http://elj.warwick.ac.uk/jilt/02-2/naples.html).

Vatis, M. 2001. *Cyber attacks during the war on terrorism: A predictive analysis*. Hanover, NH: Institute for Security Technology Studies, Dartmouth College (available at: http://www.ists.dartmouth.edu/ISTS/counterterrorism/cyber_a1.pdf).

Chapter 9: Cyberstalking and the Law

Ellison, L., and Akdeniz, Y. 1998. Cyber-stalking: The regulation of harassment on the Internet. *Criminal Law Review* (December special edition: *Crime, Criminal Justice and the Internet*), 29–48 (available at: http://www.cyber-rights.org/documents/stalking_article.pdf).

Sorokin, E. 2000. Anti-stalking laws usually are unable to protect targets. *The Washington Times*, 17 April 2000 (available at: http://www.lizmichael.com/antistal.htm).

Wallace, H. 1998. Stalking and preventative measures. *American Association of Behavioral and Social Sciences Journal* [online] (Fall 1998) (available at: http://www.aabss.org/journal1998/wallace.htm).

Chapter 10: Dealing with Cyberstalking

Gross, L. 2000. *Surviving a stalker: Everything you need to know to keep yourself safe*. New York: Marlowe and Company.

Klinkhart, G. 2002. *A CyberCop's guide to Internet child safety*. Anchorage, AK: CyberCop Guides (available at: http://www.cybercopguide.com).

Medlin, A. 2002. *Stalking to cyberstalking, a problem caused by the Internet* [online]. Atlanta: Georgia State University College of Law (available at: http://gsulaw.gsu.edu/lawand/papers/fa02/medlin/).

Pathé, M. 2002. *Surviving stalking*. Cambridge: Cambridge University Press.

Pettinari, D. 2000. *Cyberstalking investigation and prevention* [online]. Pueblo, CO: Pueblo County Sheriff's Office (available at: http://www.crime-research.org/eng/library/Cyberstalking.pdf).

INTERNET RESOURCES

Chapter 1: What Is Cyberstalking?

The U.S. government operates an official web site devoted to identity theft. The site contains information describing how a person's identity can be stolen and provides advice on dealing with identity theft:

http://www.consumer.gov/idtheft

The Privacy Rights Clearinghouse provides a wealth of information about identity theft, including fact sheets, case studies, and links to online resources:

http://www.privacyrights.org/identity.htm

The Network for Surviving Stalking is a UK charity that provides information and advice about stalking. The site was established by Tracey Morgan and contains a fascinating account of her experience of stalking. The material is extremely compelling since it describes Morgan's experience from the point of view of her family, friends, and even the police officer who dealt with the case. Although not directly relevant to cyberstalking, this material provides valuable background information on stalking and helps to show how it affects victims and their families:

> http://www.nss.org.uk

The National Center for Victims of Crime maintains a comprehensive web site containing information on stalking and cyberstalking. The site provides access to a huge amount of information, including definitions, statistics, advice for victims, selected readings, and more:

> http://www.ncvc.org/special/stalking.htm

The National Criminal Justice Reference Service provides links to thousands of full-text documents drawn from a number of U.S. government agencies. A search engine can be used to access hundreds of stalking-related documents. A search engine that can be used to locate full-text documents can be found at:

> http://fulltextpubs.ncjrs.org/content/FullTextPubs.html

Chapter 2: Stalking or *Cyber*stalking?

A hoax message concerning the Slavemaster occasionally circulates around the Internet. The details of this hoax can be found at:

> http://urbanlegends.about.com/library/blslavemaster.htm

This article describes a case in which the threat of cyber-smearing was used to solicit telephone sex and cybersex. This provides a good example of the harm that can be caused by cyber-smearing:

> http://net4tv.com/voice/story.cfm?storyid=2931

This page from SafetyEd discusses the problems with insisting that a "credible threat" must be made when dealing with cases of cyberstalking:

> http://www.safetyed.org/help/stalking/stalkusa.html

Chapter 3: The Incidence and Prevalence of Cyberstalking

Statistics Canada provides a wealth of official statistics on Canadian demographics, such as crime and unemployment:

> http://www.statcan.ca/start.html

NUA Internet Surveys provides a regular e-mail newsletter containing the latest facts and figures about the Internet. The company's web site also provides statistics on surveys dealing with privacy, security, entertainment, education, and Web demographics:

> http://www.nua.com

The Australian Bureau of Statistics provides access to official government statistics on various subjects, including crime:

http://www.abs.gov.au

The U.S. Census Bureau's main web site is located at:

http://www.census.gov/index.html

The U.S. Census Bureau maintains a Web page with links to the statistical agencies of dozens of countries:

http://www.census.gov/main/www/stat_int.html

The United Kingdom's official statistics can be accessed via the National Statistics Online site:

http://www.statistics.gov.uk

Fedstats provides links via a simple search page to all major U.S. federal agencies involved in law enforcement. In addition to linking directly to every agency, the results page also links directly to some of the key statistics produced by each agency:

http://www.fedstats.gov/programs/crime.html

The Women Halting Online Abuse (WHOA) web site contains some interesting statistics on the organization's cases:

http://www.haltabuse.org/resources/stats/index.shtml

InterGOV's statistics about the incidents reported to the Web Police organization can be found at:

http://www.intergov.org/public_information/general_information/latest_web_stats.html

Chapter 4: Who Are the Cyberstalkers?

The Group for the Advancement of Psychiatry (GAP) has a number of psychiatry-related documents on its web site. GAP's main web site is located at:

http://www.groupadpsych.org

Of particular interest on the site is a discussion of stalking typologies:

http: //www.groupadpsych.org/pdf%20files/Stalking%20112402.pdf

Lorrain Sheridan, a researcher at the University of Leicester in the United Kingdom has proposed a new typology of stalkers that includes the category of the sadistic stalker. Brief details of this work can be found at:

http://www.le.ac.uk/press/ebulletin/archive/speaker_sheridan.html

Davis, Ace, and Andra (2000) discuss stalking in the context of relationship breakups. The complete article can be downloaded in Adobe Acrobat format from:

http://www.cla.sc.edu/PSYC/faculty/daviske/stalk11davisace.pdf

This article from the National Violence Against Women Prevention Research Center provides a brief discussion of stalking as a form of abuse. This is an important issue given that research has shown a link between domestic violence and stalking:

http://www.vawprevention.org/research/defining.shtml

The Lancet is a highly respected journal that publishes cutting-edge medical research. The web site's eResearch Archive provides access to several stalking-related articles when the search term *stalking* is used. Note that you are required to register with the site before you can access articles; however, registration is free. Two articles are of particular interest. "Association between Violence, Psychosis, and Relationship to Victim in Stalkers" is a brief article that looks at stalking and mental illness, and "Intimate Partner Violence: Causes and Prevention" looks at stalking in the context of domestic violence:

http://www.thelancet.com

Although it repeats some of the information given in this chapter, some people may find it helpful to read "Anatomy of a Stalker" from *Police Magazine* (May 2000):

http://www.polfed.org/magazine/05_2000/05_2000_stalker.htm

Chapter 5: Who Are the Victims of Cyberstalkers?

Cyber-Stalking.net provides a brief but informative discussion of the harm suffered by stalking and cyberstalking victims:

http://www.cyber-stalking.net/victimimpact.htm

The Australian Institute of Criminology has a number of academic papers on stalking available to download from its web site. One of the papers available is titled "Stalking and the Infliction of Mental Harm" and deals with how legislation sees the harm caused by stalking:

http://www.aic.gov.au/conferences/stalking/Wiener.html

The National Violence Against Women Survey has been referred to a number of times in this chapter and the previous one. The official report is titled *Full Report of the Prevalence, Incidence, and Consequences of Violence Against Women* and can be downloaded free of charge. Although the report is mainly concerned with domestic violence, stalking is also considered in some detail:

http://www.ncjrs.org/pdffiles1/nij/183781.pdf

Chapter 6: What Motivates Cyberstalkers?

This link leads to an interesting essay by Catherine Waerner that discusses sexual harassment on the Internet. The material explains how harassment may be motivated by a desire for attention and includes a discussion of how to deal with it:

> http://www.uow.edu.au/arts/sts/bmartin/dissent/documents/
> Waerner1.html

NetSafe, an Internet safety organization, has published a paper titled "Disinhibition on the Internet: Implications and Intervention" on its site. The paper can be accessed from this address:

> http://www.netsafe.org.nz/resources/resources_disinhibition.asp

This article by Yaara Di Segni Garbasz offers an account of how and why people display aggression when using the Internet:

> http://www.personal.u-net.com/~yandy/papers/PSA.html

The entire content of Howard Rheingold's book *The Virtual Community* is available to read online. Chapter 5 is devoted to a discussion of online identity:

> http://www.rheingold.com/vc/book

Chapter 7: Threats to Young People

A fascinating personal account of an adult camgirl is provided in the dissertation of Theresa Senft, a doctoral student in the Department of Performance Studies at New York University. At the time of writing, the index page was not available, but individual chapters can be accessed directly by substituting the number of the chapter in the address below (e.g., 1.pdf, 2.pdf, etc.):

> http://www.echonyc.com/~janedoe/diss/1.pdf

Donna Hughes has published a great deal of work about the Internet and the sexual exploitation of women and children. A number of articles are available from her web site:

> http://www.uri.edu/artsci/wms/hughes/hughes.htm

AntiChildPorn.org is a nonprofit organization that campaigns against child pornography. The organization's web site contains a great deal of information for parents and young people, including fact sheets, activities, posters, and links to other resources:

> http://www.antichildporn.org

The Office for Victims of Crime at the U.S. Department of Justice published a bulletin in 2001 dealing with Internet crimes against young people. The bulletin can be read online (http://www.ojp.usdoj.gov/ovc/publications/

bulletins/internet_2_2001/) or can be downloaded as an Adobe Acrobat file from:

> http://www.ojp.usdoj.gov/ovc/publications/bulletins/
> internet_2_2001/NCJ184931.pdf

This article from ABC News describes some of the harm caused to young people by pornography:

> http://abcnews.go.com/sections/us/DailyNews/
> internetporn_kids020626.html

Although fairly brief, this article from Child and Family Canada outlines how pedophiles select and victimize young people. The article also lists some of the signs that may indicate a child has come into contact with an online predator:

> http://www.cfc-efc.ca/docs/mnet/00001239.htm

Answers Investigation has made available a complete transcript of real chatroom conversations between an online predator and an investigator posing as a teenage girl. The investigation was done for a BBC news report in late 2002. Although some people may find the content of the transcript disturbing, it provides a fascinating insight into how pedophiles and others use the Internet to select and groom victims:

> http://www.answers.uk.com/services/chatscript.htm

Chapter 8: Cyberstalking and Organizations

The full text of a RAND publication entitled *Networks and Netwars: The Future of Terror, Crime, and Militancy* can be downloaded in Adobe Acrobat format. This is a comprehensive text that looks at how the Internet has been used for political protest. There are three chapters that deal with well-known hacktivism cases, including the World Trade Organization "virtual sit-in":

> http://www.rand.org/publications/MR/MR1382/

The Chilling Effects Clearinghouse is a joint project of the Electronic Frontier Foundation and Harvard, Stanford, Berkeley, University of San Francisco, and University of Maine law school clinics. The organization's aim is to provide Internet users with information and advice about their online rights. On the Chilling Effects web site, the organization is described as follows: "Chilling Effects aims to help you understand the protections that the First Amendment and intellectual property laws give to your online activities. . . . The website offers background material and explanations of the law for people whose websites deal with topics such as fan fiction, copyright, domain names and trademarks, anonymous speech and defamation." The web site address is:

> http://www.chillingeffects.org

A good introduction to hacktivism is provided in an article titled "Hacktivists of the World, Divide" by Kirsten Weisenburger of SecurityWatch.com. The article provides a great deal of background information and offers many links to additional sources:

http://www.securitywatch.com/TRE/042301.html

The Hacktivist is an online resource that provides news, articles, and links related to hacktivism. The site describes itself as follows: "The Hacktivist is dedicated to examining the theory and practice of hacktivism and electronic civil disobedience while contributing to the evolution of hacktivism by promoting constructive debate, effective direct action, and creative solutions to complex problems in order to facilitate positive change." The web site address is:

http://thehacktivist.com/index.php

Chapter 9: Cyberstalking and the Law

Information on U.S. legislation dealing specifically with cyberstalking can be found at the WiredPatrol web site:

http://www.wiredpatrol.org/stalking/us-states/us_stalkinglaw.html

The World Wide Legal Information Association operates a web site that provides information about legislation in the United States, Canada, the United Kingdom, New Zealand, and Australia. Information on Canadian stalking legislation can be found at:

http://www.wwlia.org/ca-stalk.htm

The Canadian Journal of Psychiatry published a two-part article by Karen Abrams and Gail Robinson. The first part provides an overview of stalking and the harm that it can cause. The second part looks at the victims' difficulties with the legal system. Both parts can be found at:

http://www.cpa-apc.org/Publications/Archives/CJP/1998/June/abrams.htm

http://www.cpa-apc.org/Publications/Archives/CJP/1998/June/abrams-2.htm

The National Center for Victims of Crime maintains a comprehensive web site that provides detailed information on federal laws, state-by-state legislation, case law, and other material:

http://www.ncvc.org/src/legislation/state/index.html

A paper by Shonah Jefferson and Richard Shafritz provides a survey of cyberstalking legislation. However, the material may be a little dated as the paper was published in 2000:

http://gsulaw.gsu.edu/lawand/papers/fa00/jefferson_shafritz

Chapter 10: Dealing with Cyberstalking

The GuardianAngel.com web site (not related to Curtis Sliwa, the Guardian Angels, or Cyberangels.org) offers a number of articles dealing with Internet safety and also provides links to a variety of other resources:

http://www.theguardianangel.com/internet_safety_articles.htm

An extremely detailed tutorial describing the history of computer viruses, how they are transmitted, and how to deal with them is available from Computer Knowledge:

http://www.cknow.com/vtutor/vtintro.htm

Trend Micro's online virus scanning service, HouseCall, is available free of charge from:

http://housecall.trendmicro.com

The SysAdmin, Audit, Network, Security (SANS) Institute is a leading organization in the area of in information security research, certification, and education. The SANS web site features a reading room that provides access to over 1,300 articles on information security. Although much of the information provided is geared toward technical and business users, it should be possible to locate easily any information needed.

http://www.sans.org

WiredKids.org provides a wide range of information related to Internet safety for parents and their children:

http://wiredkids.org/parents

The Digital Freedom Network has published a two-part tutorial that explains how to trace the origin of an e-mail message. The tutorial is available at:

http://www.dfn.org/focus/internet/trace-email.htm

Notes

CHAPTER 1: WHAT IS CYBERSTALKING?

1. Jayne Hitchcock's experiences are documented on her own web site at http://www.jahitchcock.com.

2. Flaming usually occurs in response to what are seen as rude, foolish, or insensitive comments made in a newsgroup or chat room. Typically, a person who makes such comments receives abusive or insulting messages (called "flames") from other users. As Jayne Hitchcock's story shows, it is relatively easy to cause an innocent person to be flamed.

3. For instance, according to Conry-Murray (2002), two well-known viruses, Code Red and Nimda, were responsible for losses valued at a staggering $13.2 billion in 2001.

4. This is an important report since it outlines the official U.S. position on cyberstalking. Interested readers should consider downloading the report and reading it in full. The report can be accessed from various sites, including http://www.harassment-law.co.uk/book/cyberep.htm.

5. See, for example, Blaauw et al. (2002, p. 51), who state: "Despite controversy over the precise boundaries of stalking behaviors, there is consensus that such behaviors can include loitering nearby, following, harassment by telephone or mail, ordering goods on the victim's behalf, making threats, physical and sexual assaults, and even murder attempts or actual murder."

6. The Johns Hopkins University web site contains information for students regarding issues such as stalking and cyberstalking: http://www.jhu.edu/news_info/report/violence/relationships/stalk.html.

7. Instant messaging allows two or more people to take part in a conversation simultaneously. A more detailed explanation of instant messaging is given in both chapter 7 and the glossary.

8. Real-time monitoring is the process of monitoring people or computer systems "live," that is, watching events as they actually happen.

9. The Dating Detectives web site is located at http://www.dating-detectives.net/harastalk/cyberstalkers.html.

10. See the *Cambridge International Dictionary*, available via the Internet at http://dictionary.cambridge.org.

11. A good example concerns a group known as the United Phone Losers, who published an article in 2000 describing how to use various web-based services to automate the process of making crank telephone calls. The article states: "You can go about your daily life doing more important and productive things while your victim's phone rings forever. And I mean forever. You need only spend minutes a day (if even that) keeping the process going and it'll last for months, even years."

12. CyberAngels is arguably the largest and best-known Internet safety organization and claims to be the oldest Internet safety organization in the world: http://www.cyberangels.org/stalking/index.html.

13. This material appeared on the CyberAngels web site in December 2000, just before the site underwent a significant redesign. Fortunately, much of the material discussed here can still be found on the site or elsewhere on the Internet. For instance, most of the cyberstalking definition used by Cyber-Angels can also be found on the Wired Patrol web site at http://uk.wiredpatrol.org/stalking/definition.html.

14. See also the following reference for a brief discussion of the material offered by CyberAngels: B. H. Spitzberg and G. Hoobler. 2002. Cyberstalking and the technologies of interpersonal terrorism. *New Media & Society*, 14 (1), 71–92.

15. The case of Patrick Naughton is described in the following articles: http://abcnews.go.com/sections/business/DailyNews/naughton990918.html and http://abcnews.go.com/sections/tech/DailyNews/naughton000317.html.

16. Two incidents in which cyberstalkers accused their victims of harassing them are described in the cases dealing with David Cruz (chapter 4) and Pamela Gilbert (chapter 10).

17. For example, see Bocij and McFarlane, 2002; Bocij, Bocij, and McFarlane, 2003; Bocij, 2002; Bocij, Griffiths, and McFarlane, 2002.

18. An anonymous remailer can be used to make it difficult—if not impossible—to trace the sender of an e-mail message. Anonymous remailers are discussed in more detail in later chapters and are also described in the glossary.

19. IRC is a form of instant messaging, providing a forum for people to hold conversations in real time. IRC and instant messaging are discussed in more detail in later chapters and are also described in the glossary.

20. Cynthia Armistead's experiences are documented on her own web site at http://www.technomom.com/harassed.

CHAPTER 2: STALKING OR *CYBER*STALKING?

1. For a detailed account of Robinson's case, see J. Glatt, *Internet slavemaster*. 2001 (New York: St. Martin's Press).

2. See the Hoaxbusters web page at http://hoaxbusters.ciac.org.

3. See, for instance, Burgess and Baker (2002), who state, "Cyberstalking may be viewed . . . as a regular stalking behaviour using new, high-technology tools."

4. Low-cost airfares of this kind are easily found using a search engine such as Google.

5. Boyer's parents maintain a web site dedicated to the memory of their daughter at http://www.amyboyer.org.

6. A reproduction of the web site created by Liam Youens can be viewed at http://www.amyboyer.org/liamsite.htm. Some people may find the content of the site disturbing.

CHAPTER 3: THE INCIDENCE AND PREVALENCE OF CYBERSTALKING

1. The results of the survey have been published by the National Institute of Justice under the title *Stalking and Domestic Violence: The Third Annual Report to Congress under the Violence Against Women Act*. This report can be downloaded in Adobe Acrobat format from http://www.ojp.usdoj.gov/vawo/grants/stalk98/welcome.html.

2. Canada's population was estimated at 31,485,623 in October 2002 (Statistics Canada, http://www.statcan.ca/start.html, 14 February 2003).

3. The NUA Internet Surveys web site has a page entitled "How Many Online?" that provides figures for the number of people online in different countries. Since the page draws on many different sources, it is considered relatively accurate. The page can be found at http://www.nua.com/surveys/how_many_online/index.html.

4. NUA's figures are drawn from their own estimates and figures provided by Nielsen//NetRatings for April 2002.

5. This figure has been reported on the WHOA web site as part of the Online Harassment Statistics the organization publishes each year.

6. Available at http://www.intergov.org/public_information/general_information/latest_web_stats.html.

CHAPTER 4: WHO ARE THE CYBERSTALKERS?

1. An additional analysis of the records of stalkers referred to clinics in New York is given in B. Rosenfeld and R. Harmon. 2002. Factors associated with violence in stalking and obsessional harassment cases. *Criminal Justice and Behavior*, 29 (6), 671–91.

2. See the previous section on classifications of stalking for a brief explanation of Harmon, Rosner, and Owens's (1995) typology of stalkers.

3. Although it may be uncommon to come across senior offline stalkers, it is not so unusual to learn of senior cyberstalkers. For instance, in 2001, news sources reported on the case of New Zealand writer Rhonda Bartle, who was cyberstalked by Peggy Phillips, an eighty-four-year-old California publicist (Carter and Nzpa, 2001).

CHAPTER 5: WHO ARE THE VICTIMS OF CYBERSTALKERS?

1. WHOA's online harassment statistics are published at http://www.haltabuse.org/resources/stats/index.shtml.

2. At the time of this writing, WHOA's figures did not provide averages for the period 2000 to 2002. It is also worth noting that the figures for 2002 were not substantially different from those for other years.

3. WHOA has speculated that these values may be skewed because the organization is based in the United States, and its web site is only available in English.

4. The "flaming monitor virus" and many other urban myths regarding computer viruses are described in detail at Vmyths.com (http://vmyths.com). Although it is theoretically possible to construct a computer program capable of causing physical damage to computer equipment, the author is unaware of any evidence suggesting that any such program has ever been produced and disseminated.

5. It is possible to compare some of the figures given here with those obtained from some additional research carried out by Purcell, Pathé, and Mullen. In general, the findings of this additional study support the findings reported in Purcell, Pathé, and Mullen. 2000. The incidence and nature of stalking victimisation. *Stalking: Criminal Justice Responses Conference*, 7–8 December 2000 (Sydney: Australian Institute of Criminology).

CHAPTER 6: WHAT MOTIVATES CYBERSTALKERS?

1. NUA Internet Surveys publishes estimates of the number of people online worldwide on its web site at http://www.nua.com/surveys/how_many_online/index.html.

2. See NUA Internet Surveys (http://www.nua.com/surveys/how_many_online/index.html) for data on worldwide Internet use.

3. Not all hacking is illegal or motivated by criminal intent. However, the popular image of the hacker is of someone who uses his or her skills in order to commit various crimes, ranging from stealing government secrets to damaging the computer systems of large companies.

4. A full description of the workings of anonymous e-mail is beyond the scope of this book. However, some simple explanations can be found at http://www.loompanics.com/cgi-local/SoftCart.exe/Articles/AnonymousEmail.html?E+scstore and http://www.andrebacard.com/remail.html.

5. QuickSilver is produced by Benchmark Software (http://quicksilver.skuz.net).

6. The process of "chaining" involves sending a message through a series of different anonymous e-mail servers. Each server that a message passes through adds an additional layer of security, making it harder to identify the real source of the e-mail. For all practical purposes, it becomes impossible to identify the real source of a message once it has passed through four or more servers.

7. BestCrypt is produced by Jetico, Inc. (http://www.jetico.com).

8. Evidence Eliminator is produced by Robin Hood Software Ltd. (http://www.evidence-eliminator.com).

9. Definition from YourDictionary.com (http://www.yourdictionary.com).

10. A good definition of *deindividuation* can be found via the online glossary provided by the AlleyDog psychology web site at http://www.alleydog.com/glossary/psychology-glossary.cfm.

11. The Stanford Prison Experiment is described in detail at a dedicated web site belonging to Philip Zimbardo at http://www.prisonexp.org.

12. A study by Alexa Research in 2001 found that "sex" was the most popular search term entered into ten of the most popular search engines, including Yahoo!, Google, AltaVista, and MSN (Pastore, 2001). Of the twenty most popular search terms, five were related to sex or pornography.

13. A succinct explanation of cognitive dissonance, together with suggestions for further reading, can be found online at http://tip.psychology.org/festinge.html.

14. The difficulties involved in dealing with criminal activities perpetrated via the Internet have been dealt with by many writers and are not discussed again here. Those interested in an introduction to cybercrime that deals with many of these issues might find the following texts useful: D. Thomas and B. Loader, eds. 2000. *Cybercrime: Law enforcement, security and surveillance in the information age* (London: Routledge) and S. Furnell. 2002. *Cybercrime: Vandalizing the information society* (London: Addison Wesley).

15. It is considered inappropriate to give the name of this discussion group since this would make it easier to locate. However, the group described is publicly accessible and is wholly dedicated to cyberstalking.

CHAPTER 7: THREATS TO YOUNG PEOPLE

1. For the purposes of this chapter, a young person is defined as a person under eighteen years of age.

2. The term *child pornography* is used to describe any material (pictures, audio, video, etc.) depicting a young person engaged in sexually explicit conduct. In general, this term is used in the same way as defined by legislation, such as U.S. Code 18, Section 2256.

3. It is recognized that some people prefer other terms to describe those who sexually abuse children. Lanning (1992), for example, prefers to use the term *child molester*. However, the word *pedophile* is used within this chapter as it is felt that readers will be more familiar with it.

4. The full report, entitled *Young Canadians in a Wired World*, can be found at http://www.media-awareness.ca/english/special_initiatives/surveys/students_survey.cfm.

5. The Australian Bureau of Statistics web site is located at http://www.abs.gov.au.

6. National School Boards Foundation, 2002. The full report of the survey can be accessed online at http://www.nsbf.org/safe-smart/full-report.htm.

7. The NCPCF web site is located at http://www.nationalcoalition.org.

8. PedoWatch maintains a web site at http://www.pedowatch.com.

9. The NAMBLA web site is located at http://www.nambla1.de.

10. A good introductory guide to newsgroups and how they work is available from HowStuffWorks.com (http://computer.howstuffworks.com/newsgroup.htm).

11. The Internet Watch Foundation web site is at http://www.iwf.org.uk.

12. A web site operated by Andreas Gelhausen provides continuously updated statistics on the number of IRC servers, channels, and users. The site is located at http://irc.netsplit.de/networks/ and, as of mid-2003, reported the existence of 587,000 channels.

13. These rules are normally set by the ISP or are agreed on by the members of the group. Copies of the rules are posted to the group at regular intervals so that newcomers can learn how the group works. The set of rules is normally called an FAQ (Frequently Asked Questions) list or, more formally, an acceptable use policy.

14. A detailed explanation of instant messaging can be found at HowStuffWorks.com (http://computer.howstuffworks.com/instant-messaging.htm).

15. A good explanation of how file sharing works is provided by HowStuffWorks.com (http://computer.howstuffworks.com/file-sharing.htm).

16. Information on Freenet can be found at http://freenetproject.org.

17. The web site for Kazaa Media Desktop is located at http://www.kazaa.com.

18. The Filetopia web site is located at http://www.filetopia.org.

19. Blogger is produced by Pyra Labs and is available from http://new.blogger.com.

20. Teen Open Diary is located at http://www.teenopendiary.com and Deardiary.net is located at http://www.deardiary.net.

21. Information about the domain owner can be withheld if the owner specifically requests it.

22. The choice of Anne Frank's diary as a comparison is an interesting one. The diary has recently been cited in the debate about child pornography since the unexpurgated edition contains her thoughts and feelings on sexuality. It has been argued that some of Anne Frank's writings can be seen as pornography, and there have been attempts to ban her diary in some places in the United States.

23. For obvious reasons, examples of the names and locations of such sites have not been provided.

CHAPTER 8: CYBERSTALKING AND ORGANIZATIONS

1. For obvious reasons, the employee's real name has not been used nor has the name of the company been provided.

2. The EFF's formal response to allegations made by the Lyons Partnership with regard to the use of the Barney character can be viewed at http://www.eff.org/Privacy/SLAPP/IP_SLAPP/20010706_eff_ barney_response.html. Additional information regarding the dispute is also available at the site.

3. Virga's account of her experience with the company is contained within her protest site at http://www.syix.com/emu/index.htm.

4. A detailed account of incidents involving alleged harassment perpetrated by supporters of Scientology can be found at http://www.factnet.org/briefing.htm#1.

5. A detailed account of Zeman's allegations about the behavior of GeoCities can be found at http://www.angelfire.com/mo/geocensored.

6. Interestingly, one of the definitions of *distress* given by the online version of the *American Heritage Dictionary* (accessible from http://www.yourdictionary.com) is "to constrain or overcome by harassment."

7. Detailed accounts of GRC's experiences are provided by Barwise (2001) and by Steve Gibson (2002) at the company's web site.

8. A detailed account of Jonathan Lebed's case, including interviews with Lebed and his parents, is provided in a *New York Times Magazine* article by Michael Lewis, available online at http://www.williamgaddis.org/jr/jlebedbyalewis2-25-2001.shtml.

9. The full story of Zeigletics can be read at The Motley Fool web site: http://www.fool.com/School/Zeigletics/Zintro.htm.

10. Electrohippies maintain a web site at http://www.fraw.org.uk.

11. The page was originally distributed via http://www.fraw.org.uk/ehippies/iraq/iraq_distro.html. However, shortly after the end of the conflict, it seemed to have been removed from the web site.

12. In order to make the material clearer, the addresses of the pages mentioned have been removed.

13. The Electrohippies have made the tools they use available on their web site. Brief descriptions of how each program works—together with information on how they can be adapted for other protests—can be found at http://www.fraw.org.uk/ehippies/tools.shtml.

14. The cDc's arguments are summarized in a document available via the Electrophippie's web site at http://www.fraw.org.uk/ehippies/papers/op1a.html.

15. Article 19 of the Universal Declaration of Human Rights states: "Everyone has the right to freedom of opinion and expression; this right includes freedom to hold opinions without interference and to seek, receive

and impart information and ideas through any media and regardless of frontiers." A summary of the Universal Declaration of Human Rights can viewed at the United Nations web site (http://www.un.org/Overview/rights.html).

16. Many organizations plan how services can be restored as quickly as possible following a major interruption, such as an equipment breakdown, labor dispute, or natural disaster (such as a fire). This kind of planning is normally known as business continuity planning but is occasionally called disaster recovery planning.

17. A detailed account of Mishkoff's case, including copies of legal documents and correspondence, can be found at one of the protest sites he created: http://www.taubmansucks.com/condensed.html.

18. Mishkoff's web site is located at http://www.taubmansucks.com.

19. The Open Source Initiative's web site is located at http://www.opensource.org.

CHAPTER 9: CYBERSTALKING AND THE LAW

1. The names of those involved have been changed.

2. This case is described in detail by Valenzi (2002).

3. Details on stalking-related legislation throughout the United States can be viewed via the National Conference of State Legislatures at http://www.ncsl.org/programs/lis/cip/stalk99.htm.

4. The full text of the Malicious Communications Act (1988) can be accessed at the official Her Majesty's Stationery Office (HMSO) web site: http://www.hmso.gov.uk/acts/acts1988/Ukpga_19880027_en_1.htm.

5. The full text of the Protection from Harassment Act (1997) can be accessed at the official HMSO web site: http://www.hmso.gov.uk/acts/acts1997/1997040.htm.

6. Details on U.S. and Canadian legislation can be found at the WiredPatrol web site: http://www.wiredpatrol.org/cyberstalking_harassment/canada/ca_stalkinglaw.html.

7. The Ontario Women's Justice Network maintains a web site at http://www.owjn.org.

CHAPTER 10: DEALING WITH CYBERSTALKING

1. A listserv is a kind of newsletter sent by e-mail.

2. Finger is a small program that can be used to return information about an e-mail address. Some finger programs report only if a user is currently logged on, but others can provide more detailed information, such as the user's address and telephone number.

3. The DejaNews service was the forerunner of Google Groups. This service provides a sophisticated search tool allowing users to search Usenet discussion groups. The service can be accessed via http://groups.google.com.

4. NetDetective is a software application that can be used to gather information on a given individual. The program is produced by the Harris Digital Publishing Group and is available via http://www.netdetective2001.com.

5. AnyWho is a service of AT&T and can be accessed via http://www.anywho.com.

6. See Netlingo for a definition of *lurker*: http://www.netlingo.com/lookup.cfm?term=lurker.

7. See Webopedia for a definition of *troll*: http://networking.webopedia.com/TERM/T/troll.html.

8. An online guide to netiquette can be found at http://www.albion.com/netiquette. This web site contains the complete text of a book on netiquette written by Virgina Shea.

9. Numerous free anonymous e-mail services are available, each offering different facilities and levels of security. For instance, the Riot anonymous remailer allows messages to be sent by completing a simple on-screen form and can be accessed via https://riot.eu.org/anon/remailer.html.en. Anonymous.To is an advertising-supported service that allows users to create an anonymous e-mail account from which they can both send and receive messages. The service can be accessed at http://anonymous.to.

10. You can place "X-No-archive: yes" (without quotation marks) as the first line of your message to instruct Google not to archive the message.

11. More information on removing newsgroup posts from Google Groups can be found in the help file available at http://www.google.com/googlegroups/help.html.

12. See http://www.fdle.state.fl.us/Fc3/cyberstalking.htm.

13. Some simple guides to e-mail etiquette can be found at http://www.emailreplies.com and http://www.iwillfollow.com/email.htm.

14. Thawte's web site is located at http://www.thawte.com.

15. Various versions of PGP are available. An international version can be downloaded from http://www.pgpi.org. A-Lock is produced by PC-Encrypt, Inc. A free version of the program can be downloaded via http://www.pc-encrypt.com/_site/alock/index.mhtml. Crypto Kong provides a simplified way of using digital signatures and encryption. The program can be used free of charge and is available via http://www.echeque.com/Kong/Kong.htm. Cryptext integrates with Windows Explorer, adding the ability to encrypt or decrypt files by right-clicking on them. The program can be used free of charge and is available from http://www.pcug.org.au/~njpayne.

16. Detailed information on computer viruses and how they work can be found online at http://computer.howstuffworks.com/virus.htm. Alternatively, a more business-oriented discussion is provided in chapter 15 of Bocij et al. 2002. *Business information systems: Technology, development and management for the e-business,* 2nd ed. (London: Financial Times and Prentice-Hall).

17. A good description of Trojan horse programs can be accessed via IRCHelp.org at http://www.irchelp.org/irchelp/security/trojan.html.

18. AVG is available from Grisoft, Inc., and can be downloaded from http://www.grisoft.com. AntiVir is available from H+BEDV and can be downloaded from http://www.free-av.com/index.htm.

19. Trend Micro's HouseCall service can be accessed via http://housecall.trendmicro.com. A range of tools, including an online virus scanner, is available from Symantec's main web page under the heading of Symantec Security Check (http://www.symantec.com).

20. A good example of a free backup program is My Own Backup. This program, together with a selection of other popular backup programs, can be downloaded from http://www.freestuffer.com/software/backup.html.

21. MooSoft Development produces The Cleaner, which can be downloaded via http://www.moosoft.com.

22. The IP address is a unique number that identifies the location of a specific computer.

23. Surveillance software is sometimes called spyware. However, spyware is also used to describe commercial programs that return information to a company without the user's knowledge. For instance, a free MP3 player might send usage statistics back to the developer's web site without the user's knowledge or permission.

24. Workplace surveillance is discussed in more detail at http://computer.howstuffworks.com/workplace-surveillance.htm. The discussion deals with a variety of topics, including privacy laws.

25. Full instructions on disabling file and print sharing for Windows 95, 98, ME, NT, 2000, and XP can be found at the AttackDenied.com web site: http://www.attackdenied.com/disable_file_sharing.htm.

26. The Shields Up! service can be accessed via GRC's web site at http://grc.com/default.htm. The Hack Yourself service can be accessed via HackerWhacker.com at http://www.hackerwhacker.com.

27. A personal version of Zone Alarm is available free of charge from the Zone Labs web site at http://www.zonelabs.com.

28. The FBI publishes *A Parent's Guide to Internet Safety*, available at http://www.fbi.gov/publications/pguide/pguidee.htm.

29. The entire book is available online at http://www.boran.com/security.

30. See the CyberAngels web site at http://www.cyberangels.com/stalking/response.html.

31. See the WiredPatrol web site at http://www.wiredpatrol.org/cyberstalking_harassment/stalking_self_help/break_contact.html.

32. WinGrab is available from http://home.no.net/wingrab/index.html and Screen Grab Pro is available from http://www.traction-software.co.uk/screengrabpro/index.html.

33. In general, the pages that can be difficult to save are those that are generated dynamically, use scripting (that is, contain program code), contain applets or ActiveX controls, or are protected in some way.

34. HTTrack is an open source program and is available via http://www.httrack.com. WebStripper is advertising-supported and is available via

http://webstripper.net. WebReaper can be used free of charge for noncommercial use and is available via http://www.webreaper.net.

35. A good introductory guide to interpreting e-mail headers can be found at http://www.stopspam.org/email/headers/headers.html.

36. The AllWhoIs service can be accessed via http://www.allwhois.com.

37. The services offered by Sam Spade can be accessed via http://www.samspade.org.

Glossary

Acceptable use policy (AUP). A formal document that sets out rules describing how a computer system or a service may be used. The AUP also defines what behaviors are not allowed and the penalties that may be imposed if the rules are broken. Many organizations have AUPs, including Internet Service Providers, schools, colleges, large companies, and government departments. In many organizations, the AUP forms part of a formal security policy. See **formal security policy.**

Anonymous e-mail. All e-mail messages contain information that identifies where the message originated. There are a number of ways in which this information can be removed from a message so that the sender cannot be identified (or located). Messages that have had this identifying information removed are called anonymous e-mail. See **header.**

Anonymous remailer. All e-mail messages contain information that identifies the sender and the Internet Service Provider used to relay the message. Anonymous remailers strip away this information before sending the message on to its destination, effectively obscuring the identity of the sender.

AUP. See **acceptable use policy.**

Bashing. See **cyber-smearing.**

Blog. A short form of web log. This term has become popular because of a software package called Blogger that helps people to publish their web logs more easily. See **web log.**

Bot. Short for robot. Bots are automated programs that can be used for a variety of purposes, from carrying out searches on the Internet to sending out advertising messages by e-mail. Bots are often used to carry out distributed denial of service attacks, which flood a company's web or e-mail service with so much fake traffic that they become overloaded. See **denial of service.**

Buddy list. See **contact list.**

Business continuity planning. There are many problems that an organization may face, ranging from labor disputes and natural disasters to cash flow problems and hacking. Each of these can affect the organization's operations and may result in significant losses. Business continuity planning involves trying to predict the problems that may affect the organization and then planning how best to overcome these difficulties.

Camgirl (or **camboy**). Many young people publish their diaries online. These web sites are often quite sophisticated, featuring online polls, guest books, and live video feeds. The teenagers who create sites containing video are usually known as camgirls or camboys. See **webcam.**

Censorware. A category of software used to control Internet access by preventing entry to inappropriate web sites. Typically, a censorware program intercepts requests for web pages from a web browser and then checks an internal database of banned web sites to see if the web site is listed. If the site is listed in the database, access is prevented and an error message is displayed. Many programs also examine the content of any web pages requested before allowing the browser to display them. If the web page contains any banned words or phrases, the page is not shown.

Chaining. In order to make it harder to trace the source of an anonymous e-mail message, it can be sent through a series of different anonymous remailers before reaching its destination. The more servers the message passes through, the harder it becomes to find the origin of the message. See **anonymous remailer.**

Chat room. A web site or part of a web site where people can hold conversations in real time. In most chat rooms, users communicate with each other by typing messages. However, some chat rooms allow users to speak to each other (using microphones attached to the sound cards in their computers), and some allow video conferencing (using webcams). There are thousands of chat rooms available, catering to all users and all interests. Many chat rooms are supervised by moderators who make sure that users follow rules governing acceptable behavior. See **video conferencing,** and **webcam.**

Computer virus. A small computer program that copies itself from one computer to another. A single computer maybe capable of "infecting" many others within a very short time. Many viruses are programmed to carry out various actions, such as deleting data, once a set of specific conditions is met. All computer viruses should be considered destructive.

Contact list. Sometimes called a buddy list, this can be thought of as a personal e-mail directory that holds the e-mail addresses of friends and relatives.

Corporate cyberstalking. This involves an organization as either the victim or the perpetrator of cyberstalking. The motivations behind corporate cyberstalking can be very different from those behind offline stalking and "normal" cyberstalking and may involve fraud, cyberterrorism, and anticompetitive behavior.

Cyber-smearing. Sometimes called "bashing," this damages a company's reputation by posting false information to the Internet. Cyber-smearing may also be used to harm the reputation of an individual by sending rumors and false information to the victim's friends, relatives, or colleagues.

Cyber-squatting. Registering a domain name that might be sought after by a large company and then offering to transfer ownership to the company for a fee. In the United States and many other countries, cyber-squatting is illegal. In countries where cyber-squatting is not illegal, there are likely to be arbitration and mediation services that can deal with disputes, such as the World Intellectual Property Organization. See **domain name.**

Cyberterrorism. The use of Internet to further political or ideological goals, usually through attacking web sites and computer systems belonging to governments and large organizations. Most cyberterrorism is restricted to activities such as hacking, web site defacements, denial of service attacks, and the dissemination of computer viruses. See **denial of service,** and **web site defacement.**

Data theft. Any attempt to gain access to confidential data. Often, data theft is done with the intention of destroying the data once it has been copied so that the legitimate owner cannot access it.

Denial of service (DoS). A denial of service attack tries to disrupt a network system, usually by creating massive amounts of traffic. A typical DoS attack floods an organization's e-mail servers with millions of e-mail messages or overloads a web page server with millions of requests for pages. The victims of DoS attacks are usually large companies, Internet Service Providers, and government agencies. However, a DoS attack also may be used to force an Internet Service Provider into closing an individual's account by constantly attacking that account. A distributed denial of service attack uses other computers on the Internet to generate fake Internet traffic that is directed toward a specific company. These computers are often used without the knowledge or consent of their owners, having been compromised by specialized programs that can generate e-mail or web traffic when activated by the attacker. These programs, often called bots or zombies, can be placed on computers many weeks or months before they are needed. See **bot** and **zombie.**

Digital divide. Just as there is a division between the rich and the poor, many people feel that there is a division between those who have access to computer technology and those who do not. This division means that some people are disadvantaged because they do not have access to news, information services, educational resources, and so on. It can also be argued that there is a digital divide between countries as well as within them. Some poorer countries, for example, have only a few thousand Internet users, whereas others have many millions.

Digital signature. See **personal e-mail certificate.**

Domain name. Web sites need to be identified by a unique name. The domain name usually identifies the owner of the web site. For instance, a domain name such as greenwood.com indicates that the web site belongs to Greenwood Publishing Group.

DoS. See **denial of service.**

E-mail bombing. A type of denial of service attack that attempts to interrupt a specific e-mail account by sending a large number of messages to it. In many cases, the messages are made up of meaningless data and may contain large file attachments. By bombarding the account with what may amount to millions of messages, it is effectively made unusable. See **denial of service.**

E-mail filter. Filters mark e-mail messages for special attention. In general, a filter checks for a series of conditions, such as if the message contains certain words or if it comes from a specific e-mail address. Any messages matching the filter conditions can be dealt with in different ways; for example, they can be deleted or automatically moved to a different place.

Encryption. Encodes the contents of a message or data file using a password or passphrase. An encrypted message appears as gibberish and is completely meaningless until it is decrypted (decoded) by someone with the correct password.

FAQs. See **frequently asked questions.**

File attachment. E-mail messages can be accompanied by data files, such as word-processing documents, databases, or spreadsheet files. Any data file attached to an e-mail message is usually called a file attachment.

File encryption. The process of encrypting one or more files using a password or passphrase. See **encryption.**

File shredder. When a file is deleted from a disk drive, the data it contains is not erased until a new file overwrites it. This means that it is often possible to recover the contents of a file even months after it has been deleted. File shredders overwrite a deleted file with randomly generated data, ensuring that the content of the file cannot be recovered.

Finger. A small program that can be used to return information about an e-mail address. Some finger programs report only if a user is currently logged on. Depending on the data stored on the computer—which must be entered by the user—some finger programs can provide more detailed information, such as the user's address and telephone number.

Firewall. Monitors and controls all traffic entering or leaving a network. If any unauthorized traffic is detected, it is automatically stopped and an alert is issued. Personal firewalls monitor Internet traffic entering or leaving a personal computer. Again, unauthorized traffic is stopped automatically and the user is alerted. In addition to monitoring traffic, some firewalls also provide "stealth" functions that effectively make the computer invisible to the tools used by hackers.

Flame war. When a person receives abusive or insulting messages in a chat room or newsgroup, it is called being flamed. Typically, a person is flamed when he or she makes a rude, insensitive, or foolish comment in a newsgroup. When the person being flamed retaliates, it is usually called a flame war.

Formal security policy. A document that describes an organization's security arrangements. The document tends to be very detailed and contains the procedures for dealing with a broad range of issues, from monitoring network activity to making backups of data.

Forums. See **message board.**

Freeware. Software that can be obtained and used free of charge.

Frequently asked questions (FAQs). A document that aims to anticipate and respond to the questions most likely to be asked by new users. In a newsgroup, for instance, the FAQ will set out basic information, such as the purpose of the newsgroup, how posts should be formatted, the rules governing behavior, and any other background information that might be needed to use the newsgroup correctly. FAQs usually follow a question-answer format and are provided as downloadable text documents.

Guest book. Many web sites allow visitors to post comments and greetings in a guest book that can be viewed by other visitors and the web site's owner.

Hacking. Traditionally, hackers were people who were able to cobble together complex computer programs very quickly and easily. Nowadays, hackers are commonly thought of as computer criminals—people who break into computer systems or cause all kinds of other damage. However, not all hackers are criminals and not all hacking is illegal.

Hacktivism. Politically motivated hacking. Some people believe that hacktivism is a genuine and useful means of expressing political views. Others, however, claim that hacktivists are little more than computer terrorists.

Header. A line of text that appears at the beginning of an e-mail message. A typical message will contain a number of headers that store information such as the name of the sender, the address to reply to, the date and time of the message, details of the route taken by the message, and so on.

History. All web browsers maintain a list of the web sites visited over a period of time.

Hosting. Many companies provide a range of services that allow organizations and individuals to operate a web site. These services can include providing storage space for web pages, e-mail facilities, and technical support. Many companies offer hosting services at very low cost, enabling almost anyone to operate his or her own web site.

ICT. See **information and communications technology.**

Identity theft. Impersonating another person, usually (but not always) with the intention of committing fraud. In cyberstalking cases, identity theft is often used to damage the victim's reputation by posting false information to chat rooms, bulletin boards, and so on.

I-jacking. "Hijacking" a web address so that people intending to visit a specific web site are redirected elsewhere. Typically, i-jacking is used to direct people to web sites devoted to a political protest or a protest against a company.

Information and communications technology (ICT). A collective term used to describe any form of computer technology or any form of technology used for communications, such as fax machines and cellular phones.

Information warfare. Deprives an opponent of important information, usually by destroying equipment or disrupting services. The term has different meanings according to the context. Information warfare can include a wide variety of acts, from deliberately infecting a computer with a virus to making denial of service attacks.

Instant messaging. Allows two or more people to hold a conversation. Conversations are instant because they take place in real time, with none of the delays associated with e-mail. Typically, most users communicate with each other by typing text messages, but some programs also allow them to speak to each other or use video conferencing.

Internet filter. A category of software used to screen out inappropriate Internet content, such as pornography. Packages for home use are intended to protect children from bad language, violence, and other unsuitable materials. Programs suitable for use across company networks are also available. See **censorware** and **parental controls.**

Internet Relay Chat (IRC). IRC is arguably the most popular chat system in use. In order to use IRC, a client program must be installed on the user's computer. There can be many discussions taking place at one time and each is called a channel.

Internet Service Provider (ISP). A company that provides clients with access to the Internet. Customers access e-mail, the World Wide Web, Usenet, and other services via a modem that connects to the ISP's computer systems.

IP address. All domain names can be translated into a number that acts as a unique address for that domain. For instance, www.greenwood.com might translate to 65.202.179.238. A web browser can accept IP addresses as well as the normal URLs most users are familiar with. See **domain name.**

IRC. See **Internet Relay Chat.**

ISP. See **Internet Service Provider.**

Key logger. A computer program that records every keystroke made on a given computer system. Recording keystrokes allows someone to monitor passwords, outgoing e-mails, documents, and so on.

Listserv. A system of mailing lists that operates via e-mail. There are many different lists, each dealing with a different topic. Users can subscribe to a list so that whenever a message is posted to a mailing list, a copy is automatically sent to them.

Lurking. The act of entering and watching a chat room without taking part in the conversation. Watching newsgroups and message boards without posting any messages is also sometimes described as lurking.

Macro virus. Most major software applications feature built-in programming languages that can be used to customize the software or automate routine tasks. Once a program has been created, it can be stored within a data file so that it can be reused or sent to other users. In addition, a program attached to a data file can be made to run automatically as soon as the file is loaded. Virus writers have taken advantage of this functionality to create new kinds of viruses that can be transmitted within word-processing documents, spreadsheet files, databases, and even e-mails. See **computer virus.**

Mail bombing. See **e-mail bombing.**

Message board. Like a newsgroup, a message board provides a forum for computer users to exchange ideas and discuss common interests. Users are able to read messages posted by other people and can post their own messages in response.

MMS. See **multimedia messaging services.**

Moderator. Many chat rooms, newsgroups, and message boards have rules governing how users should behave. Moderators oversee a chat room, newsgroup, or message board and ensure that users behave appropriately. Moderators usually have the power to delete or edit offensive messages and can ban people from using the service.

Monitor. See **moderator.**

Multimedia messaging services (MMS). Modern cellular phones can send messages containing multimedia data to other users. These messages can include pictures, sound, and even video.

Netiquette. A set of informal rules that describes how a person should behave when using Internet services, such as e-mail and newsgroups. These rules tend to reflect practices that experienced Internet users commonly agree are both responsible and polite.

Newsgroup. The Internet is made up of many different resources, of which the World Wide Web is just one. A newsgroup is a forum where people can read messages posted by others, reply to them, or post their own comments. There are many newsgroups available, and they can accessed via the web or using a special program called a newsreader. The whole system of newsgroups is often referred to as Usenet.

Offline web browser. A program that can be used to copy individual web pages or entire web sites to a computer's hard disk so that the material can be viewed later on. One of the advantages of an offline browser is that it allows users to make a permanent copy of a web site for future reference.

Parental controls. A range of services offered by Internet Service Providers that can be used to protect young people from inappropriate content, such as pornography. Many Internet Service Providers provide tools that allow parents to screen out bad language, violence, and other unsuitable materials. Although parental control software can be helpful, it is not completely effective and should not be relied on as the only way of dealing with unsuitable content. See **censorware.**

Peer to peer (P2P). A way of connecting two computers together so that they can share files. There are many P2P services that allow users to locate specific files stored on other computers. Once the file has been found, a direct connection is made between the user's computer and the computer holding the file. The file can then be copied quickly and easily.

Personal e-mail certificate. Sometimes called a digital signature, a personal e-mail certificate is a security measure that can be used to confirm that an e-mail message originated from a specific person. The certificate is a small, encrypted data file that can be automatically attached to outgoing e-mail messages.

PGP. This stands for Pretty Good Privacy and is the name of a powerful encryption package that can be obtained free of charge. Note that there is also a commercial version of PGP. See **encryption.**

Poll. Many web sites ask visitors to take part in opinion polls by answering short surveys (usually a single question). The results of the poll are automatically recorded and displayed on the web site, usually as a simple graph.

Port scanning. A common method used by hackers to locate computers connected to the Internet. Once a computer has been located, it is checked to see if it is vulnerable in some way. If it is, the hacker may try to access the computer in order to copy files, gather information, and so on. Typically, port scanning done using automated tools that allow thousands of computers to be checked each hour.

P2P. See **peer to peer.**

Pump and dump. A type of stock market fraud that uses financial newsgroups, chat rooms, and message boards to manipulate share prices. Typically, an individual buys a large quantity of shares in one or more companies at a very low price. The share prices are then inflated artificially by posting rumors and other misinformation via the Internet. As soon as prices have increased sufficiently, the shares are sold at a substantial profit.

Real time. The actual time over which events happen. For instance, a person watching an event as it actually happens ("live") would be said to be watching in real time.

Reverse engineering. Re-creating a product or piece of software by examining its functions. The result is a product or software application that produces exactly the same results as the original, even though different methods are used to achieve those results.

Screen capture utility. A small program that can be used to record the contents of the screen at a given moment. This can be thought of as taking a photograph of the screen, except that the picture is saved to the computer's hard disk drive instead of a negative.

Script. A simple type of computer program normally created using Englishlike commands.

Shareware. Often described as being distributed on a "try before you buy" basis. Typically, the software is distributed free of charge and can be used for a set period of time in order to evaluate it. After the trial period, users must either pay for the software or remove it from their computers.

Signature. The name given to a standard block of text that is automatically added to the end of an outgoing e-mail message. Although most signatures contain further contact details, such as a telephone number, they can be used to hold any kind of information.

SLAPP. See **Strategic Lawsuits Against Public Participation.**

Software audit. The process of cataloging all of the software and data stored on a personal computer or a network with the aim of identifying any unauthorized items.

Spam. Normally used to describe unsolicited e-mail, especially messages intended to advertise goods and services that have been sent out indiscriminately. This term is also used to describe advertisements posted to newsgroups that do not normally allow advertising.

Spyware. Normally used to describe a program that returns information to the software developer without the user's knowledge. Although this information is often gathered anonymously and there may be legitimate uses for it, many people are concerned that it is an invasion of privacy. Spyware is sometimes also used to describe surveillance software. See **surveillance software.**

Steganography. A way of hiding information within a message or data file. Typically, a message is encrypted and then hidden within a picture file, such as a JPEG image. Since the picture does not appear to be distorted, the hidden message is unlikely to be detected. Even if the message is found, it will not be possible to read it because it is encrypted.

Strategic Lawsuits Against Public Participation (SLAPP). A frivolous or unwarranted lawsuit that is used by an organization to silence its critics. Most SLAPPs are issued by companies against individuals or small organizations. Usually, the costs associated with defending against a SLAPP are so high that the individual is forced to give in to the organization's demands. Although the United States has enacted anti-SLAPP legislation, few other countries have followed suit.

Style sheet. Contains a set of instructions that describes how a web page should be displayed. The same style sheet can be applied to a group of web pages at the same time, helping them to appear consistent. A change made to the style sheet is reflected within all of the web pages that use it, making it easier to develop and maintain web sites.

Surveillance software. Describes a category of software that can be used to observe and record activity on one or more computer systems. The programs available vary in complexity and sophistication. Surveillance software is sometimes called spyware.

Trojan horse. This term comes from the mythological Trojan horse used to gain entry into the city of Troy. A Trojan horse is a program hackers and others use to infiltrate a computer system. A Trojan horse program is usually disguised as something innocent, like an electronic greeting card, so that the person who receives it will be tempted to run the program. Once the program has been run, the Trojan is installed on the computer system and can carry out various actions, such as transmitting passwords, copies of e-mail messages, and other sensitive data to the sender. Some programs allow the sender to take over the target computer system by remote control. Others destroy data a little at a time. Usually by the time the program is detected, a great deal of damage has been done. Still other programs simply monitor the computer system, periodically sending out reports that contain confidential information, such as every e-mail message sent or received by the computer.

Troll. A person who deliberately makes inflammatory remarks in the hope of beginning an argument. Typically, a troll posts an abusive or controversial message to a chat room, newsgroup, or message board in the hope that other users will respond. As soon as an argument develops, the troll withdraws to watch the outcome.

Usenet. See **newsgroup.**

Video conferencing. Video conferencing allows two or more people in different locations to see and hear each other. Each person taking part in a discussion uses a personal computer equipped with a video camera (webcam), microphone, and sound card. Special software is used to connect the computers together via the Internet. See **webcam.**

Virus. See **computer virus.**

Web-based remailer. A type of anonymous remailer that can be accessed via a form on a web page. Users simply complete the form and submit it in order to send an anonymous message. See **anonymous remailer.**

Web browser. The name given to a program that can be used to view web pages. Examples of web browsers include Internet Explorer, Mozilla, and Opera.

Webcam. A camera that can be connected to a personal computer and used to transmit images via the Internet. Webcams are often used for live two-way communications, such as video conferencing and instant messaging, since they allow people to see and hear each other in real time. Many webcams are set up so that they broadcast continuously, and people can view the broadcast by visiting a special web page. These kinds of broadcasts are often used to provide adult services, such as interactive pornography. In some cases, webcams have been used by pedophile rings to broadcast images of child abuse to members. A recent trend has been the emergence of camgirls and camboys: young people who use webcams to broadcast images of their lives, often with the intention of soliciting gifts from visitors to their web sites. See **camgirl.**

Web log. A web log is a journal that is frequently updated and posted to a personal web site. Often, specialized software is used to make it easier to publish the journal, for example by automatically posting new entries to the author's web site. Once published to a web site, many web logs provide visitors with special features, such as a search facility.

Webmaster. The name given to the person who is responsible for maintaining and overseeing a web site. Complaints or comments regarding the content of a web site are usually sent directly to the webmaster.

Web ring. A group of web sites that share a common theme. Each web site contains links to some of the other sites in the web ring. Users follow the links to view sites related to a topic of interest, eventually returning to the first site visited.

Web site defacement. Changing or replacing the web pages belonging to an organization or government department so that political messages or other material is displayed.

WhoIs. A special type of search that finds the registration information for a specific domain name or IP address. This registration information will normally contain contact details for the owner of the domain. See **domain name** and **IP address.**

Wish list. A list of items a young person would like to receive as gifts. Many teenagers publish their wish lists on their personal web sites in the hope that visitors to the site will send them the gifts listed.

Worm. A worm is similar to computer virus in that it attempts to copy itself from one computer to another. Worms also perform functions similar to computer viruses, such as deleting data. However, unlike a computer virus, a worm does not attach itself to programs or data files and exists as a separate entity. All worms should be considered destructive. See **computer virus.**

Zombie. Often used to describe a bot used for a distributed denial of service attack. See **bot** and **denial of service.**

Bibliography

As one might expect with a subject that deals with modern technology, many of the information sources used here are located on the Internet. Unfortunately, Internet sources are sometimes unreliable as pages may be moved or deleted whenever a web site is updated. Readers unable to locate an Internet resource listed here are invited to contact the author via the publisher for further information.

ABCNews.com. 2000a. Investigating the "Slavemaster" [online], 7 June 2000. New York: ABCNews.com. Available at: http://abcnews.go.com/sections/us/DailyNews/slavemaster000607.html.

ABCNews.com. 2000b. Victimized . . . Internet style [online], 13 January 2000. New York: ABCNews.com. Available at: http://archive.abcnews.go.com/onair/2020/2020_000111_stalking_feature. html.

ABCNews.com. 2003. Dos Reis pleads guilty to federal charges in Internet death case [online], 17 April 2003. New York: ABCNews.com. Available at: http://abclocal.go.com/wabc/news/WABC_041703_internetdeath.html.

Abrams, K., and Robinson, G. 1998. Stalking part II: Victims' problems with the legal system and therapeutic considerations. *Canadian Journal of Psychiatry*, 43 (June 1998). Available at: http://www.cpa-apc.org/Publications/Archives/CJP/1998/June/abrams-2.htm.

Abrams, K., and Robinson, G. 2002. Occupational effects of stalking. *Canadian Journal of Psychiatry*, 47, 468–72.

Aftab, P. 2001. CyberAngels handling stalking cases [online]. Allentown, PA: CyberAngels. Available at: http://www.cyberangels.com/net-ed/classes/HandlingStalking.htm.

Ahuja, A. 2000. Inside the mind of a stalker. *The* (London) *Times*, 28 January 2000. Available at: http://www.harassment-law.co.uk/book/stlkmnd.htm.

Allen, N. 2002. Police in 10 countries hold paedophile ring suspects. *The Independent*, 21 March 2002.

Ames, S. 2001. Teen settles in online stock fraud case [online], 21 September 2000. San Francisco: CNET Networks, Inc. Available at: http://news.com.com/2100-1023-246013.html?legacy=cnet.

Anderiesz, M. 2002. Caught in the net [online]. London: Independent Digital (UK) Ltd. Available at: http://news.independent.co.uk/digital/features/story.jsp?story=325826.

Anderssen, E. 2002. Camgirls: Empowerment or predator enticement? [online], 19 October 2002. Toronto: (globetechnology.com) Bell Globemedia Interactive, Inc. Available at: http://www.globetechnology.com/servlet/ArticleNews/gtnews/TGAM/20021019/UCAMMN.

Arce, R. 2003. 30-year sentence in Internet-linked sex death [online], 7 May 2003. Atlanta, GA: CNN.com. Available at: http://www.cnn.com/2003/LAW/05/06/internet.sex.death/.

Ashcroft, J. 2001. *Stalking and domestic violence*. NCJ 186157. Washington, DC: U.S. Department of Justice.

Asher, T. 2002. Girls, Sexuality, and Popular Culture. *Off Our Backs*, 32 (5/6), 22–25.

Au, S. 2002. New study shows girls are driving on the information superhighway without a license [online]. New York: Girl Scouts of the United States of America. Available at: http://www.girlscouts.org/news/archive/2002/net_effect.html.

Baker, D. 1999. When cyberstalkers walk. *ABA Journal*, 85 (12), 50–54.

Bandura, A. 1999. Moral disengagement in the perpetration of inhumanities. *Personality and Social Psychology Review* (3), 193–209.

Barry, R. 2001a. Chatroom Danger: Opinion—When online chat leads to the Crying Rooms [online], 15 March 2001. London: ZDNet UK. Available at: http://news.zdnet.co.uk/story/0,,t269-s2085044,00.html.

Barry, R. 2001b. Chatroom Danger: The making of the Tina Bell Diaries [online], 15 March 2001. London: ZDNet UK. Available at: http://news.zdnet.co.uk/story/0,,t269-s2085051,00.html.

Barry, R. 2001c. Chatroom Danger: The making of the Tina Bell Diaries Pt. II [online], 15 March 2001. London: ZDNet UK. Available at: http://news.zdnet.co.uk/story/0,,t269-s2085052,00.html.

Barwise, M. 2001. Are you an unwitting accomplice? ComputerWeekly.com, 12 July 2001. Sutton, United Kingdom: ComputerWeekly.com Ltd.

Bassett, G. 2000. Developing a computer security proposal for small businesses—How to start [online]. Bethesda, MD: SANS Institute. Available at: http://www.sans.org/rr/policy/cssb.php.

BBC News. 2000. Love Bug may have been accident [online], 11 May 2000. London: BBC News. Available at: http://news.bbc.co.uk/1/hi/sci/tech/744537.stm.

BBC News. 2001a. "Internet abduction" girl heads home [online], 5 February 2001. London: BBC News. Available at: http://news.bbc.co.uk/1/hi/world/americas/1153513.stm.

BBC News. 2001b. Woman "confesses to Internet murder" [online], 25 February 2001. London: BBC News. Available at: http://news.bbc.co.uk/1/hi/world/middle_east/1189804.stm.

BBC News. 2003. Text message stalker jailed [online], 20 May 2003. London: BBC News. Available at: http://news.bbc.co.uk/1/hi/england/london/3043743.stm.

BBC News Interactive, 2003. Anti-war hackers target websites [online]. London: BBC News Interactive. Available at: http://news.bbc.co.uk/1/hi/technology/2871985.stm.

BBC Online Network. 1999. Business: The company file bitter taste of airline feud [online], 14 July 1999. London: BBC Online Network. Available at: http://news.bbc.co.uk/1/hi/business/the_company_file/394647.stm.

Beder, S. 1995. SLAPPs—Strategic Lawsuits Against Public Participation: Coming to a controversy near you. *Current Affairs Bulletin*, 72 (3), 22–29.

Beloit Daily News. 1997. Victims call for new laws on Internet harassment [online], 1 April 1997. Beloit, WI: Beloit Daily News. Available at: http://www.beloitdailynews.com/497/onln1.htm.

Berensen, A. 2000. Investigators arrest a suspect in stock manipulation case [online], 1 September 2000. New York: New York Times. Available at: http://www.nytimes.com/library/financial/090100 emulex-plunge.html.

Berg, T. 2001. Confronting evil on the Internet: The challenge of taming the electronic frontier. *America* (18–25 June 2001), 15–19.

Bicknell, C. 1999. Strange corporate hacking saga [online], 12 November 1999. San Francisco: Wired News. Available at: http://www.wired.com/news/business/0,1367,32488,00.html.

Blaauw, E., et al. 2002. The toll of stalking: The relationship between features of stalking and psychopathology of victims. *Journal of Interpersonal Violence*, 17 (1), 50–63.

Blacharski, D. 2000. Emerging technology: Create order with a strong security policy [online], 10 July 2000. S.l.: Network Magazine. Available at: http://www.networkmagazine.com/shared/article/show Article.jhtml?articleId=8702862.

Blom, E. 1998. These predators are no longer isolated [online], 11 October 1998. Portland: Press Herald Online. Available at: http://www.press-herald.com/specialrpts/danger/predators.htm.

Bocij, P. 2002. Corporate cyberstalking: An invitation to build theory. *First Monday* [online], 7 (11). Available at: http://firstmonday.org/issues/issue7_11/bocij/index.html.

Bocij, P. 2003. Victims of cyberstalking: An exploratory study of harassment perpetrated via the Internet. *First Monday* [online], 8 (10). Available at: http://www.firstmonday.dk/issues/issue8_10/bocij/index.html.

Bocij, P., Bocij, H., and McFarlane, L. 2003. Cyberstalking: A case study concerning serial harassment in the UK. *British Journal of Forensic Practice*, 5 (2), 25–32.

Bocij, P., et al. 2002. *Business information systems: Technology, development and management for the e-business*, 2nd ed. London: Financial Times and Prentice Hall.

Bocij, P., et al. 1999. *Business information systems: Technology, development and management*. London: Pitman Publishing.

Bocij, P., and McFarlane, L. 2002a. Online harassment: Towards a definition of cyberstalking. *Prison Service Journal*, 139, 31–38.

Bocij, P., and McFarlane, L. 2002b. Cyberstalking: Genuine problem or public hysteria? *Prison Service Journal*, 140, 32–35.

Bocij, P., and McFarlane, L. 2003a. The Internet: A discussion of some new and emerging threats to young people. *The Police Journal*, 76 (1), 3–13.

Bocij, P., and McFarlane, L. 2003b. Cyberstalking: the technology of hate. *The Police Journal*, 76 (4), 20–37.

Bocij, P., McFarlane, L., and Sutton, M. 2003. Cyberstalking and the misuse of hi-technology: Findings and issues for future research and crime reduction. *Hate Crimes*, 21–22 February 2003. Nottingham, United Kingdom: SOLON and Nottingham Centre for Study and Reduction of Hate Crimes.

Bonisteel, S. 2002. ACLU backs Yahoo, "Cybergriper" in free-speech cases [online], 7 May 2002. Washington, DC: WashTech.com. Available at: http://emoglen.law.columbia.edu/CPC/archive/civil-liberties/ACLU%20backs%20two%20cases.html.

Bowen, J. 1993. Computer hacking of flight details "was illegal." *The Risks Digest* [online], 14 (26). Available at: http://catless.ncl.ac.uk/Risks/14.26.html.

Brewster, M. 2001. Legal help—Seeking experiences of former intimate-stalking victims. *Criminal Justice Policy Review*, 12 (2), 91–112.

Bubaš, G. 2001. Computer mediated communication theories and phenomena: Factors that influence collaboration over the Internet. Third CARNet Users Conference, 24–26 September 2001. Zagreb, Croatia: CARNet.

Budd, T., and Mattinson, J. 2000. Stalking: Findings from the 1998 British Crime Survey. *Research Findings*, 129, 1–4.

Budd, T., Mattinson, J., and Myhill, A. 2000. *The extent and nature of stalking: Findings from the 1998 British Crime Survey*. London: Home Office Research, Development and Statistics Directorate.

Burgess, N. W., et al. 1997. Stalking behaviors within domestic violence. *Journal of Family Violence*, 12 (4), 389–403.

Burgess, W. A., and Baker, T. 2002. Cyberstalking. In J. Boon and L. Sheridan, eds., *Stalking and psychosexual obsession: Psychological perspectives for prevention, policing and treatment*. London: John Wiley & Sons, pp. 201–19.

Burke, L. 2000. Huge kid porn ring busted [online], 14 April 2000. San Francisco: Wired News. Available at: http://www.wired.com/news/print/0,1294,35684,00.html.

Carter, B., and Nzpa. 2001. It began with an e-mail then turned into terror [online], *The New Zealand Herald*, 23 June 2001. Auckland: The New Zealand Herald. Available at: http://www.nzherald.co.nz/storydisplay.cfm?storyID=196374.

Cassel, D. 2000. Hacktivism in the cyberstreets [online], 30 May 2000. San Francisco: AlterNet.org. Available at: http://www.alternet.org/story.html?StoryID=9223.

CBSNews.com. 2002a. The two faces of a 13-year-old girl [online], 21 May 2002. New York: CBSNews.com. Available at: http://www.cbsnews.com/stories/2002/05/31/national/main510739.shtml.

CBSNews.com. 2002b. Web of seduction [online], 4 September 2002. New York: CBSNews.com. Available at: http://www.cbsnews.com/stories/2002/01/04/48hours/main323129.shtml.

Cha, A. E. 2001. Dear web diary, SO much to tell! *The Washington Post*, 2 September 2001, p. A01.

Chan, R. 2000. The dangers of online relationships, stalking, and pedophiles: How true love or tragedy is only a click away [online]. Palo Alto, CA: Stanford University. Available at: http://www.stanford.edu/~mrubens/pornsite2/relations.htm.

Childnet International. 2001. *Online grooming and UK law: A submission by Childnet International to the Home Office*. London: Childnet International.

City of Santa Monica. 2002. Online safety [online]. Santa Monica, CA: City of Santa Monica. Available at: http://santamonicapd.org/CrimePrevention/OnlineSafety/OnlineSafetyopen.htm.

Clancy Systems International. 2001. Clancy Systems International, Inc. gets court judgement against basher [online]. Denver, CO: Clancy Systems International. Available at: http://www.clancysystems.com/newsite/20011101.htm.

Cnews. 2000. Net "slavemaster" suspected in slayings [online], 6 June 2000. Toronto, Canada: Canoe. Available at: http://www.canoe.ca/CNEWSLaw0006/06_slavemaster.html.

CNN Interactive. 1997. Internet sting identifies 1,500 suspected child pornographers [online], 30 September 1997. Atlanta, GA: CNN Interactive. Available at: http://www.cnn.com/US/9709/30/cybersting/.

Coman, J. 2003. Crime scene investigation [online], 7 February 2003. Melbourne, Australia: The Age Company Ltd. Available at: http://www.theage.com.au/articles/2003/02/07/1044579926881.html.

Computer Weekly. 2001. Security booming despite economic downturn. *Computer Weekly*, 18 September 2001.

Conry-Murray, A. 2002. Strategies & issues: Deciphering the cost of a computer crime. *Network Magazine* [online], 4 April 2002. Available at: http://www.networkmagazine.com/article/NMG20020401S0003.

CourtTV.com. 2003. Kansas man sentenced to death for killing two women, stuffing bodies into barrels [online], 20 March 2003. New York: CourtTV.com. Available at: http://www.courttv.com/trials/robinson/012103_death_ap.html.

Cyberspace Research Unit. 2002. *Young people's use of chat rooms: Implications for policy strategies and programs of education.* Preston, UK: Home Office Internet Task Force/University of Central Lancashire.

Dating Detectives. 2003. Cyber-stalking in detail [online]. Aldershot, UK: Dating Detectives & Trafalgar Consultancy Ltd. Available at: http://www.datingdetectives.net/harastalk/cyberstalkers.html.

Dean, K. 2000. The epidemic of cyberstalking [online], 1 May 2000. San Francisco: Wired Digital, Inc. Available at: http://www.wired.com/news/politics/0,1283,35728,00.html.

Deirmenjian, J. 1999. Stalking in cyberspace. *Journal of the American Academy of Psychiatry and the Law,* 27 (3), 407–13.

Delio, M. 2001. This hack's sights set on AIM [online], 24 September 2001. San Francisco: Wired News. Available at: http://www.wired.com/news/technology/0,1282,47072,00.html.

Denning, D. 2001. Activism, hacktivism, and cyberterrorism: The Internet as a tool for influencing foreign policy. In J. Arquilla and D. Ronfeldt, eds., *Networks and netwars: The future of terror, crime, and militancy.* Santa Monica, CA: RAND, pp. 239–88.

Denning, D., and Baugh, W. 2000. Hiding crimes in cyberspace. In D. Thomas and B. Loader, eds., *Cybercrime: Law enforcement, security and surveillance in the information age.* London: Routledge, pp. 103–31.

Department of Health. 2001. *National plan for safeguarding children from commercial sexual exploitation.* London: Department of Health.

Department of Justice, Equality and Law Reform. 1998. *Illegal and harmful use of the Internet.* Dublin, Ireland: The Stationery Office.

Donald, M. 2003. It doesn't suck.com [online], 20 February 2003. Dallas, TX: DallasObserver.com. Available at: http://www.dallasobserver.com/issues/2003-02-20/news.html/1/index.html.

Duffy, D. 2000. Prepare for the worst [online], December 2000. Framingham, MA: Darwinmag.com. Available at: http://www.darwinmag.com/read/120100/worst_content.html.

DuPree, C., and Miller, N. 1999. 1999 violence against women legislation [online]. Alexandria, VA: Institute for Law and Justice. Available at: http://www.ilj.org/dv/99SessionLaw.htm.

Dussuyer, I. 2000. Is stalking legislation effective in protecting victims? Stalking: Criminal Justice Responses Conference, 7–8 December 2000. Sydney: Australian Institute of Criminology.

Evers, L. 2000. Hacked websites could face libel threat [online], 27 September 2000. London: VNUnet.com. Available at: http://www.vnunet.com/News/1111742.

Feather, M. 1999. Internet and child victimisation. Children and Crime: Victims and Offenders Conference, 17–18 June 1999. Brisbane: Australian Institute of Criminology.

Felson, M. 2002. *Crime and everyday life*, 3rd ed. Thousand Oaks, CA: Sage Publications.

Festa, P. 2003. Opera: Microsoft is hurting our style [online], 6 February 2003. San Francisco: ZDNet. Available at: http://zdnet.com.com/2100-1104-983500.html.

Finch, E. 2002. Stalking: A violent crime or a crime of violence? *The Howard Journal*, 41 (5), 422–33.

Finkelhor, D., Mitchell, K., and Wolak, J. 2000. *Online victimization: A report on the nation's youth*. Arlington, VA: National Center for Missing & Exploited Children.

Fleet, M. 1999. Stalker sent back to jail after fresh harassment [online]. London: Electronic Telegraph. Available at: http://www.telegraph.co.uk/htmlContent.jhtml?html=%2Farchive%2F1999%2F01%2F05%2Fnstalk05.html.

Frauenfelder, M. 2002. Cam girls [online]. Yahoo! Internet Life, June 2002. S.l.: Yahoo! Available at: http://boingboing.net/camgirls.html.

Fremouw, W. J., Westrup, D., and Pennypacker, J. 1997. Stalking on campus: The prevalence and strategies for coping with stalking. *Forensic Science*, 42 (4), 666–69.

Gallagher, R., 2002. *I'll be watching you: True stories of stalkers and their victims*. London: Virgin Books Ltd.

Gardiner, J. 2000. "Be secure or be sued" businesses warned [online], 16 November 2000. London: Silicon.com (CNET Networks UK). Available at: http://www.silicon.com/news/500013/1/1020900.html.

Gaudin, S. 2003. Analysts: Child porn hidden on corporate networks [online], 14 February 2003. South Darien, CT: Datamation. Available at: http://itmanagement.earthweb.com/secu/article.php/1584551.

George, W., and Norris, J. 1996. Alcohol, disinhibition, sexual arousal, and deviant sexual behavior [online]. Bloomington, IN: Indiana University. Available at: http://www.drugs.indiana.edu/publications/ncadi/radar/misc/sexual.html.

Gibson, S. 2002. The Strange tale of the denial of service attacks against GRC.com [online]. Laguna Hills, CA: GRC.com. Available at: http://grc.com/dos/grcdos.htm.

Giddens, A. 2001. *Sociology*, 4th ed. London: Polity Press.

Gilbert, P. 2002. On space, sex and stalkers. *Women and Performance* [online], 17. Available at: http://www.echonyc.com/~women/Issue17/art-gilbert.html.

The Glasgow Herald. 2001. Thousands of children were abused and the evidence was damning so why did Andrew Aspinall walk free? *The Glasgow Herald*, 18 November 2001.

The Glasgow Herald. 2002. Children must be protected: Fighting porn takes precedence over internet freedom. *The Glasgow Herald*, 26 February 2002.

Gossett, J., and Byrne, S. 2002. "Click here": A content analysis of Internet rape sites. *Gender and Society*, 16 (5), 689–709.

Gouda, N. 2000. Legislative and criminal justice responses to stalking in the context of domestic violence. Stalking: Criminal Justice Responses Conference, 7 8–December 2000. Sydney: Australian Institute of Criminology.

Graham, W. 2000. Uncovering and eliminating child pornography rings on the Internet: Issues regarding and avenues facilitating law enforcement's access to "Wonderland." *The Law Review of Michigan State University Detroit College of Law*, (2), 457–84.

Gregorie, T. 2001. Cyberstalking: Dangers on the information superhighway [online]. Washington, DC: National Center for Victims of Crime. Available at: http://www.ncvc.org/src/help/cyberstalking.html.

Grice, C., and Ard, S. 2000. Hoax briefly shaves $2.5 billion off Emulex's market cap [online], 25 August 2000. San Francisco: CNET Networks, Inc. Available at: http://news.com.com/2100-1033-244975.html?legacy=cnet.

Griffiths, M. 2000. Excessive Internet use: Implications for sexual behavior. *Cyberpsychology and Behaviour*, 3 (4), 537–52.

Griffiths, M. 2001. Sex on the Internet: Observations and implications for Internet sex addiction. *The Journal of Sex Research*, 38 (4), 1–10.

Gross, L. 2000. *Surviving a stalker: Everything you need to know to keep yourself safe*. New York: Marlowe and Company.

Grossman, M. 1997. Cyberstalking—The newest form of terror [online]. Miami, FL: Becker & Poliakoff. Available at: http://www.ecomputerlaw.com/articles/1997/cyberstalking.htm.

Grossman, M. 1999. Cyberstalking [online]. Miami, FL: Becker & Poliakoff. Available at: http://www.ecomputerlaw.com/articles/1999/cyberstalking.htm.

Groves, P. 2001. Perspective: Sick web of corruption. *Birmingham Post*, 3 December 2001.

Gustafson, S. 2001. Cyber tussle [online], 19 December 2001. Detroit, MI: MetroTimes.com. Available at: http://www.metrotimes.com/editorial/story.asp?id=2773.

Hansen, E. 2000. ICQ hack raises security concerns [online], 24 February 2000. San Francisco: News.com (CNET). Available at: http://news.com.com/2100-1023-237255.html?legacy=cnet.

Harmon, R., Rosner, R., and Owens, H. 1995. Obsessional harassment and erotomania in a criminal court population. *Journal of Forensic Sciences*, 40 (2), 188–96.

Harmon, R., Rosner, R., and Owens, H. 1998. Sex and violence in a forensic population of obsessional harassers. *Psychology, Public Policy, and Law*, 4 (1–2), 236–49.

Her Majesty's Stationery Office. 1988. Malicious Communications Act [online]. Available at: http://www.legislation.hmso.gov.uk/acts/acts1988/Ukpga_19880027_en_1.htm.

Her Majesty's Stationery Office. 1997. Protection from Harassment Act [online]. Available at: http://www.legislation.hmso.gov.uk/acts/acts1997/1997040.htm.

Hight, M. 2000. Suspect arrested in murder of Texas A&M student [online],

28 April 2000. Chicago: U-Wire. Available at: http://www.uwire.com/content/topnews042800000.html.

Hines, M. 2003. War spotlights need for hardy Web sites [online], 10 April 2003. Needham, MA: SearchCIO.com. Available at: http://searchcio.techtarget.com/originalContent/0,289142,sid19_gci893136,00.html.

Hirsh, L. 2001. The boss is watching: Workplace monitoring on the rise [online], 29 June 2001. Sherman Oaks, CA: NewsFactor.com. Available at: http://www.newsfactor.com/perl/story/11634.html.

Hitchcock, J. 2000. Cyberstalking and law enforcement: Keeping up with the web [online]. S.l.: Compute Me. Available at: http://computeme.tripod.com/cyberstalk.html.

Hook, P. 2000. Internet safety awareness. Riverside, CA: TheGuardian Angel.com. Available at: http://www.theguardianangel.com/internet_safety_cyberstalking.htm.

Hughes, D. 1998. Use of the Internet for global sexual exploitation of women and children [online]. Kingston, RI: Coalition Against Trafficking in Women. Available at: http://www.uri.edu/artsci/wms/hughes/internet.pdf.

Hughes, D. 1999. Pimps and predators on the Internet: Globalizing sexual exploitation of women and children [online]. Kingston, RI: Coalition Against Trafficking in Women. Available at: http://www.uri.edu/artsci/wms/hughes/pprep.htm.

Hughes, D. 2000. The Internet and sex industries: Partners in global sexual exploitation. *Technology and Society Magazine* [online] (Spring 2000). Available at: http://www.uri.edu/artsci/wms/hughes/siii.htm.

Hughes, D. 2001. *The impact of the use of new communications and information technologies on trafficking in human beings for sexual exploitation: A study of the users.* Strasbourg, France: Committee for Equality between Women and Men/Council of Europe.

Hughes, D. 2002a. The use of new communication and information technologies for the sexual exploitation of women and children. *Hastings Women's Law Journal*, 13 (1), 129–48.

Hughes, D. 2002b. *Trafficking of children for prostitution.* Washington, DC: U.S. Department of Justice.

Hughes, D. 2003. *Group of specialists on the impact of the use of new information technologies on trafficking in human beings for the purpose of sexual exploitation.* EG-S-NT (2002) 9. Strasbourg, France: Council of Europe.

Hulme, G., and Garvey, M. 2001. Terror attack brings renewed emphasis on security [online], 17 September 2001. New York: Information Week. Available at: http://www.informationweek.com/story/IWK20010916S0013.

Humphreys, A. 2000. Statistics show stalking rising rapidly. *The National Post*, 30 November 2000. Available at: http://fact.on.ca/news/news0011/np001130.htm.

Hyman, G. 2001. Two Beverly Hills men sentenced for securities fraud [online],

24 January 2001. South Darien, CT: InternetNews.com. Available at: http://siliconvalley.internet.com/news/article.php/5321_568551.

The Information Centre. 2000. *Stalking and Harassment* (Research Notes). RN 00-58. Edinburgh, Scotland: The Scottish Parliament.

InterGOV International. 2003. Latest web statistics [online]. Lutz, FL: InterGOV International. Available at: http://www.intergov.org/public_information/general_information/latest_web_stats.html.

Internet Crime Forum. 2001. *Chat wise, street wise—Children and Internet chat services*. London: Internet Watch Foundation.

Joinson, A. 1998. Causes and implications of disinhibited behavior on the Internet. In J. Gackenbach, ed., *Psychology and the Internet: Intrapersonal, interpersonal, and transpersonal implications*. San Diego, CA: Academic Press, pp. 43–60.

Jordan, C., et al. 2003. Stalking: An examination of the criminal justice response. *Journal of Interpersonal Violence*, 18 (2), 148–65.

Junnarkar, S. 2001. MSN.com won't play nice with others [online], 25 October 2001. San Francisco: ZDNet. Available at: http://zdnet.com.com/2100-1106-274944.html.

Kamphuis, J., and Emmelkamp, M. 2000. Stalking—A contemporary challenge for forensic and clinical psychiatry. *British Journal of Psychiatry*, 176, 206–9.

Kaplan, C. 2001. Can hacking victims be held legally liable? [online], 24 August 2001. Cambridge, MA: Mazu Networks, Inc. Available at: http://www.mazunetworks.com/news/n-nyt.html.

Karp, H. 2000. Angels online. *Reader's Digest* [online], April 2000. Available at: http://www.tcs.org/ioport/aug00/cyberstalking.htm.

Kienlen, K., et al. 1997. A comparative study of psychotic and nonpsychotic stalking. *Journal of the American Academy of Psychiatry and the Law*, 25 (3), 317–34.

Kiesler, S., Siegel, J., and McGuire, T. 1984. Social psychological aspects of computer-mediated communication. *American Psychologist*, 39, 1123–34.

King, B. 2001. Claire Swire: Everyone remembers but few have changed their ways [online], 19 July 2001. London: Silicon.com. Available at: http://www.silicon.com/news/500021/1/1025866.html.

Kirby, C. 2000. Hacking with a conscience is a new trend [online], 20 November 2000. San Francisco: SFGate.com. Available at: http://sfgate.com/cgi-bin/article.cgi?file=/chronicle/archive/2000/11/20/BU121645.DTL.

Kirk, E. 1998. Slapped? Slapp back [online]. Redway, CA: Civil Liberties Monitoring Project. Available at: http://www.civilliberties.org/spring98slapp.html.

Klein, M. 1998. Stalking situations. *American Demographics*, 20 (3), 32.

Knight, W. 2001. Hackers become terrorists under UK law [online], 20 February 2001. Pyrmont, Australia: ZDNet Australia. Available at: http://www.zdnet.com.au/newstech/news/story/0,2000025345,20205108,00.htm.

Ko, M. 2000. Where do you live? *The Report/Newsmagazine* (Alberta edition), 28 August 2000, p. 54.

Ko, M. 2001. Still in a hi-tech closet—barely. *The Report*, 11 June 2001, pp. 34–36.

Koch, L. 2000a. Commentary box: The cyberstalking hype [online], 13 December 2000. London: ZDNet UK (CNET Networks, Inc.). Available at: http://comment.zdnet.co.uk/story/0,,t479-s2113983,00.html.

Koch, L. 2000b. Cyberstalking hype. *Inter@ctive Week*, 7 (21), 28.

Konrad, R., and Junnarkar, S. 2001. Rival browsers benefit from MSN gaffe [online], 1 November 2001. London: ZDNet UK. Available at: http://news.zdnet.co.uk/story/0,,t269-s2098460,00.html.

Lanning, K. 1992. *Child molesters: A behavioral analysis*, 3rd ed. Arlington, VA: National Center for Missing & Exploited Children.

Law, G. 2003. 10 Downing St. Web site hacked [online], 25 March 2003. Framingham, MA: ComputerWorld. Available at: http://www.computerworld.com/securitytopics/security/story/0,10801,79689,00.html.

Lea, M., and Spears, R. 1991. Computer-mediated communication, de-individuation and group decision-making. *International Journal of Man-Machine Studies*, 34, 283–301.

Lee, D. R. 2001. Developing effective information systems security policies [online]. Bethesda, MD: SANS Institute. Available at: http://www.sans.org/rr/policy/effective.php.

Lee, E. 2002. Browser wars [online]. London: LabourStart. Available at: http://www.labourstart.org/ssv08.shtml.

Lettice, J. 2003. MSN deliberately breaks Opera's browser, claims company [online], 6 February 2003. Southport, UK: The Register. Available at: http://www.theregister.co.uk/content/6/29219.html.

Lewis, M. 2001. Jonathan Lebed: Stock manipulator, S.E.C. nemesis—and 15. *New York Times Magazine*, 25 February 2001.

Livingstone, S. 2001. *Online freedom and safety for children*. IPPR/Citizens Online, Research Publication No. 3. Norwich, CT: Citizens Online and IPPR.

Lopez, R. 1999. Corporate strategies for addressing Internet "complaint" sites [online]. San Francisco: Thelen Reid & Priest LLP. Available at: http://www.constructionweblinks.com/Resources/Industry_Reports__Newsletters/August_1999/august_1999.html.

Mahoney, D., and Faulkner, N. 1997. *Brief overview of pedophiles on the web*. Submitted by request to the Child Advocacy Task Force on the Internet Online Summit: Focus on Children, 1 December 1997. Washington, DC: Child Advocacy Task Force.

Major, L. 2001. University investigates paedophilia research project [online], 10 September 2001. London: Guardian Unlimited. Available at: http://education.guardian.co.uk/specialreports/postgrad/story/0,5500,549727,00.html.

Malamuth, N., Addison, T., and Koss, M. 2000. Pornography and sexual aggression: Are there reliable effects and can we understand them? *Annual Review of Sex Research*, 11, 26–94.

Mann, D., Sutton, M., and Tuffin, R. 2003. The evolution of hate: Social dynamics in white racist newsgroups. *The Internet Journal of Criminology*. An online, peer-reviewed journal available at www.flashmouse publishing.com.

Martin, L. 2001. Inquiry into student's child sex research. *The Glasgow Herald*, 10 September 2001, p. 7.

Massachusetts Medical Society. 2000. Prevalence and Health Consequences of Stalking—Louisiana, 1998–1999. *Morbidity and Mortality Weekly Report*, 49 (29), 653–55.

McAuliffe, W. 2001a. Chatroom danger: The Tina Bell diaries [online], 15 March 2001. London: ZDNet UK. Available at: http://news.zdnet.co.uk /story/0,,s2085043,00.html.

McAuliffe, W. 2001b. Chatroom danger: The 60 second route to abuse [online], 15 March 2001. London: ZDNet UK. Available at: http://news.zdnet.co.uk/story/0,,t269-s2085045,00.html.

McAuliffe, W. 2001c. Chatroom "victim" to return home [online], 5 February 2001. London: ZDNet UK. Available at: http://news.zdnet.co.uk/story/0,,t269-s2084192,00.html.

McCord, V. 1998. Author's real-life story is cyberspace nightmare [online], 19 February 1998. Washington, DC: The Washington Times. Available at: http://members.tripod.com/~cyberstalked/washtimes.html.

McFarlane, L., and Bocij, P. 2003. An exploration of predatory behaviour in cyberspace: Towards a typology of cyberstalkers. *First Monday* [online], 8 (9). Available at: http://firstmonday.org/issues/issue8_9/mcfarlane/index.html.

McGrath, M., and Casey, E. 2002. Forensic psychiatry and the Internet: Practical perspectives on sexual predators and obsessional harassers in cyberspace. *Journal of the American Academy of Psychiatry and the Law*, 30 (1), 81–94.

McNamee, M. 2000. Commentary—Stocks: What you can and can't say in chat rooms [online], 16 October 2000. Boulder, CO: BusinessWeek Online. Available at: http://www.businessweek.com/2000/00_42/b3703126.htm.

Meloy, J. 1998a. The psychology of stalking. In J. Meloy, ed., *The psychology of stalking: Clinical and forensic perspectives*. San Diego, CA: Academic Press, pp. 2–21.

Meloy, J., ed. 1998b. *The psychology of stalking: Clinical and forensic perspectives*. San Diego, CA: Academic Press.

Messmer, E. 2003. Dealing with deviants on your network [online], 31 March 2003. Southborough, MA: Network World Fusion. Available at: http://www.nwfusion.com/news/2003/0331porn.html.

Metro Times. 2003. Amendment doesn't suck. *Metro Times* [online], 12 February 2003. Detroit: Metro Times. Available at: http://www.metrotimes.com/editorial/story.asp?id=4589.

Milburn, J. 2000. More deaths are linked to suspected "slavemaster" [online], 16 June 2000. Athens, Greece: Online Athens. Available at: http:// www.onlineathens.com/stories/061600/new_0616000027.shtml.

Milgram, S. 1963. Behavioral study of obedience. *Journal of Abnormal and Social Psychology* (67), 371–78.

Milgram, S. 1965. Some conditions of obedience and disobedience to authority. *Human Relations* (65), 57–76.

Milgram, S. 1974. *Obedience to authority.* New York: Harper & Row.

Miller, N. 1999. *Report on a 1998 national survey of law enforcement and prosecution initiatives against stalking.* Alexandria, VA: Institute for Law and Justice.

Mingo, J. 1996. Caught in the Net: An online posse tracks down an Internet stalker [online], Phoenix: NewTimes, Inc. Available at: http:// www.phoenixnewtimes.com/extra/cyberstalk.html.

MostlyCreativeWorkshop. 2002. News: Man kills daughter of police officer after meeting in chat room [online], 6 December 2002. Oxnard, CA: MostlyCreativeWorkshop. Available at: http://www.mostlycreative workshop.com/modules.php?op=modload&name=News&file= article&sid=118.

MSNBC. 2001. Cyberstalking rears its head in the workplace [online], 24 April 2001. San Francisco: CNET Networks, Inc. Available at: http:// zdnet.com.com/2100-11-529416.html.

MSNBC. 2002. Police: San Diego man kills girl he met in chat room [online], 6 December 2002. Redmond, WA: MSNBC. Available at: http:// www.msnbc.com/local/knsd/a1413476.asp.

Mullen, P., and Pathé, M. 1994. Stalking and the pathologies of love. *Australian and New Zealand Journal of Psychiatry* (28), 469–77.

Mullen, P., Pathé, M., and Purcell, R. 2000. *Stalkers and their victims.* Cambridge: Cambridge University Press.

Mullen, P., Pathé, M., and Purcell, R. 2001. Stalking: New constructions of human behaviour. *Australian and New Zealand Journal of Psychiatry*, 35, 9–16.

Mullen, P., Pathé, M., Purcell, R., and Stuart, G. 1999. A study of stalkers. *American Journal of Psychiatry*, 156, 1244–49.

Museum of Tolerance. 1997. Racism and politics [online]. Los Angeles: The Simon Wiesenthal Center. Available at: http://motlc.wiesenthal.org/ text/x32/xm3258.html.

National Children's Homes. 2002. 1 in 4 children are the victims of "on-line bullying" [online], 15 May 2002. London: National Children's Homes. Available at: http://www.nch.org.uk/news/news3.asp?ReleaseID=125.

National Conference of State Legislatures. 2002. *State computer harassment or "cyberstalking" laws.* Washington, DC: National Conference of State Legislatures. Available at: http://www.ncsl.org/programs/lis/cip/ stalk99.htm.

National School Boards Foundation. 2002. *Safe and smart: Research and guidelines for children's use of the Internet.* Alexandria, VA: National School Boards Foundation.

National Telecommunications and Information Administration. 2002. *A nation online: How Americans are expanding their use of the Internet*. Washington, DC: NTIA and Economics and Statistics Administration.

NBCSandiego.com. 2002. FBI searches local home for clues in Arkansas teen murder [online], 6 December 2002. San Diego, CA: NBCSandiego.com. Available at: http://ia.nbcsandiego.com/news/1825655/detail.html.

The News Herald. 2002. Greek jailed for Internet affair with teen still in contact. *The News Herald* [online], 2 February 2002. Available at: http://www.newsherald.com/articles/2002/02/02/st020202i.htm.

Nichols, M. 2001. Sick club that pandered to perverts. *The Scotsman*, 16 November 2001.

Ninemsn Pty Ltd. 2002. Japanese Internet dating crime doubles [online], 22 August 2002. Sydney, Australia: Ninemsn Pty Ltd. Available at: http://news.ninemsn.com.au/Sci_Tech/story_37762.asp.

Nordland, R., et al. 2001. The web's dark secret. *Newsweek*, 19 March 2001, 37 (12), 44–51.

North County Times. 2002. Friends: Girl felt she was being followed [online], 8 December 2002. S.l.: North County Times. Available at: http://www.nctimes.net/news/2002/20021208/wwww.html.

NUA Internet Surveys. 2003. How many online. Dublin, Ireland: Computerscope Ltd. Available at: http://www.nua.com/surveys/how_many_online/index.html.

Ogilvie, E. 2000a. Stalking: Criminal justice responses in Australia. Stalking: Criminal Justice Responses Conference, 7–8 December 2000. Sydney: Australian Institute of Criminology.

Ogilvie, E. 2000b. Stalking: Policing and prosecuting practices in three Australian jurisdictions. *Trends and Issues in Crime and Criminal Justice* No. 176. Canberra: Australian Institute of Criminology.

Ontario Women's Justice Network. 2002. Stalking questions and answers [online]. Ontario, Canada: Ontario Women's Justice Network. Available at: http://www.owjn.org/issues/stalking/qa.htm.

Ornstein, C. 2001. 2 AIDS activists accused of stalking: They admit late-night calls to S.F. officials and reporters but deny making threats [online], 29 November 2001. Los Angeles: Los Angeles Times. Available at: http://www.aegis.com/news/Lt/2001/LT011107.html.

Out-Law.com. 2003. "Sucks" domains are OK, says US appeals court [online]. Glasgow, Scotland: Out-Law.com. Available at: http://www.out-law.com/php/page.php?page_id=sucks1044887636&area=news.

Pastore, M. 2001. Study says users are ignorant of browsers and URLs [online], 15 February 2001. S.l.: ISP-Planet. Available at: http://www.isp-planet.com/research/2001/whats_a_browser.html.

Pathé, M. 2002. *Surviving stalking*. Cambridge: Cambridge University Press.

Pathé, M., and Mullen, P. 1997. The impact of stalkers on their victims. *British Journal of Psychiatry*, 170, 12–17.

Penenberg, A. 1998a. Reverse hack [online], 17 April 1998. New York:

Forbes.com. Available at: http://www.forbes.com/1998/04/17/feat_side1.html.

Penenberg, A. 1998b. The enforcers [online], 17 April 1998. New York: Forbes.com. Available at: http://www.forbes.com/1998/04/17/feat_side2.html.

Perlman, J. 2000. Securities fraud [online], 23 February 2000. Alexandria, VA: The Motley Fool. Available at: http://www.fool.com/specials/2000/sp000223fraud.htm.

Petherick, W. 1999. Cyber-stalking: Obsessional pursuit and the digital criminal [online]. S.l.: s.n.. Available at: http://www.crimelibrary.com/criminology/cyberstalking/index.html.

Posey, J. 2003. Child pornography: Is it so bad? [online]. S.l.: PedoWatch. Available at: http://www.pedowatch.com/pedowatch/porn.htm.

Preston, M. 2001. Dear diary, I really need a DVD player. *The Independent*, 5 October 2001.

Purcell, R., Pathé, M., and Mullen, P. 2000. The incidence and nature of stalking victimisation. Stalking: Criminal Justice Responses Conference, 7–8 December 2000. Sydney: Australian Institute of Criminology.

Purcell, R., Pathe, M., and Mullen, P. 2002. The prevalence and nature of stalking in the Australian community. *Australian and New Zealand Journal of Psychiatry*, 36, 114–20.

Quayle, E., and Taylor, M. 2002. Paedophiles, pornography and the Internet: assessment issues. *British Journal of Social Work*, 32, 863–75.

Raikow, D. 2000. New legal storm on Net horizon [online], 6 July 2000. London: ZDNet UK. Available at: http://comment.zdnet.co.uk/story/0,,t479-s2114368-p1,00.html.

Raphael, R. 2000a. Precocious "pump and dumper"? [online], 21 September 2000. New York: ABCNews.com. Available at: http://abcnews.go.com/sections/business/DailyNews/teen000920.html.

Raphael, R. 2000b. Stalking in cyberspace: New medium, old crime [online], 13 July 2000. New York: ABCNews.com. Available at: http://abcnews.go.com/onair/2020/2020_000713_cyberstalker_feature.html.

Raymond, P. 2000. "Love Bug" virus to cost businesses billions [online], 5 May 2000. London: Silicon.com. Available at: http://www.silicon.com/news/500013/1/1017303.html.

Reno, J. 1999. *Cyberstalking: A new challenge for law enforcement and industry* [online]. Washington, DC: U.S. Department of Justice. Available at: http://www.usdoj.gov/criminal/cybercrime/cyberstalking.htm.

Reno, J., et al. 1998. *Stalking and domestic violence: The third annual report to Congress under the Violence Against Women Act*. NCJ 172204. Washington, DC: Office of Justice Programs.

The Reporters Committee for Freedom of the Press. 2002. Court permits mall critic site to stay online [online]. Arlington, VA: The Reporters Committee for Freedom of the Press. Available at: http://www.rcfp.org/news/2002/0321taubma.html.

Ricciuti, M. 1998. Memo angers open source advocates [online], 4 November 1998. San Francisco: CNET Networks, Inc. Available at: http:// news.com.com/2100-1001-217522.html.

Rosenfeld, B., and Harmon, R. 2002. Factors associated with violence in stalking and obsessional harassment cases. In *Criminal justice and behavior*, pp. 671–91.

Rouse, A. 2003. Opera turns MSN into a bunch of muppets [online], 14 February 2003. London: The Inquirer. Available at: http:// www.theinquirer.net/?article=7814.

Rowan, D. 2002a. Every parent's worst nightmare. *The Observer*, 7 July 2002.

Rowan, D. 2002b. Police probe paedophile links to teen "camgirl" sites. *The Observer*, 7 July 2002.

TheSanDiegoChannel.com. 2002. Police: Local man meets girl via 'net, kills her [online], 6 December 2002. San Diego, CA: TheSanDiegoChannel.com. Available at: http://www.thesandiegochannel.com/news/1824677/ detail.html?treets=sand&tid=2652207299813&tml=sand_4pm&tmi= sand_4pm_790_06000112062002&ts=H#.

Sauer, M. 2000. A web of intrigue: The search for Curio leads cybersleuths down a twisted path [online], 24 September 2000. San Diego, CA: Union-Tribune Publishing Co. Available at: http://users.cybercity.dk/ ~ccc44406/smwane/Curio.html.

Sauer, M. 2002. Stalking suspect to undergo more psychological tests [online], 31 December 2002. San Diego, CA: SignOnSanDiego.com. Available at: http://www.signonsandiego.com/news/metro/20021231- 9999_1m31stalker.html.

Savino, L. 2001. Kid porn Web sites lead to 100 arrests [online], 9 August 2001. Detroit, MI: Detroit Free Press. Available at: http://www.freep.com/ news/nw/kids9_20010809.htm.

Schwimmer, M. 2003. 6th Circuit: SHOPSATWILLOWBEND.COM and gripe site decision [online], 7 February 2003. New York: The Trademark Blog. Available at: http://trademark.blog.us/blog/2003/02/07.html.

The Scotsman. 2002. 90 held for child porn, 19 March 2002.

Shepardson, D. 2003. Court rules for critic of Taubman [online], 9 February 2003. Detroit, MI: DetNews.com. Available at: http:// www.detnews.com/2003/business/0302/10/b01-80220.htm.

Sheridan, L., Davies, G., and Boon, J. 2001. The course and nature of stalking: A victim perspective. *The Howard Journal*, 40 (3), 215–34.

SignOnSanDiego.com. 2003. Love Hewitt stalker committed to state hospital [online], 10 March 2003. San Diego, CA: SignOnSanDiego.com. Available at: http://www.signonsandiego.com/news/metro/20030310- 1100-lovestalker.html.

Sinwelski, S., and Vinton, L. 2001. Stalking: The constant threat of violence. *Affilia*, 16 (1), 46–65.

Smith, A. 2000. Stock shenanigans: The cybersmear [online], 28 August 2000.

Washington, DC: USNews.com. Available at: http://www.usnews.com/usnews/nycu/tech/articles/000828/nycu/stocks.htm.

Smith, K. 2002. Sex offender charged in obscene phone calls, threats from jail [online], 20 September 2002. Las Vegas, NV: Las Vegas Sun. Available at: http://www.lasvegassun.com/sunbin/stories/lv-crime/2002/sep/20/514014807.html.

Smith, R. 1998. Criminal exploitation of new technologies. *Trends and Issues in Crime and Criminal Justice*, No. 93. Canberra: Australian Institute of Criminology.

South London Press. 2003. Terrorised by sick stalker [online], 20 May 2003. London: icSouthLondon. Available at: http://icsouthlondon.icnetwork.co.uk/0100news/0200southlondonheadlines/content_objectid=12976482_method=full_siteid=50100_headline=Terrorised-by-sick-stalker-name_page.html.

Spencer, S. 2002. An online tragedy [online], 23 March 2000. New York: CBSNews.com. Available at: http://www.cbsnews.com/stories/2000/03/23/48hours/main175556.shtml.

Spitzberg, B. 2002. The tactical topography of stalking victimization and management. *Trauma, Violence & Abuse*, 3 (4), 261–88.

Spitzberg, B. H., and Hoobler, G. 2002. Cyberstalking and the technologies of interpersonal terrorism. *New Media & Society*, 14 (1), 71–92.

Stangret, L. 2001. Cyber-stalking omen [online], 9 February 2001. Toronto, Canada: National Post Online. Available at: http://www.degrassi.ca/Press-Releases/feb9th-2001.htm.

Starrs, C. 2001. Scots firm uncovers hidden internet messages. *The Glasgow Herald*, 11 October 2001.

Statistics Canada 2001. *Canadian crime statistics 2000*. Ottawa: Minister of Industry and Canadian Center for Justice Statistics.

Stewart, B. 2001. How to protect against computer viruses [online], 12 February 2001. San Francisco: ZDNet. Available at: http://www.zdnet.com/products/stories/reviews/0,4161,2248291-1,00.html.

Suler, J. 2003. *The psychology of cyberspace* [online]. Lawrenceville, NJ: Rider University. Available at: http://www.rider.edu/~suler/psycyber/index.html.

Sutton, M. 2003. Finding the rar-right online: An exploratory study of white racialist web sites. In P. Taylor and D. Wall, eds., *Global deviance in the information age*. London: Routledge.

Talamo, A., and Ligorio, B. 2001. Strategic identities in Cyberspace. *CyberPsychology & Behavior*, 4 (1), 109–22.

Taylor, D. 2001. IT management: Life style [online], 8 March 2001. London: Computer Weekly. Available at: http://www.computerweekly.com/articlesarticle.asp?liArticleID=26725&liArticleTypeID=13&liCategoryID=2&liChannelID=29&liFlavourID1&sSearch=&nPage=1.

Taylor, M., Quayle, E., and Holland, G. 2001. Child pornography, the Internet and offending. *Canadian Journal of Policy Research*, 2 (2), 94–100.

Thomas, D., and Loader, B., eds. 2000. *Cybercrime: Law enforcement, security and surveillance in the information age*. London: Routledge.

Tjaden, P., and Thoennes, N. 1998. *Stalking in America: Findings from the National Violence Against Women Survey*. No. 93-IJ-CX-0012. Washington, DC: U.S. Department of Justice.

Topham, G. 2000. Email boaster gets his comeuppance [online]. 15 December 2000. London: Guardian Unlimited. Available at: http://www.guardian.co.uk/internetnews/story/0,7369,411910,00.html.

Travis, J. 1996. *Domestic violence, stalking, and antistalking legislation: An annual report to Congress under the Violence Against Women Act*. NCJ 160943. Washington, DC: Department of Justice.

Turow, J., and Nir, L. 2000. *The Internet and the family 2000*. Washington, DC: The Annenberg Public Policy Center of the University of Pennsylvania.

U.S. Attorney. 2001. Thomas Reedy sentenced to life imprisonment in child porn case [online], 6 August 2001. Dallas, TX: U.S. Department of Justice. Available at: http://www.usdoj.gov/usao/txn/PressRel01/reedy_sent_pr.htm.

USA Today. 2002a. Body of 13-year-old Connecticut girl found [online], 21 May 2002. McClean, VA: USA Today. Available at: http://www.usatoday.com/news/nation/2002/05/21/conn-girl.htm.

USA Today. 2002b. Teen's death places spotlight on Net dangers [online], 22 May 2002. McClean, VA: USA Today. Available at: http://www.usatoday.com/tech/news/2002/05/22/teen-net-dangers.htm.

Valenzi, K. 2002. The terrifying reality of cyberstalking. *Virginia.edu* [online], 6 (2). Available at: http://www.itc.virginia.edu/virginia.edu/fall02/stalking/home.html.

Valetk, H. 2002. A guide to the maze of cyberstalking laws [online]. Atlanta, GA: GigaLaw.com. Available at: http://www.gigalaw.com/articles/2002-all/valetk-2002-07-all.html.

Valetk, H. 2003. Teens and the Internet: Disturbing "camgirl" sites deserve a closer look [online], 23 January 2003. Mountain View, CA: FindLaw. Available at: http://writ.news.findlaw.com/commentary/20030123_valetk.html.

Vatis, M. 2001. *Cyber attacks during the war on terrorism: A predictive analysis*. Hanover, NH: Institute for Security Technology Studies, Dartmouth College.

Vorderman, C. 2001. Chatroom danger: Carol Vorderman speaks out [online], 15 March 2001. London: ZDNet UK. Available at: http://news.zdnet.co.uk/story/0,,s2085041,00.html.

Ward, M. 2000. Nike website is hijacked [online], 22 June 2000. London: BBC News. Available at: http://news.bbc.co.uk/1/hi/sci/tech/801334.stm.

Weisman, R. 2001a. Internet deathtrap in the Holy Land [online], 19 January

2001. Sherman Oaks, CA: NewsFactor.com. Available at: http://sci.newsfactor.com/perl/story/6861.html.

Weisman, R. 2001b. Palestinian woman confesses to Internet romance murder [online], 26 February 2001. Sherman Oaks, CA: NewsFactor.com. Available at: http://sci.newsfactor.com/perl/story/7757.html.

Weisman, R. 2001c. Sex and death on the Internet [online], 23 January 2001. Sherman Oaks, CA: NewsFactor.com. Available at: http://sci.newsfactor.com/perl/story/6912.html.

Westhead, J. 2003. "I was groomed online" [online], 6 February 2003. London: BBCi. Available at: http://news.bbc.co.uk/2/hi/uk_news/2733989.stm.

Whittle, S. 2002. Online: Why sex still leads the Internet: Battling paedophilia. *The Guardian*, 28 February 2002.

WHOA. 2003. Online harassment statistics [online]. S.l.: WHOA. Available at: http:// www.haltabuse.org/resources/stats/index.shtml.

Wilcox, J., and Junnarkar, S. 2001a. MSN lockout fuels antitrust cry [online], 26 October 2001. San Francisco: ZDNet. Available at: http://zdnet.com.com/2100-1106-274998.html.

Wilcox, J., and Junnarkar, S. 2001b. Microsoft backs down on MSN browser block [online], 26 October 2001. London: ZDNet UK. Available at: http://news.zdnet.co.uk/story/0,,t269-s2098075,00.html.

Wilkins, L. 2003. Stalker had sophisticated cyber plan [online], 20 May 2003. London: BBC News Online. Available at: http://news.bbc.co.uk/2/hi/uk_news/3040623.stm.

Willison, R. 2001. *The unaddressed problem of criminal motivation in IS security: Expanding the preventive scope through the concept of readying.* Working Paper Series. London: London School of Economics.

Wiltz, S. M. 2002. Kansas v. Robinson: Internet "Slavemaster" murder trial [online], 23 September 2002. New York: CourtTV.com. Available at: http://www.courttv.com/trials/robinson/background.html.

WiredPatrol. 2002. US federal laws [online]. S.l.: WiredPatrol. Available at: http://www.wiredpatrol.org/stalking/federal.html.

WiredSafety. 2003. Canadian stalking law. S.l.: WiredPatrol. Available at: http://www.wiredpatrol.org/stalking/canadian/can_stalkinglaw.html.

Wright, J., et al. 1996. A typology of interpersonal stalking. *Journal of Interpersonal Violence*, 11 (4), 487–502.

Wu Song, F. 2002. Virtual communities in a therapeutic age. *Society* (January/February 2002), 39–45.

ZDNet UK. 2003. Cyber-war rages over Iraq [online], 10 April 2003. London: ZDNet UK. Available at: http://news.zdnet.co.uk/story/0,,t269-s2132670,00.html.

Zillman, D. 1986. Effects of prolonged consumption of pornography. Surgeon General's Conference on Pornography and Public Health, 22–24 June 1986. Arlington,VA: Office of the Surgeon General.

Zimbardo, P. 1969. The human choice: Individuation, reasons, and order versus deindividuation, impulse and chaos. In W. Arnold. and D. Levine, eds., *Nebraska symposium on motivation*, vol. 17. Lincoln: University of Nebraska Press.

Zimbardo, P. 1973. On the effects of intervention in human psychological research: With special reference to the Stanford Prison Experiment. *Cognition*, 2, 243–56.

Zona, M., Sharma, K., and Lane, J. 1993. A comparative study of erotomanic and obsessional subjects in a forensic sample. *Journal of Forensic Sciences*, 38 (4), 894–903.

Index

Acceptable use policy, 191–192
Affectionate/amorous stalker, 54–55
Anonymity, 23, 67, 94–95, 97, 100, 102, 103
Anonymous e-mail, 11, 23, 94–95, 105. *See also* Anonymous remailer
Anonymous remailer, 23, 95, 182–183
Anti-stalking legislation, 165–171
Armistead, Cynthia, 11, 16–17, 100
Assault, 14, 15, 21, 24–25, 27, 61, 62, 84
Australia: anti-stalking legislation, 171, 175; characteristics of stalkers, 60–61; characteristics of stalking victims, 74; extent of stalking, 39, 74; impact of stalking on victims, 84–86; Internet use by young people, 110

Bashing. *See* Cyber-smearing
Behaviors associated with cyber-stalking, 8–9, 10, 12–14, 26–27, 63–67, 79

Behaviors associated with stalking, 6–7, 58–59, 75, 82, 83
Blog. *See* Web log
Boehle family, 89–90, 100, 176
Boyer, Amy, 25, 30–31
Business continuity planning, 153, 192

Camboys. *See* Camgirls
Camgirls, 129–134
Canada: anti-stalking legislation, 170–171; extent of stalking, 39; number of Internet users, 92; proportion of cyberstalking victims, 77; use of Internet by young people, 110
Chain letter, 20
Characteristics of cyberstalkers, 63–68
Characteristics of cyberstalking victims, 76–80
Characteristics of stalkers, 58–62
Characteristics of stalking victims, 73–76

Chat rooms, 111–112, 119, 121, 126–129, 182; corporate cyberstalking, 28, 142; definitions of cyberstalking, 9; inability to record conversations, 127; moderated, 105, 126; pedophile activity, 11, 29, 111, 119, 127; precautions against cyberstalking, 182–184; recording conversations, 196; reporting incidents, 199; Tina Bell diaries, 116–117; use in stock fraud, 142, 150

Child abuse. See Sexual abuse of children

Child pornography, 44–45, 105, 113–116; causing abuse at a distance, 100; chat rooms, 126–129; difficulties in prosecuting, 115; ease of access via Internet, 109; encryption, 95; growth in cases involving Internet, 114; legal implications for companies, 154; newsgroups, 125–126; P2P, 129; size of industry, 113; specialized services, 115; use in grooming, 119

Companies. See Corporate cyberstalking

Compensated dating, 133

Computer literacy, 63, 66

Computer virus. See Virus

Contacting the cyberstalker, 194–195

Controlling access to information, 81, 180–182

Corporate cyberstalking, 28–29, 138–139; as a competitive strategy, 143; cost of cyberstalking incidents, 148, 158; as a means of dealing with critics, 140–141; for political reasons, 144–145; for profit, 142–143; stalking-by-proxy, 143; as an unwitting accomplice, 139

Credible threat, 7, 15, 26–27, 167, 172

Cruz, David, 55, 68–70, 100

Curio. See Napolis, Diana

CyberAngels, 9–11, 40–43, 194–195, 200

Cyber-identity. See Strategic identities

Cyber-smearing, 25, 26, 30, 142

Cybersquatting, 155

Cyberstalkers: behaviors, 63–65, 66–67; computer literacy, 63, 66; distance from victims, 4, 28; gender, 77–78; number active in world, 42; organized groups, 66, 105–106; relationship to victim, 67–68; sentencing, 175–176; typologies, 50, 142

Cyberstalking: behaviors associated with, 9, 12–14; as a crime, 173–174; definitions, 7–12, 14–15; as distinct from offline stalking, 11, 15, 36; as an extension of offline stalking, 21–22; extent of, 40–46; false accusations, 8; frequency of incidents, 9; identifying cases, 192–193; linked with pornography, 109; mental health, 22–23, 28; moving offline, 15, 78; sexual abuse of children, 11, 29; young people, 132–133. See also Corporate cyberstalking

Cyberterrorism, 144, 152–153

Definitions of cyberstalking, 7–12, 14–15

Definitions of stalking, 5–7

Dehumanizing others, 99

Deindividuation, 98

Delusional stalkers, 55–56

Denial of service, 140, 143, 148–149, 150–153

Digital camera. See Web cam

Digital divide, 94

Digital signature, 185

Directories. See White pages

Disinhibition, 97–98

Distance between cyberstalker and victim, 25, 27–28, 100

Domain name, 130, 155, 200; as an expression of free speech, 157
Domestic stalking, 55–56
Domestic violence, 59

E-mail, 184–185; bombing, 2; certificates, 185; computer viruses, 186; file attachments, 186; filters, 195; message headers, 197–198; reporting offensive messages, 197–199; threats, 8, 12, 111, 168; tracing messages, 121, 198–199, 200. *See also* Anonymous e-mail
Emotional distance, 97, 100, 102, 104
Emotional distress/harm, 14, 24, 25, 81–82, 114, 165–166
Encryption, 95–96, 121, 129, 185
Erotomania, 56
Erotomanics, 54
Evidence of cyberstalking, gathering, 195–197

False accusations/rumors, 8, 12, 14, 25, 28
Felson, Marcus, 20–21, 104–105
File attachments, 186
File encryption. *See* Encryption
File shredder, 96
Filters, 195
Financial costs of cyberstalking and stalking: individuals, 82, 148; organizations, 148, 158
Firewall, 79, 188–189, 192
Flame war, 26, 181, 183
Formal security policy, 191
Forums. *See* Message boards

Gilbert, Pamela, 177–179
Grooming, 118, 119
Group stalking and cyberstalking, 61, 62, 105–106

Hackers/hacking, 29, 147, 152–153, 187
Hacktivism, 152

Harassment, 3–4, 6–8, 10, 14, 45, 75; as a crime, 173–174; duration of, 75, 79, 82; escalation, 78; legal definitions, 165–166, 169–170; reporting, 197–200; serial stalking, 62; young people, 111–112. *See also* Cyberstalking; Stalking
Headers, 197–198
Hitchcock, Jayne, 1–3, 12, 100, 138

Identity theft, 15, 67, 169, 171, 181
ICQ, 23–24, 126–127
ICT (Information and Communications Technology), 3, 14–15, 79, 94, 191
Identity, 27, 56, 61–62, 67–68, 78, 103–104; cyberstalkers creating or using false identities, 20, 50, 187. *See also* Anonymity
Identity theft, 15, 67, 169, 171, 181
I-jacking, 153
Impact of harassment, 80–87
Incompetent stalker, 57
Inhibitions, 97
Instant messaging, 126–129, 187
Internet: difficulties in policing, 104–105; ease of access to, 92–94; number of users in Canada, 92; number of users in United Kingdom, 92; number of users in United States, 42, 92–94; number of users worldwide, 42; rape sites, 101–102; use by young people, 110–111
Internet rape sites, 101–102
Intimacy seeker, 57
Intrusion. *See* Hackers/hacking
IP address, 187, 200
IRC, 126, 127
ISP (Internet Service Provider), 10, 125, 167, 195, 197–198

Key logger, 188
Kujawa, Kerry, 49–50, 57

Legal responses to stalking, effectiveness of, 83, 174–176, 201–202
Legislation, 165–171
Lifestyle changes, 84, 85–87
Long, Christina, 135–136
Love bombing, 112
Love obsessional, 54
Lurking, 182

Macro virus, 186
Mental health of stalkers and cyberstalkers, 23, 28, 60
Mental health of stalking victims, 80–83, 85
Message boards, 118, 125, 199
Milgram, Stanley, 102
MMS (Multimedia Messaging Services), 172
Mona, Amana, 137–138

NAMBLA (North American Man Boy Love Association), 123–124
Napolis, Diana, 33–35, 43
Netiquette, 182
Newsgroups: definitions of cyberstalking, 9; pedophile activity, 125–126; reporting offensive messages, 199; trolls, 182; use of racist terms, 99
Nondomestic stalkers, 55–56

Obsessional behavior, 22–23, 51, 54–55, 133
Offline stalking. See Stalking
Offline web browser, 196
Organizations and stalking. See Corporate cyberstalking
Organized stalkers, 55–56

Paranoia, 8
Parental controls, 190
Pedophiles, 11, 29; adoption of new technology, 120–122; approaches to young people, 29, 110, 111, 112, 116; characteristics of, 112; chat

rooms, 105, 127–128; formation of organized groups, 26, 105–106, 118–120; grooming, 118, 119; hysteria regarding, 116–117; newsgroups, 125–126; Tina Bell diaries, 116–117; travelling to meet young people, 116; use of encryption, 95, 121; use of Internet, 114, 118; use of pornography, 118–119; web sites, 121–124
Peer to peer (P2P) networking, 129, 188
Persecutory/angry stalker, 54–55
Personal information, protecting, 81, 180–182
Physical assault. See Assault; Sexual assault
Poison pen letters, 15, 21, 25–26
Police/policing, 83, 104–105, 121, 174–175, 194; reporting harassment to, 201–203
Pornography, 95; degrading women, 101; disinhibition, 97–98; harm caused by, 114–115; newsgroups, 125; P2P, 129; use by young people, 113. See also Child pornography
Port scanning, 187
Power, 57, 99–102
Predatory stalker, 57
PTSD (Post-Traumatic Stress Disorder), 80, 85
Pump and dump, 142–143, 149–150

Rape, 97, 101, 102, 133, 175. See also Internet rape sites
Reasonableness, test of, 15, 170
Rejected stalker, 56–57, 61
Reporting cyberstalking, 197–200
Resentful stalker, 57, 61, 142
Restraining orders, 174–175, 202
Robinson, John. See Slavemaster
Rumors and false accusations, 8, 12, 14, 16, 25, 28

Screen capture software, 196
Script kiddies, 147

Scripts and scripting, 94–95, 151, 186–187
Secondary victims, 54, 62, 82
Serial cyberstalking, 23–24, 36, 43, 62
Sex tourist, 100, 124–125
Sexual abuse of children, 11, 29, 100, 113–116, 118, 120, 125
Sexual assault, 15, 84, 101, 120. *See also* Rape
Shamrock, Lindsay, 27, 107–109, 125
Signature, e-mail, 184, 185
Silent telephone calls, 38–39, 56
Simple obsessional, 54
SLAPP (Strategic Lawsuit Against Public Participation), 140–141, 157–158
Slavemaster, 19–20, 25, 27; chain letter hoax, 20
Social factors that encourage cyberstalking, 96–106
Software audits, 191
Stakeholders, 5, 14
Stalkers: age, 59, 62; ethnicity, 60; gender, 59, 61; mental health, 60; relationship with victim, 61, 62; typologies, 51–58; violence against victims, 61, 62
Stalking by proxy, 13, 25–26, 66, 100–101, 103
Stalking, 5; age of victims 37, 38, 39–40; becoming cyberstalking, 15; behaviors, 5–6, 57–58, 75; definitions of, 6–7; as distinct to cyberstalking, 4; domestic violence, 59; extent of in Australia, 39–40; extent of in Canada, 39; extent of in United Kingdom, 37–39; extent of in United States, 36–37; gender of victims, 37, 38, 39–40; legal definitions, 166; typologies, 51–58
Steganography, 121
Stock fraud, 142–143
Strategic identities, 103–104

Surveillance software, 139, 171, 188

Technological factors that encourage cyberstalking, 92–96
Technology: adoption by cyber-stalkers, 22; adoption by pedo-philes, 120–122
Threats, 8, 12, 111, 168
Thresholds for number of incidents, 9, 170
Tina Bell diaries, 116–117
Travelers, 124–125
Trojan horse, 36, 146, 185–186, 188
Troll, 182
Typologies: of cyberstalkers, 50, 142; of stalkers, 51–58

Vandalism, 15, 26
Virus, 3, 26, 80, 185–186, 195

United Kingdom: anti-stalking legislation, 168–170; characteristics of stalkers, 61–62; characteristics of stalking victims, 73–74; duration of stalking, 75; extent of cyberstalking, 38–39; extent of stalking, 37–38; number of Internet users, 92; use of Internet by young people, 110
United States: anti-stalking legislation, 27, 165–168; attacks on military web sites, 152–153; characteristics of stalkers, 58–61; characteristics of stalking victims, 73; effectiveness of restraining orders, 174–175; extent of cyberstalking, 40–41; extent of stalking, 36–37; legislation dealing with child pornography, 154; number of Internet users, 42, 92–94; size of adult industry, 113; use of Internet by young people, 110
Usenet. *See* Newsgroups

Victims of cyberstalking: age, 76–77; behaviors experienced, 63–65, 66–67; computer literacy, 63, 66, 79–80; duration of harassment, 79; ethnicity, 77; gender, 77–78; Internet use, 78; location, 77; relationship with cyberstalker, 77

Victims of stalking: additional risk factors, 74; age, 73–74; duration of harassment, 75, 82, 83; effects of harassment, 80–87; effects of harassment on health, 85; employment status, 75–76, 86; ethnicity, 73–74; gender, 73–74; lifestyle changes, 84, 85–87; reluctance to approach police, 201–202

Virtual sex tourist, 100

Virtual sit-in, 150–151

Web cam, 120–121, 131, 134

Web log, 130–134, 196, 199

Web Police, 44–45

Web site defacements, 152, 153

Web sites: adult sites, 110, 113; attacks on sites, 151–153; complaining about, 199–200; created by camgirls, 130–134; created by cyberstalkers, 12; pedophile sites, 121–122; rape sites, 101–102; recording sites, 196; reporting offensive content, 199–200; used to victimize others, 101

Web site defacements, 152, 153

White pages, 23–24

WHOA (Women Halting Online Abuse), 44–45, 76–77, 200

WhoIs, 130, 200

WiredPatrol, 167, 195

Wish list, 131

Woody, Kacie, 71–72, 82

Young people: approaches by pedophiles, 110–111; harassment by, 112–113; Internet use, 110; placing themselves at risk, 130–131; pornography, 113; signs of victimization, 193

Zimbardo, Philip, 99

Zombie, 146, 147

About the Author

PAUL BOCIJ is a former university lecturer who now works as a professional writer and consultant. He has written or contributed to more than 20 books and has authored numerous articles, magazine columns, training guides, and other materials related to information systems and information technology.